Blanc de Chine

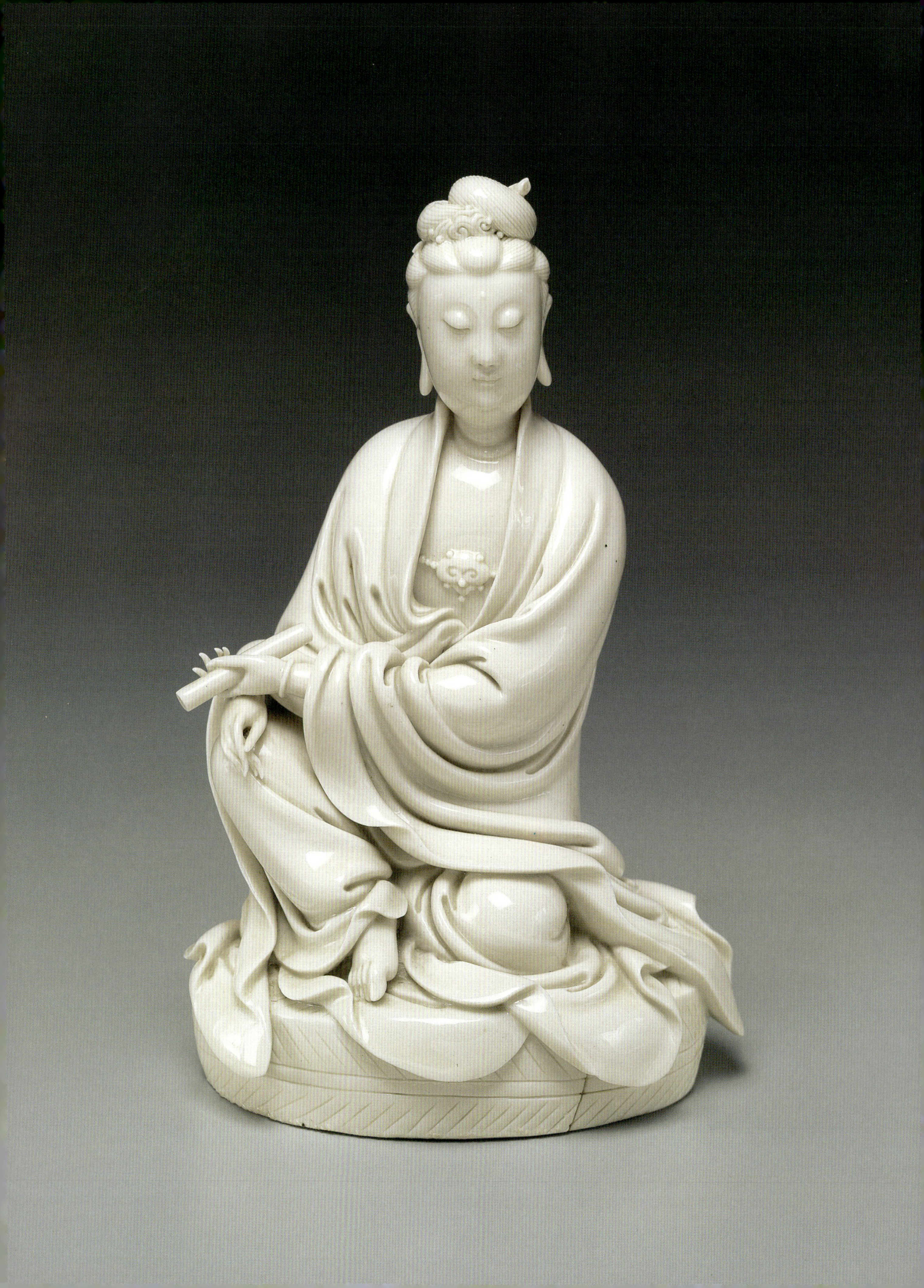

BLANC DE CHINE

DIVINE IMAGES IN PORCELAIN

John Ayers

With an essay by
Yuan Bingling

China Institute Gallery
China Institute
New York
2002

Distributed by Art Media Resources, Ltd.

This catalogue was produced to accompany the exhibition
Blanc de Chine: Divine Images in Porcelain
September 19–December 7, 2002

China Institute Gallery
125 East 65th Street
New York, NY 10021
212 744-8181

Library of Congress Control Number: 2001012345
ISBN: 0-9654270-6-4

General Editor and Project Director: Willow Hai Chang
Editor: J. May Lee Barrett
Designer: Peter Lukic
Printed by Pressroom Printer and Designer, Hong Kong

Chinese is romanized in the *pinyin* system throughout the text and bibliography except for the names of Chinese authors writing in Western languages. Chinese terms cited in Western-language titles remain in their original form and have not been converted.

China Institute was founded in 1926 by American philosopher John Dewey and Chinese educator Hu Shih, together with other prominent educators. It is the oldest bi-cultural and educational organization in the United States with an exclusive focus on China and is dedicated to promoting the understanding, appreciation, and enjoyment of Chinese civilization, culture, heritage, and current affairs through classroom teaching and seminars, art exhibitions, public programs, teacher education, lectures, and symposia.

Cover illustration (cat. no. 27)
He Chaozong (early 17th century)
Damo (Bodhidharma) Crossing the Yangzi on a Reed
Ming dynasty, early 17th century
H. 17 ⅛ in., W. 5 in.
Square seal: *He Chaozong yin*
Wang Xing Lou Collection

Back cover illustration (cat. no. 27 detail)

Frontispiece (cat. no. 34)
He Chaozong (early 17th century)
Guanyin with the Scroll of Wisdom
Ming dynasty, first half 17th century
H. 9 ⅜ in., W. 6 ⅛ in.
Gourd-shaped seal: *He Chaozong*
Private Collection

Contents

Sponsors of the Exhibition

*This exhibition and catalogue have been made possible in part through the generous support of the following exhibition supporters:**

Patrons

The Christensen Fund
Lee Foundation, Singapore

Leaders

John R. & Julia B. Curtis

Contributors

Robert T. and Kay F. Gow
Metropolitan Center for Far Eastern Art Studies

Individuals

Arnhold Foundation
Maie Lee N. Chen
The Chinese Porcelain Company
Michael E. and Winnie Feng
Edith and Joel Frankel
Alice King, Alisan Fine Arts Ltd., Hong Kong
James J. and Helen Lally
William M. Lipton
Theresa M. Reilly
Linda R. Shulsky
Peter D. Sobel
David Solo
Robert C. Tang
Marie-Hélène and Guy A. Weill
Grace Wu
Dennis C. Yang

We are also grateful for the continuing support to China Institute Gallery from

The Henry Luce Foundation
The Starr Foundation
China Institute's Friends of the Gallery

*At time of printing

Lenders to the Exhibition

Phillip Allen

Anonymous

Robert H. Blumenfield Collection

The Detroit Institute of Arts

Mr. and Mrs. Stanley F. Druckenmiller

Richard Lehman Gray

The Koger Collection, The John and Mable Ringling Museum of Art, the State Art Museum of Florida

The Metropolitan Museum of Art

Peabody Essex Museum, Salem, Massachusetts

Private Collection

Private Collection, New York

Virginia Museum of Fine Arts, Richmond

Wang Xing Lou Collection

Message From the Chairman of the Board

Porcelain, one of the monumental technological innovations of Chinese civilization, has captured the imagination of Western Europeans since the days of Marco Polo. It was not only a medium of artistic expression, but also of cultural exchange. *Blanc de Chine*, the fine white-glazed porcelain wares produced at Dehua, in Fujian province, has been received with particular enthusiasm in Europe since the seventeenth century.

Serious study of *Blanc de Chine* began in the West, fueled by the early collecting habits of the European elite. Chinese interest in Dehua wares, on the other hand, lagged behind, because they put greater value on the imperial wares from the Jingdezhen kilns. More recently, however, Chinese archaeological data and textual research have greatly advanced the study of Dehua wares.

China Institute, which has devoted itself since 1926 to fostering the understanding of Chinese culture, is proud to present this exhibition of *Blanc de Chine* in the light of the increased communication and exchange between Chinese and Western scholars in recent years.

China Institute is particularly grateful to its own board member, John R. Curtis, Jr., who with his wife, Julia, have shared their interest and profound knowledge of the ceramic arts in China with us. We are also grateful to guest curator John Ayers, formerly the keeper of the Far Eastern Art Department at the Victoria and Albert Museum in London, who has brought to this project not only his knowledge of the history of Chinese ceramics but also of the history of collecting in Europe. We are pleased to present an essay from Dr. Yuan Bingling which affords us a view of this type of ceramic art from the perspective of its producers and local users. I would also like to thank our gallery staff for their hard work in bringing this beautiful and original exhibition to fruition.

This exhibition was made possible through generous funding provided by the Christiansen Fund; the Lee Foundation, Singapore; the Metropolitan Center for Far Eastern Art Studies; and many individual patrons. We are also indebted to The Henry Luce Foundation, The Starr Foundation and China Institute's Friends of the Gallery for their continuing support.*

H. Christopher Luce

* At time of printing

Foreword

Chinese white-glazed ceramics reached its peak with the beautiful Dehua ware of the Ming dynasty, but it was born from a pursuit of perfection that may well have begun very early in Chinese history. In the Shang dynasty (16th c. B.C. to ca. 1100 B.C.), a hard-bodied white pottery decorated to resemble ritual bronze vessels was highly prized by the ruling class. During the Sui (581–618) and Tang (618–907) dynasties, white ware became the pride of northern China and was considered comparable to the celadon of southern China; this was reflected in the old expression "green in the south and white in the north." Many kilns from the Sui to the Song dynasty (960–1279) produced white ware, the most renowned ones being Xing and Ding ware from Hebei province. Xing ware was praised by Lu Yu, author of the Tang dynasty *Cha Jing* (Book of Tea), as being like "snow" and "silver," and "everyone uses it regardless of being rich or poor."

Beginning in the Five Dynasties Period (907–960), the kilns at Jingdezhen, Jiangxi province, developed an extremely refined porcelain called *yingqing*, "shadow-blue," or *qingbai*, "greenish-white," which is related to the famous *shufu* ware of the Yuan dynasty (1279–1368). An almost pure white porcelain ware covered with a slightly bluish-white opaque glaze, *shufu* was the antecedent of the Ming dynasty *tianbai* (sweet white) porcelain, made by the imperial kilns specifically for the court of the Yongle emperor. Throughout the Ming dynasty, the imperial court continued to order white ceramics from the Jingdezhen official kilns; most of them were ceremonial wares, especially offering vessels for the Yuetan (Moon Temple).

Although the Dehua kilns of Fujian province in southern China were known to have been in production since the Song dynasty, it was only in the sixteenth century during the Ming dynasty that the pure white porcelain of Dehua, known as *blanc de chine* in the West, began to achieve its fame. The ware is characterized by the dense paste of its porcelain body and a high degree of translucency. The glaze is remarkable for its purity, shininess, and softness—like frozen fat—and has a slightly pinkish or milky color that is different than the slightly yellowish glaze of white porcelains produced in northern China or the slightly bluish glaze of Jingdezhen white porcelains. Thus, Dehua ware earned such names as "Ivory White" or "Pork Fat White." In the West it was also known as "Goose Feather White" or "China White."

Dehua figural objects, known for their highly detailed features, brought the art of ceramic sculpture to a higher level. Great attention was paid to the expression and setting of each figure—the solemn Damo, the merciful Guanyin, the humorous Luohan, and others—through such refined observations as the floating quality of wind-blown garments and the movement of waves. The paste of Dehua ware is usually brittle, and thus, as Song Yingxing in his book *Tiangong kaiwu* (1637) stated, "it only makes figures and decorative objects but is not good for utensils."

Once introduced to the West through trade, Dehua ware was collected, commissioned, and copied, and the demand increased. This remarkable white porcelain represents a significant artistic and commercial output of the Minnan region in southern China during the Ming and Qing dynasties, and it continues now as it did during the peak of its fame to form a cultural bridge between East and West.

We are fortunate to have renowned scholar John Ayers, former keeper of the Far Eastern Art Department at the Victoria and Albert Museum, London, share with us his knowledge about *blanc de Chine*. Working almost solely with American collections, he was able to select examples from the fourteenth to nineteenth century and to update us with his new research on dating, function, and historical records. We are also grateful to Dr. Yuan Bingling, a scholar now at Fujian University, for contributing an essay which introduces the local culture of Fujian and provides us with the historical and social background of ceramic production at Dehua.

Our sincere gratitude goes to all the lenders to this exhibition for generously sharing their beloved works of art with the public. We cannot thank enough the sponsors of the exhibition, the Friends of the Gallery, and all the trustees of the China Institute for their continued support of the Gallery. We also take this opportunity to thank the Gallery Committee of the China Institute, especially its Chairman, Mr. John Curtis, for suggesting the theme of this exhibition and for the generous support and assistance that we have received from him and his wife, Julia Curtis.

The installation of this exhibition and the publication of this catalogue were realized through the efforts of many loyal and creative people. J. May Lee Barrett, our editor, has transformed the original manuscript, with all its parts, into a single polished publication with her knowledgeable suggestions and thorough editing. Peter Lukic once again designed a handsome catalogue and produced all the graphic materials for the installation. Perry Hu, as always, thoughtfully and tastefully designed the exhibition installation with his characteristic sense of refinement. Nicole Straus, our public relations representative deserves special thanks for her generous help. Lenette Talpins, former Gallery Manager and Registrar, handled the numerous details required for securing all the loans, photographs, and the needed information for the catalogue and the exhibition. I would like to thank Pao Yu Chen and Elaine Smollin of the gallery staff for their assistance in so many different ways and all of the gallery docents and volunteers for the unstinting offer of their time and talents. I also extend my gratitude to the entire China Institute staff for their concern and support throughout the various stages of this exhibition. Without such a great team, the Gallery could not carry on successfully. I am grateful to all of them.

Willow Hai Chang
Director
China Institute Gallery

Preface

The circumstances in which this exhibition project came into being deserve a few words of comment. As many will be aware, under the stimulus of widespread and often sensational archaeological discoveries during the last half century, the history of Chinese ceramics has been effectively rewritten, chiefly by Chinese scholars and archaeologists. However, leaving aside the uniquely important excavations at the imperial kiln at Jingdezhen, this historical review has been less sweeping in its effects for the Ming (1368–1644) and later periods, and notably so as regards more outlying parts of the country such as Fujian province, where the so-called *blanc-de-Chine* porcelains which are our current concern were made. In this area, Chinese scholarship has labored under a double handicap: firstly a lack of significant fresh evidence, whether from archaeological or documentary sources, and secondly the great extent to which the more important products of the kilns have been dispersed abroad. *Blanc de Chine* is therefore one area of study where the cooperation of outsiders may be said to be indispensable.

A pioneering stride in this direction was taken as long ago as 1969 by P.J. Donnelly, whose lengthy study (discussed in the following introduction) offers even today the most thorough investigation yet made into the surviving material; indeed, in the absence of any real alternative it has come to acquire for many the status of gospel. In recent years, however, Donnelly's study has been shown to contain flaws that undermine its reliability. An important requirement for the exhibition became therefore to avoid and, where possible, counteract the misconceptions arising from Donnelly's work, while the primary aim remains that of presenting the artistic achievement by which the Dehua kilns are particularly distinguished.

I was personally drawn more deeply into this field when, a few years ago, I became involved with the display of the Koger collection in Jacksonville, Florida. (This celebrated collection, which includes more *blanc de Chine*, it would seem, than any other collection in the United States, has lately been donated to the Florida State University, and will in due course be displayed at the Ringling Museum in Sarasota). I was thus obliged to confront problems of identification and chronology that curators, auctioneers, and dealers alike, myself included, have too often become accustomed to sidestepping by easy reliance on Donnelly's opinions. Throwing off this burden of time-honored errors took some time, and I was obliged to revisit a wide body of collections and literature until ultimately certain solutions began to present themselves as inescapable. My conclusions, incomplete as they are, are now offered for consideration by colleagues and the wider public, and at the same time I hope they will not fail to appreciate the exceptional quality of the range of pieces assembled from across the country. While laying the main emphasis on the late Ming figure models that present the peak of Dehua's achievement, I have tried to do justice also to the range of early wares exported to the West (which are so familiar a part of our historical experience of Chinese porcelain) and to cast a light on the almost unknown renaissance of the figure-modeler's art, effectively unnoticed by Donnelly, that took place in the later years of the Qing dynasty (1644–1911).

I should like to acknowledge in the first place the great debt I owe to the numerous scholars, collectors, and others whose goodwill has been indispensable to the achievement of the exhibition. In particular those notable collectors, Ira and Nancy Koger, whose enthusiasm has been from the outset a major source of encouragement. Their loans remain by far the most numerous, and their care in ensuring they remained available despite their recent donation to the University makes their contribution of unique value. The curator of their collection, Brian Shrum, has remained throughout a tower of reliable support. John and Julia Curtis have assisted my progress in more ways than I can tell; I am especially grateful also to Robert H. Blumenfield, the noted West Coast collector, for his generous participation and for allowing his recent book on *blanc de Chine* to be used as a source of information in compiling the catalogue, and to Richard L. Gray, another major lender, whose sustained interest has been a constant source of support. The Chinese Porcelain Company of New York, in the persons of Conor Mahoney and Margaret Cristina, have likewise been unfailingly helpful. Especial thanks are also due to Phillip

Allen of Bedford, England, for one loan of spectacular interest and for his continual enthusiasm and advice.

Many curators have been unstinting in their assistance, notably Suzanne Valenstein of the Metropolitan Museum of Art, William Sargent of the Peabody Essex Museum, Salem, and Joseph Dye of the Virginia Museum of Fine Arts, Richmond. My studies in European collections have been notably eased by the enthusiasm of Jessica Harrison-Hall of the British Museum, Rose Kerr and Ming Wilson at my old home, the Victoria & Albert Museum in London, and Shelagh Vainker at the Ashmolean Museum in Oxford; and no less by the help and advice received from Dr. Frances Wood of the British Library, Hincheung Lovell, and Gordon Lang. Nor must I neglect to include thanks to my friendly correspondents in the East, Chen Jianzhong of the Dehua Ceramic Museum and Heidi Tan at the Asian Civilisations Museum, Singapore.

I have also to thank Yuan Bingling for her stimulating essay on the subject of Fujian cultural life in the late Ming and Qing periods, which might otherwise have remained for many of us a closed book; and of course Willow Hai Chang and all her colleagues at the China Institute, for their ever-patient and understanding handling of all the difficulties arising from the participation of such an awkward and demanding figure as the author.

John Ayers

Summary in Chinese

中文簡介

德化窰為中國宋、元、明著名瓷窰之一，位於福建省南部的德化縣，於十世紀五代後唐長興二年（公元931年）正式置縣，轄於泉州。根據文獻記載，宋元時代的德化製瓷業已經嶄露頭角，產品以青白瓷為大宗，也有少量的純白瓷。其燒瓷遺址主要集中在城關一帶，以蓋德的碗坪侖窰址和潯中的屈斗宮窰址尤為出眾。著名的意大利旅行家馬可波羅在他的東方游記中曾記載："繁榮的剌桐（泉州港）附近，屹立著廷基（德化）城，這裏除了製造瓷杯或瓷碗碟，別無其他值得注意的地方……，大量的瓷器是在城市出售的，一個威尼斯銀幣能買到八個瓷杯。"

明清時代，德化窰以生產白瓷聞名，陶瓷界命名為"建白瓷"。它的胎體潔白細緻，俗稱"糯米胎"；釉汁晶瑩潤澤，具有玉質感。在琳琅滿目的中國瓷壇上獨樹一幟。由於所用瓷胎含鐵量低，含鉀量高，經高温燒成後，乳白如凝脂，在光照之下，釉中隱現粉紅或牙黃，有"豬油白"、"象牙白"之稱。明清德化白瓷遠銷歐洲，影響深遠。法國人又稱"鵝絨白"，"中國白"。從傳世實物觀察，器形以爐、杯、尊、鼎為多見，特別是梅花杯屬其典型物品。瓷塑工藝尤為發達，所製觀音、達摩、彌勒、文昌、關公、壽星、媽祖等像，無不形神兼備，栩栩如生。當時的名工有何朝宗、林朝景、張壽山等人。瓷簫、瓷笛在明代已為人所重。明清德化白瓷與宗教信仰，以及飲茶風尚是有密切關係的，如常見器形的香爐、燭台、花瓶，各式茶杯都是神案上的供品。至於雕塑方面，則有眾多民間喜愛的佛教和道教人物。總之，德化窰從宋代至今天已有八百多年的製瓷歷史，而明代嘉靖至清代康熙是其白瓷工藝成就最高時期，雍、乾之後雖仍燒白瓷，但其釉色與典型的明代產品相比，釉層較薄，且白中略閃青色，質量逐漸下降。之外，明代後期起，德化兼燒青花，還有少量的五彩。

張浦生

Chronology

Chinese Dynasties and Historical Periods

Golden Age of Antiquity prior to Xia dynasty	
Xia	21st–16th century B.C.
(Erlitou period)	19th–16th century B.C.
Shang	16th–11th century B.C.
Zhou	11th century–256 B.C.
Western Zhou	11th century–771 B.C.
Eastern Zhou	770–256 B.C.
Qin	221–206 B.C.
Han	206 B.C.–A.D. 220
Western Han	206 B.C.–A.D. 9
Eastern Han	A.D. 25–220
Six Dynasties	220–589
Three Kingdoms	220–280
Wu	222–280
Shu Han	221–263
Wei	220–265
Western Jin	265–317
Eastern Jin	317–420
Period of Northern and Southern Dynasties	386–581
Sui	581–618
Tang	618–906
Five Dynasties	907–960
Song	960–1279
Northern Song	960–1127
Southern Song	1127–1279
Jin	1115–1234
Yuan	1279–1368
Ming	1368–1644
Hongwu	1368–1398
Jianwen	1399–1402
Yongle	1403–1424
Xuande	1426–1435
Zhengtong	1436–1440
Jingtai	1450–1457
Tianshun	1458–1464
Chenghua	1465–1487
Hongzhi	1488–1505
Zhengde	1506–1521
Jiajing	1522–1566
Longqing	1567–1572
Wanli	1573–1620
Taichang	1620
Tianqi	1621–1627
Chongzhen	1628–1644
Qing	1644–1911
Shunzhi	1644–1661
Kangxi	1662–1722
Yongzheng	1723–1735
Qianlong	1736–1795
Jiaqing	1796–1820
Daoguang	1821–1850
Xianfeng	1851–1861
Tongzhi	1862–1874
Guangxu	1875–1908
Xuantong	1908–1911

MAP OF CHINA

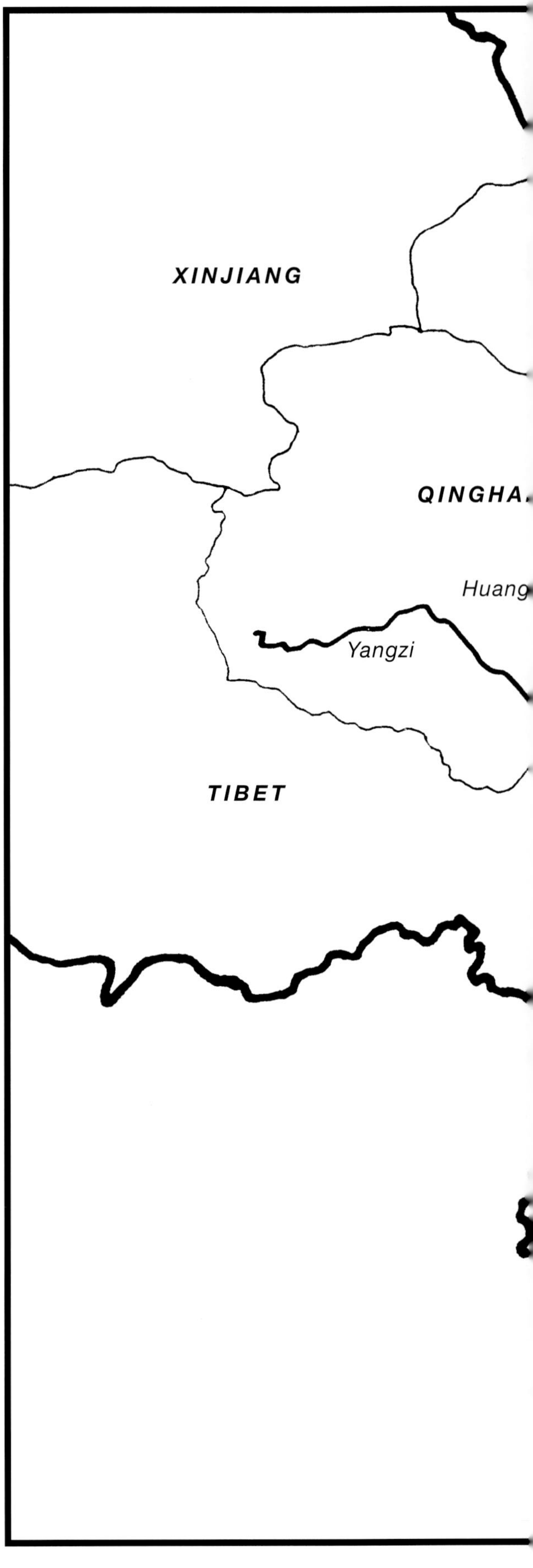

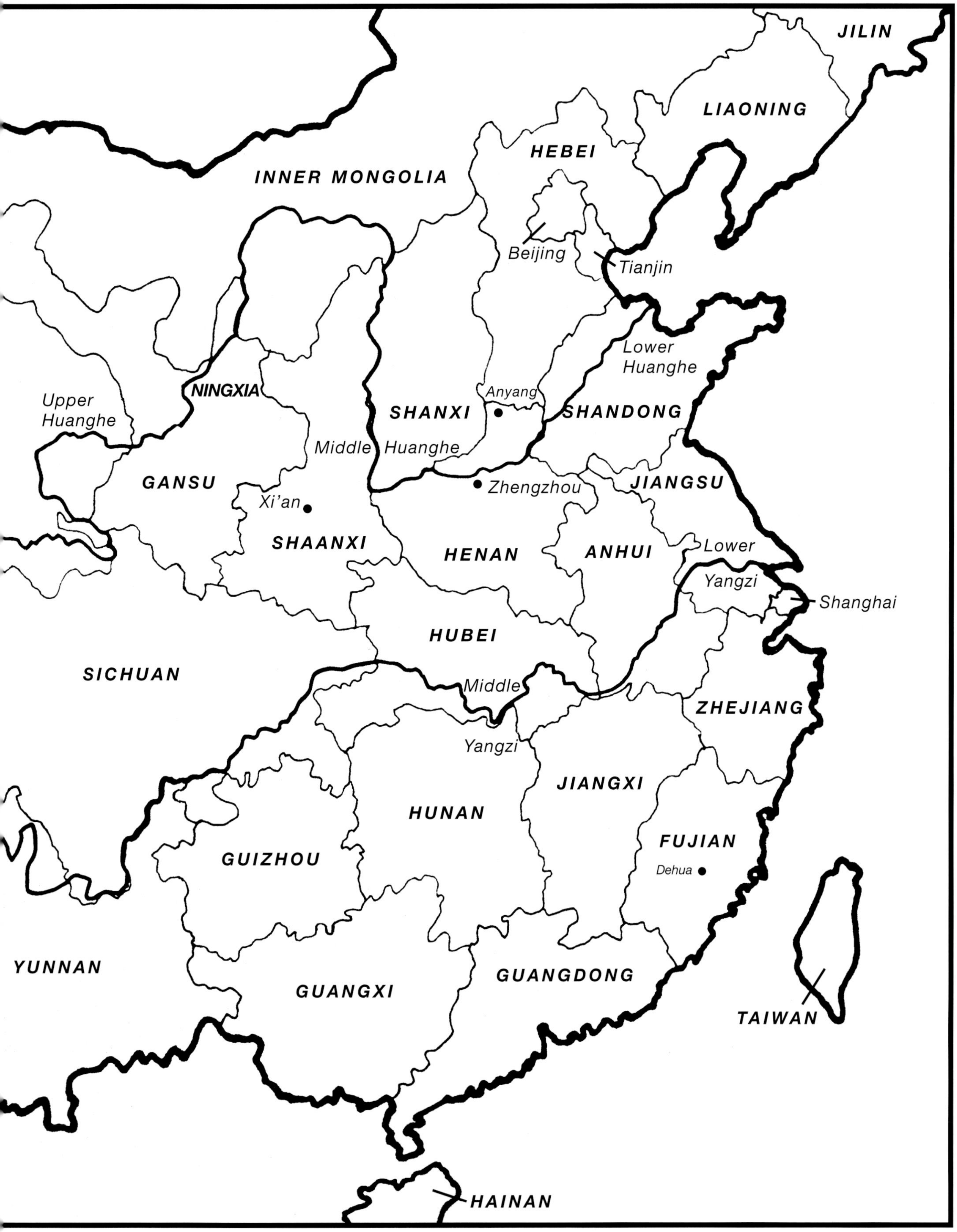
JILIN
LIAONING
HEBEI
INNER MONGOLIA
Beijing
Tianjin
Lower
Huanghe
Upper
Huanghe
NINGXIA
Anyang
SHANXI
SHANDONG
Middle
Huanghe
GANSU
Zhengzhou
JIANGSU
Xi'an
SHAANXI
HENAN
ANHUI
Lower
Yangzi
Shanghai
HUBEI
SICHUAN
Middle
Yangzi
ZHEJIANG
JIANGXI
HUNAN
FUJIAN
GUIZHOU
Dehua
YUNNAN
GUANGDONG
GUANGXI
TAIWAN
HAINAN

Blanc de Chine: Divine Images in Porcelain

John Ayers

Introduction

Among those who appreciate fine porcelain, *blanc de Chine* has always been popular. Special praise is given to its unique range of figures of Chinese divinities, which are often of Ming date and of unusual sculptural merit. The aim of the exhibition has been to assemble a representative series of the finest *blanc de Chine,* both to encourage its appreciation and to promote a reassessment of its still uncertain history. As collectors, scholars, and dealers know all too well, the existing historical picture is built on slight foundations, and the subject confused by differing opinions and unresolved doubts. To present the exhibits in their true chronological context it has been necessary to dismiss statements that are demonstrably false or misleading, and the account that follows, however partial and discontinuous, is supported by recent research and, it is hoped, is more plausible. The rigors of the selection process have been reduced by the welcome collaboration of both private lenders and museums; remarkably enough, the exhibition has been put together almost exclusively from collections within the United States.

"Blanc de Chine" is the name widely used for an especially pure and largely undecorated form of white porcelain that was made at Dehua, a pottery town in southern China, in the relatively remote maritime province of Fujian. The appeal of the wares is due in no small measure to the rare quality of the porcelain clay available in that neighborhood. In the past, leading Chinese writings on ceramics were neither very informative nor wholly complimentary about what they tended to discount as a lesser, provincial product. For example, *Jingdezhen taolu,* the compendious history published in 1815, remarks briefly that "the porcelain of Dehua is rich and lustrous but, as a rule, thick," while conceding that "the images of Buddha are very beautiful." It also provides confirmation that the factories were active in the Ming period (1368–1644).[1]

In Europe, the distinctive qualities of *blanc de Chine* were appreciated at an early date when, in the seventeenth and early eighteenth centuries, significant quantities were imported in the ships of the growing East India Companies. Groups of pieces found their way at once into the porcelain collections that were for a time almost *de rigeur* for the furnishing of large houses; at the same time some pieces were imitated at the new factories that everywhere sprang up to meet the growing demand for this unfamiliar material. Hence, the ware came to acquire a cachet that has clung to it among collectors ever since.

After a lengthy interval, *blanc de Chine* returned to favor with the renewed wave of enthusiasm for Chinese ceramics that swept the West in the late nineteenth century, and it was at this time that the term itself first became current among French collectors and international porcelain dealers.[2] Some interest in the ware's individuality is apparent in the work of the distinguished ceramic historian R.L. Hobson,[3] who joins in the praise for the figure models, "although," he remarks, "on account of their lack of decoration, there will always be difficulty in determining the date of the finest specimens, e.g., whether they are Ming or Qing." He is not tempted to enlarge on the point, but his concern seems evident when he adds, rather ominously, "Many specimens in modern collections are likely to be the exception and not, as optimistic owners would lead one to suppose, the rule." After discussing a range of pieces drawn mainly from old collections of "export" ware, the early date of which is thus beyond question, his main comment on the ware's subsequent history is also perhaps rather odd. "Brinkley asserts," Hobson writes, "without giving any authority, that the industry was virtually dissolved at the end of the eighteenth century, and revived in recent years"; he then proceeds to cite some recent reports on the modern industry.[4] Today, while *blanc de Chine* still has numerous enthusiastic admirers, doubts continue to be raised about the standing of some products: the problem being mainly that firm evidence is simply not available about essential aspects of the kilns, even the most celebrated of the potters, and the facts of their working lives. Of course the reign marks that elsewhere guide our path through the morass of chronology are here virtually absent.

Indeed, study of the subject in the West might have been further marginalized and postponed had it not been for one very determined individual, the England-domiciled Irish collector P.J. Donnelly, who devoted years of single-minded research to producing *Blanc de Chine: The Porcelain of Tehua in Fukien*, a study of the ware in all its aspects that came out in London in 1969. Although some of its conclusions about the dating of pieces and the potters whose marks they bear have since been found to be unreliable,[5] this work has remained without rival as the standard account because of its encyclopedic scope. Despite such doubts it is virtually impossible to discuss *blanc de Chine* without reference to this monumental work.[6] Before going further it needs to be said that *blanc de Chine* was not the only porcelain produced at the Dehua factories. From the seventeenth century if not earlier, they made a lesser quantity of wares painted in underglaze blue ("blue-and-white" ware), as well as some enameled wares and pieces with single-colored glazes; but no great account will be taken of any of these in the exhibition. Our subject is the beautifully pure, white ware to which the factories owe their international renown.

Donnelly was the first Westerner to begin his account of the ware with archaeological research, drawing on material that is mostly hidden away in Chinese technical journals and, because of the confused nature of many of the sites studied, led to few clear-cut conclusions. While adding only marginally perhaps to our understanding of the main body of *blanc de Chine*, this field research established beyond doubt that Dehua was in production during the Song dynasty (960–1279); white porcelains were made there mostly with the *qingbai* (greenish-white) glazes that were widely current in China at the time. Donnelly was inclined to draw a line between these early wares and the more developed *blanc de Chine*, with its generally ivory-white material and lustrous glaze, which had demonstrably emerged by middle Ming times in the early sixteenth century. As many have remarked, it is one of the most beautiful porcelains ever produced: the pure whiteness and high translucency of the body being complemented by the warm glaze tint resulting from an essentially oxidation firing. The quality of the perfected ware may well be largely due to the introduction of a more sophisticated firing technique involving use of the stepped chamber kiln, which continued to characterize production until modern times; recent visitors to Dehua report the current dependence on electrically-fired ovens.[7]

Among the merits of Donnelly's approach is the persistence with which he tracked down examples in collections around the world, studying their many variations of form, which in the book are exhaustively categorized and illustrated by photographs. He relied very much on what was preserved in early Western collections and the sure evidence of date it provides. He knew well that the greatest achievement of Dehua was its inspired development of the figure model, and today the number of these available for study is remarkably high; but to identify their various makers and trace their history in the almost total absence of records confronted him with a sterner task. He set about systematically recording and studying the impressed seals that appear on the finer models, which are the only clues we have to the potters and their artistic identities. He recognized that figures of this caliber were not available to the early trade, which was conducted at a more mundane level, and that they did not reach the West until a much later date through the rise of the modern antique trade in the late nineteenth century. This renewed traffic, however, was to introduce a great volume of figures among which were a flood of impressive-looking models that, whatever their artistic merit, had no sustainable claim to antiquity—something that, unlike Hobson perhaps, Donnelly failed sufficiently to recognize. The task of distinguishing these was one he had not the information nor perhaps the trained judgment to tackle, with the unfortunate result that sometimes they were accepted as being older than they were. The exhibition aims in particular to illuminate this problem.

It is clear from the more recent Chinese literature that certain families of potters played a leading role in the history of Dehua.[8] In recent years, renewed efforts have been made in Fujian to extract information from whatever records exist, and one recent work assembles an intriguing series of biographies of potters, modelers, and others associated with the industry over the centuries.[9] In actuality, however, very little seems to survive from the earlier periods, and on account of the lax use of uncited sources the documentary value of much of the work is to be treated as suspect. Its limitations are laid bare once it is recognized that in some instances Donnelly's book has been pressed into service as a primary source and his speculative views accepted as fact, as in the case of the entry on He Chaochun, for instance, who is declared to be the younger brother of the great Dehua modeler, He Chaozong; it is also stated quite implausibly that much of his work was exported to Europe in the reign of Kangxi (1662–1722): the period in which Donnelly decided he had worked. It has long been appreciated in the West—not least by Donnelly himself—that none of the finer models marked with their maker's seals was carried to Europe by the early porcelain trade. Further to this, it should be noted that a figure in a Singapore collection marked with the He Chaochun seal has been shown to

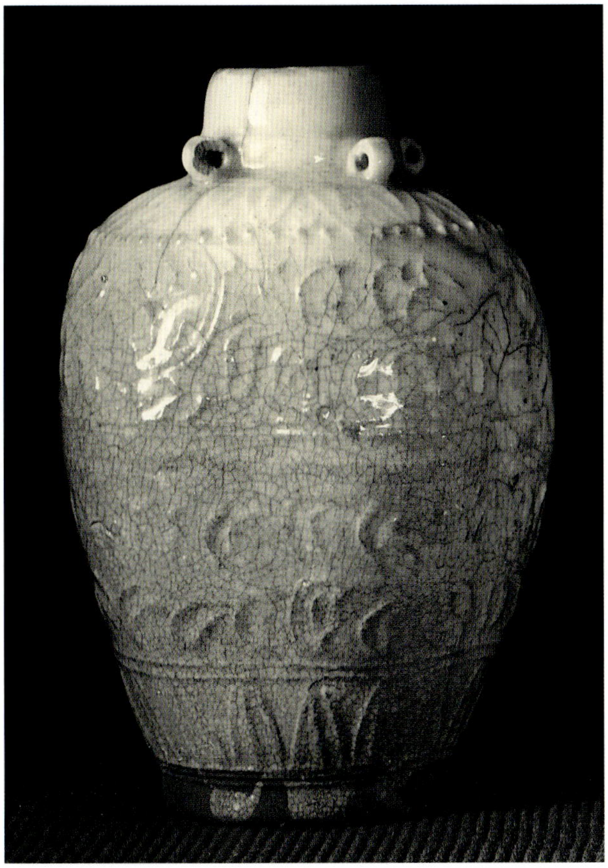

Fig. 1. The "Marco Polo" vase, Yuan dynasty, 13th century. Dehua porcelain with molded decoration, h. 4¾ in. (12.1 cm). Treasury of San Marco, reproduced with kind permission of Procuratoria Di San Marco, Venice.

have been made by the method known as slip casting: a modern manufacturing process which a Chinese scholar reports was introduced at Dehua only in 1936.[10] An examination of other He Chaochun figures from Donnelly's collection, now part of his bequest to the British Museum, does not dispel doubts of his dating of this modeler's work as a whole.

At the end of his study, Donnelly produced a list of some thirty-six potters whose names appear either on wares or on figures. In the absence of documentary evidence, he conjured up tentative working dates for them all.[11] Their various marks were carefully reproduced in facsimile in an appendix, and no less than fourteen of the potters are stated to have made figures in the course of the seventeenth century; notably, they include members of the Zhang, He, and Lin families. A bare three names, however, of potters working solely within the eighteenth century were given: Chen Nianshan, known only from a seated Guanyin in an English collection; Yi Mozi, whose otherwise unknown mark appears on an admirable and much-published Guanyin in the Victoria and Albert Museum;[12] and Puji (universal aid), perhaps a mark of commendation rather than a potter's name, noted only on a figure of Budai in the Percival David Foundation, London.[13] Three marks were judged to date from the period overlapping the late eighteenth and early nineteenth centuries: all from the Xu family (although to this period, it must be said, were also ascribed another very substantial group of figures that bear the so-called fisherman commendation mark). One potter, Su Yunyu, was judged to belong to the mid-nineteenth century; while Su Rushan was assigned to the modern era, i.e., twentieth century. Members of all five families named in the above list are represented by work in the exhibition and will be discussed below.

Dehua, its Earlier History and Trade

We return to the earlier history of Dehua, on which recent excavations have possibly thrown fresh light. Whereas few specimens of this early period are known to have survived intact on the mainland, by the thirteenth century (if not earlier) the Fujian potters were already selling their porcelains overseas, especially to their compatriots who had migrated to Southeast Asian lands in order to further their trade in the exotic produce of the tropics. Some of these exported pots were in course of time buried and have been unearthed in recent times, either by the local population or by archaeologists.[14] By singular chance one example of these early wares found its way to Europe, where it has been preserved as a relic ever since.

This is the so-called Marco Polo vase (fig. 1), now kept in the Treasury of St. Mark's in Venice, the native city of the famous merchant-traveler. It was deposited there at some time prior to 1903 together with the legend that he brought it back on his return from China in 1295, not long before the composition of the epoch-making account of his exploits, popularly known as the "Milione," which was to inspire generations of mariners to set sail in search of the marvels and potential riches it described. Polo describes his return journey by way of the port of Zayton (modern Quanzhou in Fujian province, not far from Dehua) and provides the first description in the West of the making of porcelain.

We cannot take it for granted that this vase was in fact brought from China by Polo; indeed serious scholars have doubted that he actually reached China at all.[15] The ware however, although rare, is of a type for which a date in the late thirteenth century is now known to be acceptable, and it is hard to imagine how otherwise than through him it would have come into the possession of

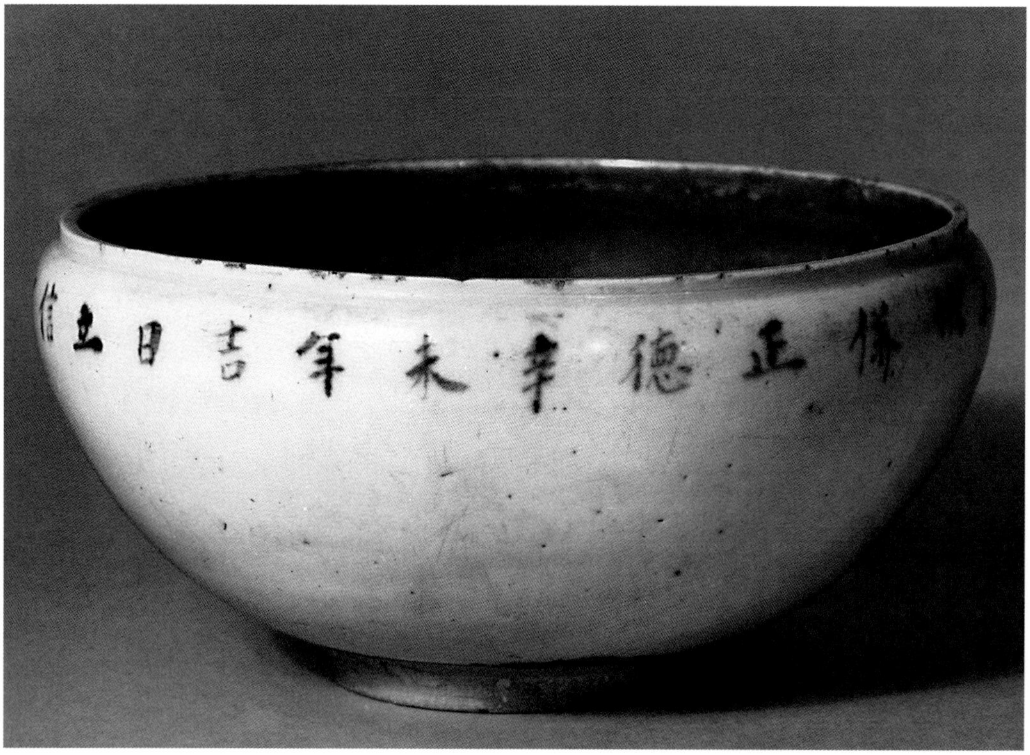

Fig. 2. Water bowl inscribed "sixth year of Zhengde," Ming dynasty, 1511. Porcelain, diam. 6½ in. (16.6 cm). British Museum, London (OA1930.7-15.1).

his descendants. The likelihood that Marco Polo did in fact own it, by whatever means he came by it, cannot be lightly rejected.

Examples of these wares found in the Philippines are the earliest items shown here. They are made of "a soft-looking, cream-white close-grained white porcelain body, with a thin glaze that is mostly of a cream-white color, and a decoration which is usually moulded in a low cord-like relief," to quote one of its earlier students in her catalogue of the Williams Collection.[16] It should be remarked that this early ware from the Philippines and elsewhere does not invariably have the *qingbai*-colored glaze, and sometimes its body material seems to be less highly fired than would merit its description as porcelain. Other factories in Fujian province appear also to have participated in its manufacture. The range of vessel forms found is limited; the ware is typified by numerous small covered boxes (e.g., cat. no. 1) characterized by simple relief-molded decoration. These were perhaps used mainly for cosmetics. Figure 87 in the above-mentioned Williams Collection catalogue illustrates a small vase of similar shape to the Marco Polo vase, while this exhibition includes a spouted vessel (cat. no. 2) in the form known as *kendi*. Sometimes described as a drinking vessel and possibly used as such, the *kendi* was originally designed for use in Muslim rituals and possibly still served this function in the Southeast Asian countries that had by this time subscribed to that faith.[17]

A brief report on some recent kiln-site excavations at Dehua draws a further distinction between the so-called *qingbai* or Marco Polo type ware and another type that is seen as an intermediary stage in the development of *blanc de Chine* proper. This is described as being thick and translucent, the glaze being white with a soft and creamy luster. Both types are said to have been made together at the Qudoukong kiln.[18]

Following this in time, we reach the earliest reliably dated piece of *blanc de Chine:* a bowl in the British Museum (fig. 2) which is dated by the inscription around the rim to the sixth year of Zhengde, i.e., 1511.[19] It is heavily stained inside, apparently through use as a container for pure water as indicated in the inscription; as Donnelly rightly observed, the relatively thick, creamy material has all the characteristics demanded of Ming *blanc de Chine*. Further examples of about this date come from Dehua itself, where tombs have been excavated containing tablets dated in accordance with 1519 and 1559.[20] The inscriptions are written on tablets in an impure underglaze blue; while the tomb contents include in each case a pair of altar vases, incense burners, and other items (the earlier set is illustrated in fig. 3).

Blanc de Chine of this middle-Ming period is scarce even in Southeast Asia, as commentators have remarked,[21] but Donnelly located a few other dateable pieces, such as altar vases with inscriptions dated to 1586

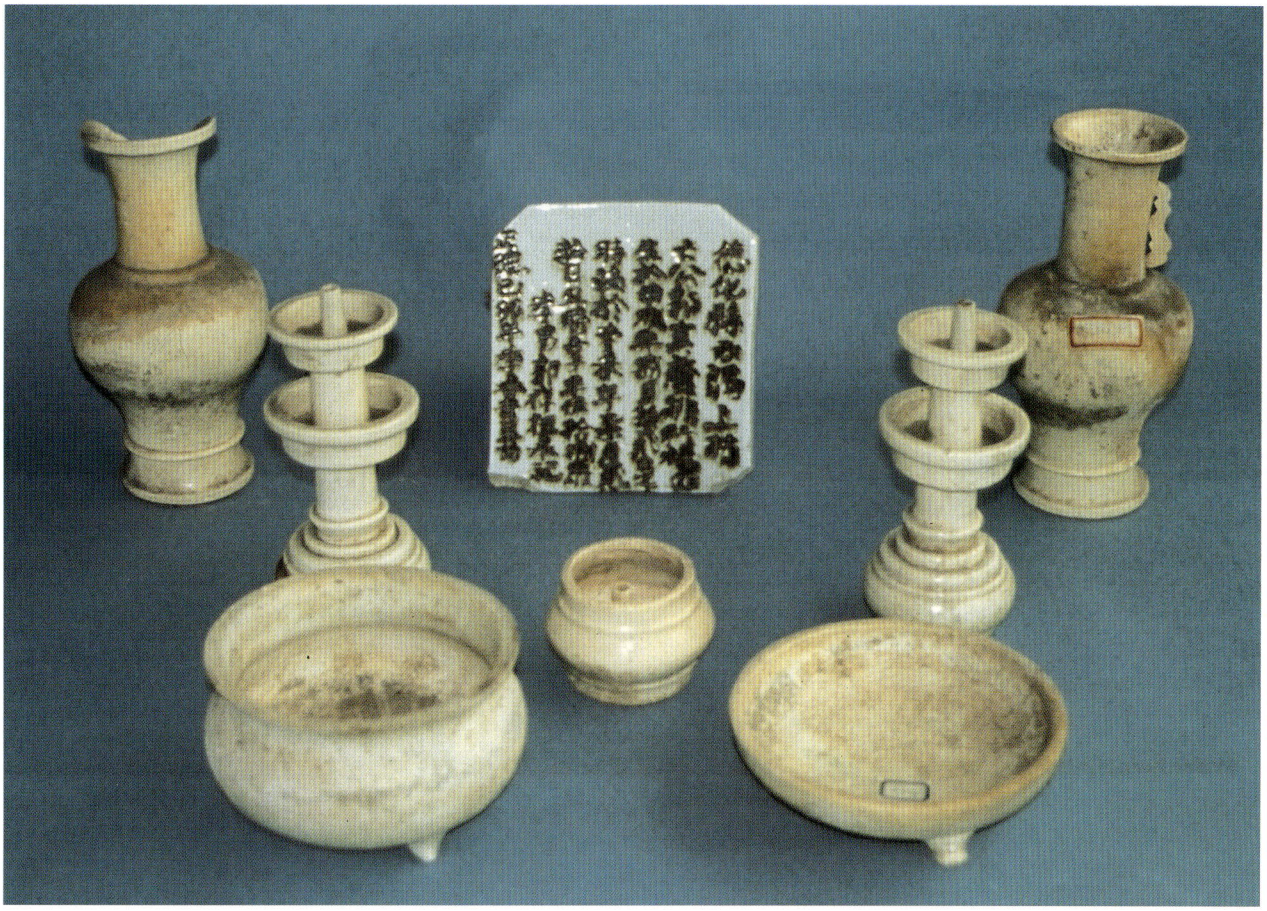

Fig. 3. *Blanc-de-Chine* vessels recovered from a tomb at Dehua, with inscribed tablet dated to 1519. Ming dynasty, early 16th century. Photo courtesy of Chen Jianzhong, Dehua Ceramics Museum.

and 1636; these show how gradual was the evolution of that particular form.[22] The vase from the Koger collection and a small dish with an unusual cut rim (cat. nos. 4 and 3) may be tentatively added to this group.

The Southeast Asian markets were no doubt of long-term importance to Dehua. However, the comfortable pattern established by the Song, Yuan, and early Ming trade was upset when, in the sixteenth century, first Portuguese, then Dutch and English ships arrived without warning from the unknown world of the West. The Dutch in particular, with their well-organized East India Company, were bent on mercantile expansion and established a powerful presence in the Indies. Increasingly intent on finding a footing in China itself, they maintained a base on the island of Formosa from 1624 to 1662; the Portuguese, however, had their foothold in Macao from 1557. All were concerned not merely with bringing oriental goods to Europe but with conducting profitable trade with other nations in Asia. There is, however, little surviving today in these countries to indicate that they were interested in the better sort of Dehua production.[23]

The Golden Age of Dehua Porcelain

There are few, if any, grounds to believe shipments of *blanc de Chine* reached Europe before 1600, and Donnelly certainly believed the golden age of Dehua did not begin until the seventeenth century. Less well founded was his conclusion that the zenith of creativity was attained during the last quarter of the seventeenth and first quarter of the eighteenth centuries. "The thick potting and smooth unctuous glaze, with their characteristic shapes," he wrote, "enable the products of this golden age to be recognised at sight. Not so with the earlier and later periods of Tehua production," he continued. "We have absolutely nothing that can be put forward with confidence before the closing years of the sixteenth century...[F]rom 1750 onwards [the problem] is different...[T]he glaze, colder in tone, thinner in texture, bluish or greenish in tinge though it may become, never loses a certain soft, pearly sheen...."[24] His description of developments in porcelain characteristics is unexceptionable, but the dates are debatable.

Frustrated by the absence of reliable information

from China itself, Donnelly concluded that the "golden age" was in the time of the emperor Kangxi (1662–1722). In this he was undoubtedly influenced by his special study of the great porcelain collection assembled at this time by King Augustus the Strong of Saxony, which contained several hundred pieces of *blanc de Chine,* and possibly his view was affected no less by the unusually distinguished place this reign occupies in the history of Chinese porcelain as a whole. Much of the King's collection was in fact of specifically export (and on that account, less than the finest) quality brought in shortly before, or soon after, 1700. But contrary to Donnelly's supposition, a part may well have been of earlier origin, either received through donations or accessed by his agents from various older sources. Further study of seventeenth-century inventories and collections lends support to alternative interpretations.[25] A review of the evidence as a whole reinforces the Chinese view that in Fujian itself the period of quality production began in the later years of the Ming dynasty and surely by the early seventeenth century; however, just how long it was sustained is harder to say.

One recent source of importance for dating is the "first Hatcher wreck," a Chinese trading vessel that sank in the South China Seas in or shortly after the year 1643.[26] Some items recovered from the wreck by Captain Michael Hatcher match types to which Donnelly gave a late-seventeenth-century date. A teapot actually recovered from the ship is exhibited here from the Koger collection (cat. no. 17). The items display similar characteristics of material and manufacture, such as a generally fine ivory-white material and rather robust, neatly finished potting.[27]

As pointed out in the following essay by Yuan Bingling, the period beginning about 1563, in which year trading with foreigners was officially permitted at its ports, was one of unparalleled prosperity in southern Fujian and is considered the "Golden Century" of that region. This newfound wealth may be considered responsible for an upsurge in the local culture which was reflected in scholarship, in architecture, and in a strong development of local secular and quasi-religious organizations; these tended to be partly Buddhist and partly Daoist in inclination. Because traditional temples were to some extent in decline, lay bodies and guilds appear to have played an important part in popular worship. At the same time many families maintained domestic altars. It seems possible that it was partly to provide the appropriate images and other furnishings for these devotions that the porcelain manufactures of Dehua were now raised to such an admirably high level.

Apart from ritual vases and incense burners, water bottles and lamps may also have been part of this altar furniture; at this period all are distinguished by the quality of material and manufacture described above (cat. nos. 12–15). Many wares seem on the other hand to be intended for the scholar's desk; the numerous brush holders, water pourers, and brush washers used in calligraphy and painting often have an archaic flavor or show a lively taste for adapting the forms of nature: the lotus leaf, the pomegranate and lichee, or the crab (cat. nos. 5–11). There are also a variety of vessels for tea and wine, and elegant drinking cups, sometimes poetically inscribed (cat. nos.16–21), which point to an atmosphere of refined sophistication that is reinforced by the presence here of a porcelain flute, apparently well-tuned musically and still playable, and a *qin* zither (which judging from its size is presumed to be a model) (cat. nos. 22–23). All these are shaped with a sensibility and technical skill that reveal the existence in the area of a thriving and cultivated clientele. The fact that wares of comparable quality are sometimes, even if only rarely, found in old European collections suggests that prior to the time when production of lesser quality items was stepped up to exploit this new market, perhaps soon after the middle of the seventeenth century, there may have been a phase during which visiting Western merchants were able to indulge in a superior choice.

The Figure Models of Dehua and their Makers

The truly unique distinction of Dehua's *blanc de Chine* is unquestionably its art of the figure model; and it is this that has dominated the interest of the modern viewer. Most of the images produced were meant for devotions, whether in public or domestic shrines, but their relatively modest size shows they cannot have been generally intended for major temple altars. Their subjects are preeminently Buddhist or Daoist, and their treatment tends to be responsive to popular perceptions of the deities concerned. The largely unrecorded sculptors who produced them had no doubt learnt their craft at the feet of model makers in other materials such as wood or clay or even soapstone, ivory, or rhinoceros horn.[28] Consideration of the art must begin with the potter who is generally recognized to have been its greatest exponent. He is known to us by the seals bearing his name that are stamped on rather too large a number of models in circulation today. But while dating, as we have seen, presents the student with recurring problems, it was disconcerting to find that virtually nothing is recorded about He Chaozong, not even the bare details of his life or indeed the fact that he was a potter. Donnelly writes with conviction: "I think he was a Kangxi potter. The evidence is slender, but it exists." In support of this he tells us that as well as figures He Chaozong made censers of a form that Donnelly dates with confidence to the second half of the seventeenth century. Finally, in issuing his list of tentative dates, he estimates that He Chaozong worked between 1665 and 1695.[29]

The gloom cast by the apparent fact that this distinguished artist lived without leaving any historical record was lifted a little when, in 1995, Professor Zeng Fan of the provincial university in Fuzhou appeared to have announced the discovery of his name in the regional gazetteer *Quanzhou fuzhi*, published during the late Ming in 1612.[30] This announcement was naturally enough taken up by other writers, but was so lacking in detail that it seemed essential to check the original. As Yuan Bingling explains in her following essay, she searched through a copy of this rare work in the university library at Fuzhou without being able to find such a passage. When another copy was found to exist in the British Library in London, a search was instituted there too; but Dr. Frances Wood, curator at the Library, who was kind enough to undertake the task, reported the same negative result. In Fuzhou, however, Yuan Bingling fortunately located and read a copy of the 1763 edition of the same work which, as she reports below, bore fruit. Here, in a section entitled "Ming specialists" (*yishu*), of whom no more than half a dozen are to be considered as artists, is the record that He Chaozong was a noted modeler of porcelain figures, lived in the Ming period, and, according to reports, came from Dehua. A meager biography indeed, but one that establishes for the first time the true nature of his craft and the time in which he worked.

The style of his output, which, it must be borne in mind, is known only from those few of the hundreds of models stamped with his seals that we have reason to believe are genuine—for there is no doubt he has been hugely plagiarized—is the main factor that leads us to place He Chaozong towards the end of the late Ming period, i.e., in the late sixteenth to early seventeenth centuries. This, of course, is to rely on an artistic judgment or on a firmly-held Chinese tradition. Can anything else enable us to fix the time of his activity? The earliest literary reference to the making of Dehua porcelain figures is the isolated one cited by Donnelly from a work dated 1604, which refers to "Buddhist figures now appearing in the market at Po-shan (Boshan)."[31] We may also of

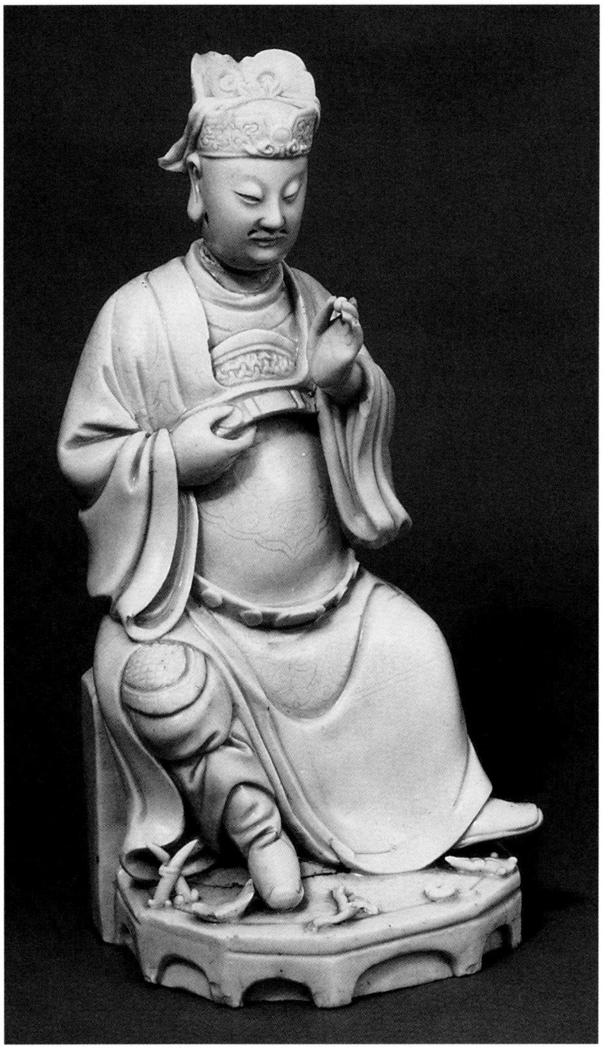

Fig. 4. Figure of God of Wealth (or perhaps Guandi) with inscription dated to the forty-seventh year of the Wanli reign, Ming dynasty, 1610. *Blanc-de-Chine* porcelain, h. 10⅜ in. (26.5 cm). British Museum, London (OA1930.11-13.1).

course compare his models with the only known *blanc-de-Chine* figure of this early period with a dated inscription, the so-called Caishen, God of Wealth, in the British Museum (fig. 4). The figure has no maker's mark, but is dated by an inscription on its back to the forty-seventh year of the Wanli reign, i.e., 1610.[32] Harrison-Hall remarks that the traditional identification of the deity as Caishen is now regarded as questionable, and that this may in fact be a representation of Guandi, a much more popular deity in late Ming times who had also come to be revered as a God of Wealth; in view of his greater popularity this may well be the more plausible interpretation. It is one of a number of unmarked early models, some of which show a relatively heavy and almost rough construction, to which those of He Chaozong would seem to be generally superior. Whether this is due to his greater natural ability or simply to his having been further down the road of technical development we can only guess; the latter alternative might support an even later dating for He, closer to that suggested by Donnelly (but nevertheless, according to the evidence just cited, still within the Ming, i.e., before 1644).

A credible model dated by He Chaozong himself would of course be most helpful, but the search proved fruitless until, in the last year of the millennium, one finally came to light in a New York collection (see cat. no. 25). Representing Guanyin enthroned in contemplation on a lotus base, dressed in voluminous white robes, and with her hands folded in her lap, this figure must count among He Chaozong's most perfect creations. His seal is stamped on the back, and the model is one of three known slightly varied examples, all of which are in collections in the United States.[33] The inscription, which appears on this example alone and consists of just three characters, was incised roughly in the porcelain on the front of the lotus base at the foot before glazing. It represents a date under the Chinese sixty-year cyclical system which, unless the reign name is also provided, is not precise and may be read variously as 1559, 1619, or 1679. Only the first two of these years fall within the Ming period, and the balance of evidence points firmly to the choice of 1619.

As we write, further evidence in this connection comes to hand in the form of the newly-published book by the leading *blanc-de-Chine* collector and lender to this exhibition, Robert H. Blumenfield, who in this work makes known to the world a Guanyin figure in his collection which has the unusual distinction of being backed by an inscribed mandorla.[34] He reports that the piece has a He Chaozong mark and that the inscription—written in an impure underglaze blue and made legible only by photography under ultraviolet light—states that the figure was made in the year of the Wanli reign corresponding to 1618. The eventual publication in full of the inscription and mark is eagerly awaited, but there can be no question that firm evidence now exists as to the activity of one who is undoubtedly Dehua's greatest figure modeler and who worked during the second decade of the seventeenth century: not, as Donnelly believed, during its later years.

We are fortunate in being able to exhibit no less than five He Chaozong marked models: an unusually rich representation of his work. In addition to the inscribed Guanyin just described are other models representing leading Buddhist deities, the subject matter to which, whether from personal choice or through demand, he seems to have been most devoted. Outstanding among these is the upright statue of Damo (Bodhidharma) (cat. no. 27), a Buddhist patriarch who, coming from the Indian subcontinent, is characteristically depicted as a bearded man with rather prominent eyes. He stands on the reed on which he is said to have crossed the Yangzi river for his meeting with the king of Wei, and his body is wrapped in long robes, the rhythmic folds of which emphasize the dignity and spiritual authority of one who is acknowledged as the founder of the contemplative Chan sect in China.

Comparable to this Damo in its refinement and majesty is another, different version of the bodhisattva Guanyin (cat. no. 26) from the collection of Ira M. Koger (now relocated to the Ringling Museum in Sarasota). In this model, the eternally popular Goddess of Mercy is shown standing with her hands beneath her elegant windswept robe; the waves lapping at her feet recall her role as the protector of seafarers. It may be appropriate to remark here on the color of the glaze of this figure, which despite its fine quality has something of the colder, less ivory appearance that is often associated with later products. The artistic and technical excellence of the model should however be enough to convince anyone who may be tempted to doubt it on these grounds. In addition, the seal stamped on the back is one of the most reliable of those found on He's works.[35] The subject of the viability of the various He Chaozong seals, of which Donnelly reproduces almost thirty, is too complex to explore here, but it is undoubtedly ripe for comprehensive research. This figure underlines an important lesson for the student, touching on something of which every experienced judge is aware: that contrary to an opinion often heard, glaze color, which may be the product of nothing more than differences in kiln atmosphere during the firing process, is no trustworthy rule-of-thumb guide to the dating of *blanc de Chine*.

While on the subject of devotional images with Buddhist subjects, it may seem remarkable that models of Sakyamuni Buddha are not among the most numerous in early *blanc de Chine,* and none is known to bear an early potter's seal. A seventeenth-century date is, however, appropriate for the unmarked model (cat. no. 32) which depicts him regally established on a lotus pedestal with a direct presence and simplicity of modeling that carry conviction. It seems unlikely that He Chaozong could have resisted the challenge of producing a Buddha image, but none is known. Another very popular image to be mentioned here on account of its Buddhist connections is that of the so-called hundred-armed Guanyin, a deity in fact of part-Hindu derivation by way of esoteric Buddhism and more properly known as Doumu, "the Dipper Mother" or "Goddess of the North Star,"[36] who has been described as the Daoist equivalent of Guanyin (cat. no. 33). Remarkably, an identical example survives today at Hampton Court Palace near London as part of a collection believed to have been formed by Queen Mary II prior to her death in 1694. Another example survived (at least until the Second World War) in the collection of her close relative, Louise Henriette, Electress of Brandenburg, and was inventoried at Oranienburg in 1688.[37] By this date, as is well known, European princely houses contained large numbers of rather crudely made figures of Guanyin. But these were models mass produced specifically for export (see fig. 5). This fantastic, many-armed image, which must have aroused much comment at the time, was probably intended originally for domestic use in China and must have won the attention of some shrewd visiting merchant on account of its curiosity value.

A further representation of Guanyin bearing He Chaozong's seal shows the merciful goddess seated on a reed mat and holding the scroll of wisdom, perhaps the Lotus Sutra (cat. no. 34). Another elegant version, bearing no mark but finely characterized and materially exquisite (cat. no. 36), again shows her in her role as patroness of seamen, enthroned on a rockwork base as at the shrine dedicated to her on the island of Putuoshan.

The figure of Wenchang (cat. no. 40), seated in august majesty on a low throne, wearing formal robes and an official's hat, and bearing the *ruyi* scepter of office, shows He Chaozong exercising his talents with an equally sure touch on a Daoist subject.[38] He's equal aptitude for the smaller sculptural format is revealed in his finely-observed treatment of the popular subject Li Taibai (cat. no. 43), a celebrated eighth-century poet depicted reclining beside his much-loved wine jar.

Apart from He Chaozong, three other modelers are represented here whose activity may well have overlapped his and whose lives also remain undocumented. Their link in time seems supported by material and technical features, and by the overall similarity of their stylistic approach. The seated figure of Damo (cat. no. 28) is marked with the otherwise unknown seal of Chen Shixin,[39] while the handling of the grizzled features at once invites comparison with He's treatment of him (cat. no. 27). A related version of the same subject from the Metropolitan Museum of Art (cat. no. 30) is another most compelling image of the patriarch, and it is a surprise to find no maker's mark on it.

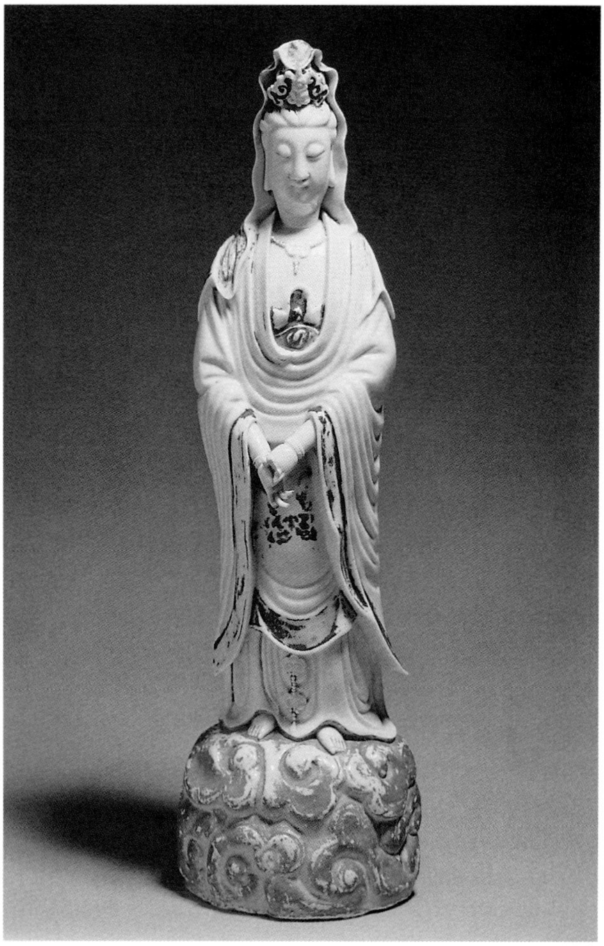

Fig. 5. Typical export figure of Guanyin (Goddess of Mercy) on the waves, Qing dynasty, ca. 1660–90. *Blanc-de-Chine* porcelain, h. 18⅝ in. (47.3 cm). Hampton Court Palace (RCIN 1101), The Royal Collection © 2002, Her Majesty Queen Elizabeth II.

A rather smaller seated figure of Damo in Chicago was made by a member of another celebrated family of potters and bears the stamped seal of Lin Chaojing.[40] The work of his presumed relative Lin Xiaozong is represented in the exhibition in the form of a distinctly appealing figure of Guanyin, charmingly conceived as seated in a lotus leaf that floats on the water (cat. no. 29). In this modeler's work, of which once again few examples are known, we are aware of a sculptural manner somewhat more distinct from that of He Chaozong: the less sharp finishing of the drapery folds contributes to a somewhat softer overall effect. There seems no particular reason, however, why he should be dated as late as the "1680–1710" ascribed to him by Donnelly.

Our fourth early figure modeler—and it will be noted that all are ascribed here to the late Ming period or soon after—is Zhang Shoushan. Donnelly located five models in England with his seal and a single one in the United

States,[41] which its present owner has generously made available. It is an entertaining study of two boys (cat. no. 42), the "Heavenly Twins" (*hehe erxian*) of Daoist mythology, who are, very suitably, the patron deities of potters. The pair are seated together in hilarious conversation, while one has on his lap a box from which a bat, an emblem of happiness, is attempting to escape. Other models by Zhang, notably the standing Damo in the Percival David Foundation,[42] seem to echo the style of He Chaozong as displayed in works such as his Damo (cat. no. 27) described above, although they perhaps lack quite the same self-assured mastery. The present *hehe erxian* group in fact bears a close resemblance to the version of this subject by He which belongs to that London collection and is little if at all inferior to it.[43]

Among other models the connotations of which can be called Daoist, or which were simply the objects of intense popular devotion, may be mentioned the Earth God, Tudi (cat. no. 48), whose image, as Yuan Bingling recounts, was everywhere to be found in roadside shrines. These models generally seem rather small and unremarkable. Other favored subjects are Zhenwu, the Dark Warrior and Lord of the North Star who defeated the legions of the demon-kings, depicted as always with the tortoise and snake associated with him in legend (cat. no. 41); and Shoulao, the much-loved God of Long Life (cat. no. 45) and convenor of the Eight Daoist Immortals, who is depicted here with his familiar crane and stag. There is also Guandi, the God of War and sanctified embodiment of General Guan Yu of the Han dynasty, who is shown seated astride his warlike charger (cat. no. 47). Less familiar or standardized models are those that represent certain of these well-loved divinities grouped in various ways with their associates, such as that involving an unknown deity and his attendant arbiters of the fortunes of mankind (cat. no. 44) or another that depicts the saintly Wenchang in an apparent state of inebriation and requiring the support of his demonic associate Kuixing (cat. no. 46).

There is still little that shows the extent to which these *blanc-de-Chine* models were appreciated in China outside the area of Fujian province in which they were produced.[44] To know more of the specific locations appropriate to particular subjects would also be of interest. It is notable that few if any of the models are approximate in size to the carved wooden images we are accustomed to find on Chinese altars. The larger and more imposing pieces may have been destined for shrines within Buddhist or Daoist temples, or in the halls of the lay guilds and associations which, as Yuan Bingling explains, flourished in southern Fujian during the golden century. It remains strange, however, that we so rarely find evidence of their being commissioned and inscribed accordingly. Many localities and institutions had their own patron deities, not all of whom might be readily identifiable to Western eyes. The lesser models were no doubt more often destined for private altars, while some of the rougher and cheaper versions were probably intended for pilgrims visiting sites such as, for example, the Putuoshan shrine to Guanyin.

The Export of *Blanc-de-Chine* Wares to the West

The *blanc-de-Chine* wares made for export to the West deserve a full separate study, although no such work (apart from Donnelly's) appears to have been undertaken. In recent years a great deal has been written about the porcelain trade between China and the outside world, most of it however concerned with the imports of Jingdezhen wares, particularly during the later centuries, when a massive trade was conducted through the port of Canton. The Dutch East India Company, with its eastern base at Batavia (present-day Djakarta in what is now Indonesia), maintained their outstation Fort Zeelandia on the island of Formosa (Taiwan) just across the straits from the ports of Fujian from 1624 until 1662, when it was overrun by the pirate/warlord Coxinga; during this period some *blanc de Chine* must surely have been shipped to Europe by this route. The English Companies, with their less secure foothold at Bantam in Java, traded where they could in the seventeenth century, and reports indicate that Amoy (modern Xiamen) on the Fujian coast, some seventy miles south of Dehua, was a favored port of call. By the early eighteenth century this place is regularly recorded as their loading point in the records of the Company in London, where in some cargoes a high proportion of the goods are readily identifiable as *blanc-de-Chine* models.

There is now mounting evidence of the extent to which imports reached collections in Europe in the course of the seventeenth century.[45] Among the most numerous of the early imports were the pairs of ceremonial Buddhist lions or "dogs of Fo" (sometimes mistakenly called "kylins," which are a different, mythical animal) (cat. no. 49), and their continuing presence on import lists of the early eighteenth century indicates their enduring popularity. The lions vary much in style and in size, but characteristically are seated on rectangular plinths, the female being distinguished by her accompanying cub and the male by an embroidered ball with which he plays. A white lion was listed among the effects of the Dutch painter Jan Blasse in the year 1637,[46] and a pair of such lions in a Hong Kong collection is dated in accordance with 1645.[47]

An inventory taken in 1641 of the contents of Tart Hall, belonging to the celebrated English art collector the Earl of Arundel, lists among the contents of the "pranketing hall" (apparently a Dutch fashion for dining arrangements) a variety of items, including a number of white figures of lions and of women, which were undoubtedly *blanc-de-Chine* models. Inventories made for diverse purposes in 1688 and 1690 at Burghley House, the home of another illustrious family, the Cecils, list a range of identifiable wares and models, a good proportion of which are still there today. Among these are "white lyons," "ffaulcons" (i.e., hawks), "2 white lyons with figures on them," and "large white ffigures with children in their lapps (Guanyin); also 2 figures sitting in Chaires" (Earth gods?) and "1 ball'd fryor sitting" (i.e., Budai).[48] The previously mentioned historic collection at Hampton Court, which has ten pieces including a Guanyin with child, and other investigated inventories of the period extend the story.[49] Among the earliest known figures of Guanyin is one bearing an inscription and dedication with the date corresponding to 1629 and which is reported to be in a Hong Kong collection.[50] The goddess is enthroned on a rocky base with the books of wisdom and an alms bowl beside her and figures of her two acolytes below her. This model was certainly not intended for export (on account of its inscription, which offers thanks for the gift of a child), has no modeler's seal, and is apparently not of the very highest quality; but there are points of marked similarity between it and another more specifically connected with the West. This is the figure represented in a drawing that appears as a marginal illustration to a map published in Blaeuw's *Nieuw Atlas* of 1655;[51] the illustration actually belonged to an atlas produced by Father Martinus, who is said to have returned from China to Europe in 1651. An undamaged example of what is evidently the original porcelain model for this drawing (illustrated alongside the model in the exhibition) is lent by the Virginia Museum of Art (cat. no. 50). It seems likely that a number of examples of this model in fact reached the West in the mid-seventeenth century.

Direct Western influence on the Dehua factories at this time is another intriguing development, indicated by a number of Christian images and other objects which must have resulted from the copying of models supplied by missionary communities in the East. A unique *blanc-de-Chine* figure of the infant Christ, closely related to models in other materials that belonged to the Portuguese missions in India in the late sixteenth century, has been preserved in Vienna; and in a recent exhibition catalogue this somewhat primitive-looking piece is ascribed (without further evidence) to that period.[52] Better known are a number of tall, slender models of the Madonna holding a child which no doubt resulted from a similar influence (cat. no. 56) and for which a date around the third quarter of the seventeenth century seems appropriate. More mysterious are some models of what appear to be church pulpits of unexplained use, with ladders on one side and a stumpy protrusion in the center (cat. no. 57). Strangely enough, the lists of cargoes up for sale in London in about 1702 include an entry for "pulpits with padries," but no one has yet produced a satisfactory explanation of where these "padries," perhaps "padres," have disappeared to.[53]

Other instances of wares made to Western order are the cups and mugs (e.g., cat. no. 64) copied from European vessels, which must date from the late seventeenth century.[54] Perhaps more ambiguous are some cases of models and groups in which Europeans or other foreigners are represented. Can we assume none of these were made to meet the curiosity of Chinese purchasers? Prominent among them is the well-known group known as "the Dutch Family" (cat. no. 58), in which the couple are seen seated by a small table with two children and a dog. The list of a cargo of porcelain for sale in London in 1703 includes in addition to these "Dutch familyes," "Dutch troupers" and "men on horses" (see cat. no. 59) among others, as well as a variety of inexpensively priced and presumably small models of figures riding on different animals (cat. no. 62), and whistles (cat. no. 63). There follows a long list of birds and animals, including lions and hawks, recalling the "ffaucons" in the 1688 inventory from Burghley.[55] The presence of all these in the cargo of the *Dashwood*, which was loaded at Amoy in the winter of 1701, is uniquely valuable evidence of date; and it is notable that all this cargo was apparently permitted as "private trade," i.e., the property not of the Company but of the ship's crew. There was hardly enough profit in such "curiosities" to interest the ship's owners, who may have called at Amoy mainly to buy tea or to collect the goods that were regularly brought there from Japan. In Europe however such baubles were all

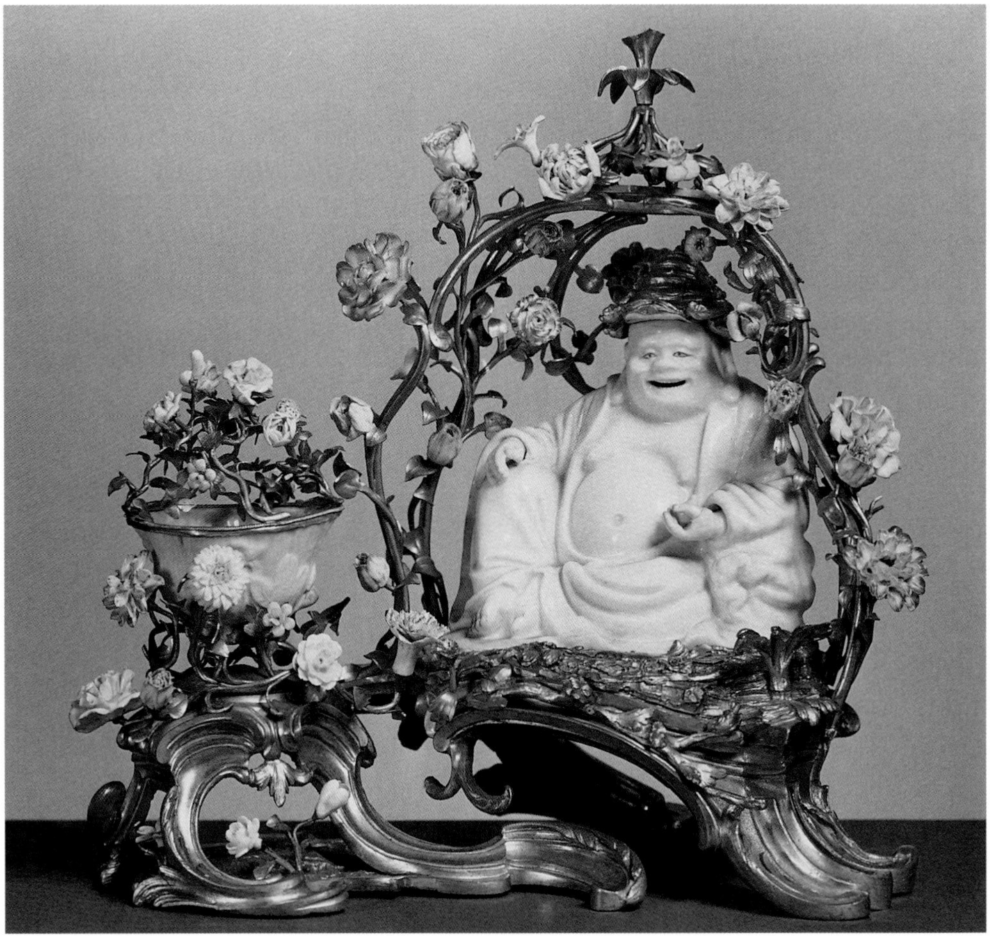

Fig. 6. *Blanc-de-Chine* figure of Budai mounted with a cup and flowers of Meissen porcelain in French ormolu with the crowned "c" mark for 1745–49. Qing dynasty, early 18th century. Porcelain with metal mount, h. 14 in. (35.6 cm). The Walters Art Museum, Baltimore.

the rage, and it would seem that Augustus the Strong was keen to possess examples of every known model.

The last English East India Company sale of which records are noted by Godden was in 1707, and thereafter references to *blanc de Chine* virtually cease for the rest of the century, the bulk of the Company's porcelain trade and that of the other Western nations now being conducted through Canton, where an officially sanctioned system of trading had been established. If *blanc de Chine* was still obtainable through the ports of Southeast Asia, we have no records of such transactions.

In Holland certainly, *blanc-de-Chine* pieces were sought after by the freelance porcelain enamelers, who were able to convert them into the equivalent of "famille verte," "famille rose," or "Kakiemon," which were always in demand. An example of this is the piece in the European form known as a porringer (cat. no. 67), to which a colorful design has been added in the form of a family coat of arms. Particularly during this period also, like other kinds of porcelain, some *blanc-de-Chine* wares were adorned with silver mounts, often of Dutch workmanship, as in the case of the mug (cat. no. 64) and the splendidly gilt teapot (cat. no. 65); while the French love of the material is revealed in their liking for mounting figures or vessels in costly ormolu for use as elegant room decorations in the rococo style (see fig. 6 for a fine example belonging to the Walters Art Gallery, Baltimore).

The Decline of the European Trade; and the Problem of the 18th Century at Dehua

The question of what happened at the Dehua kilns in the period following the decline of the European trade, which in view of its relatively modest size can hardly have been disastrous, is hard to answer because no records have been reported in China. Donnelly assigned a variety of pieces to an eighteenth-century date, usually on the basis of their style, and assumed a continuity of output that should not perhaps be taken for granted. While not confronting the question directly, he seems to have been aware of a decline in the purity of the style, expressed perhaps in a less classic perfection of form and in fussier decoration. However, there is no doubt that the production of lower quality wares for Southeast Asia went on and may well have flourished, possibly to the extent that this became their principal manufacture.

Recovery from the seabed of the contents of various ill-fated vessels engaged in this trade suggests a trend already visible in the case of a Chinese ship discovered in 1989 off the coast of Vietnam; its cargo, the so-called Vung Tao cargo, was offered for sale in Amsterdam.[56] Carrying a substantial quantity of fine Kangxi blue-and-white ware reliably dateable to the 1690s, the ship was apparently making for Batavia with a view to the onward transmission of this material to Holland. A part of its contents consisted of some hundreds of *blanc-de-Chine* porcelains possibly also intended in part for Holland; for in addition to wares of traditional Southeast Asian type they included a batch of small Guanyin figures and a few thousand coarse porcelains—mainly bowls and dishes that were catalogued for the Amsterdam sale as "provincial wares." These were plainly not made for Europe but for markets in Asia, and more than half of them are painted with simple designs in blue. If not from Dehua, these wares probably would have come from kilns in adjoining areas of Fujian. With taste in this important overseas market veering in the direction of blue-and-white ware, Dehua would surely have been obliged to match its competitors, and there is no doubt that a substantial shift towards the production of these painted wares had taken place there by the following century.[57] Confirmation of this trend in Fujian production is provided by the wreck in 1823 of the great junk *Tek Sing*, sailing from Amoy with a cargo that Captain Hatcher found to include literally thousands of blue-and-white table wares together with a proportionately minor amount of export quality *blanc de Chine*.[58]

What was happening meanwhile, one must wonder, to Dehua's other great asset: its ancient ability to produce figure models of unrivaled quality? We do not know to what extent they may have remained in demand for devotional purposes, and Donnelly's survey of figures and their marks in collections worldwide offers very few candidates for the period, apart from the large but possibly irrelevant group that bear the "fisherman" mark. It would be presumptuous indeed to conclude that no fine *blanc-de-Chine* figures at all were made during the two centuries leading up to 1890, but for the time being we are faced with few credible candidates and an almost total lack of evidence. The recently-compiled compendium of biographies[59] refers briefly to the careers of two sculptors, Deng Xiang and Xu Liangxi, who lived in the Qing period; the latter is specifically associated with Dehua, but this statement on their behalf remains unsubstantiated by any document. Their dates are not known, and no work with the signature or seals of either appears to have been recorded.

Figure Modelers of the Late Qing and Following Periods

Too little is known of the views of other scholars in China on this subject; however a few years ago, following a visit to London, Professor Zeng Fan of the provincial university in Fuzhou—better known perhaps for his work on the kiln sites of Song dynasty Jian wares—presented the Oriental Ceramic Society with a paper entitled "Additional Comments on the Dehua Kilns," a summary of which was printed.[60] After outlining the nature of late Ming production and the work of He Chaozong and others, he takes a leap across two centuries or more and says: "As well as the Ming potters, there are a considerable number of pieces made by Su Xuejin (1869–1919) and Xu Youyi (1887–1940)." He then describes the work of all three men, beginning with the statement about He Chaozong's appearance in the *Quanzhou fuzhi* that has been misread to mean he was named in the 1612 edition, which we now know is not the case. Describing the career of Su Xuejin (other names Guanquan, Wenyu) late in the Qing period, Zeng remarks that Su was the son of an established country craftsman in clay and wood carving; and that he followed the family tradition, excelling in imitating the works of He Chaozong to the extent that they are hard to distinguish. Using his name "Wenyu," Su made a wide range of legendary and historical religious figures. He also used the marks *Dehua* in seal script and *Da Ming Wanli nianzhi* in regular script. His other seals include *Su Wenyu* and *puji yuren*. Some special pieces are also inscribed "handmade by Su Xuejin." (Through an unfortunate error, the mark *puji yuren*, nowadays read as *boji yuren*, was in fact mistakenly printed as *pu yuren* in Zeng's manuscript and appears thus in the translation, a confusion arising from the fact that the character *ji*, which was added in ink, had been missed.) Another publication gives a fuller account of the work of this important modeler which, because of his relatively recent date, may be accepted with some confidence.[61] Zeng Fan continues in his paper to describe the career of Xu Youyi (Jingyong, Yunlin; 1887–1940), which brings us effectively into modern times. He too was the descendant of generations of "craft modelers of Buddhist figures and woodcarvers. He became a disciple of Su 'Wenyu' as a young man and was skilled in making delicate and intricate pieces." Xu Youyi used the gourd-shaped seal *Dehua,* the square vase-shaped seal *Xu Yunlin,* and the square seal-script mark *Xu Yuyuan zhi.* Once again this is an essentially credible account. There is information too about the descendants of these two potters, whose work won international awards and, in sum, had the character of a full-scale revival of the figure modeler's art. There is little doubt that on occasion they continued to make use of the marks introduced by their immediate predecessors, as well as those of the much-admired Ming masters. It is surely remarkable that no other aspect of Dehua's production over the preceding two centuries, apart from the work of these men, struck this native commentator as being worthy of discussion.

In view of their historical importance therefore it seemed important that the work of these two potters should be represented in the exhibition (see cat. nos. 68–77). Regarding Su Xuejin, it must be said at once that his use of the mark *boji yuren* associates him directly with the "fisherman" whose work Donnelly ascribed to the late eighteenth or early nineteenth century. The meaning of this cryptic phrase and reason for its use remain obscure, but it has been suggested that he may have adopted it as a boastful expression of the aspiration represented by his new workshop: along the lines of the modern advertising motto. That he also used the Wanli date mark probably also resolves the question about the group of pieces having that mark and which share their general material characteristics with the "fisherman" pieces; but unfortunately none of these could be located for the exhibition.

An unusual distinction belongs to Su Xuejin's elegant Guanyin figure (cat. no. 71), which has been brought from afar on account of it. This figure, which has the seal *boji yuren* stamped on the back, evidently went to England soon after it was made, and according to credible family history was given in 1897 as a wedding present to the grandparents of the present owner; it has descended unaccompanied by any written document but with its original fitted silk-lined box: an altogether satisfactory proof that the "fisherman" mark belongs to the 1890s.[62] The cold-looking glaze is characteristic of all our works by Su Xuejin, and in traditional models such as this and his Buddha (cat. no. 68), which give little scope for truly original treatment, we see him in his role as the revivalist of an honored late Ming tradition. His somewhat chilly Magu with a fawn (cat. no. 70) and the lively figure of Liu Hai with his three-legged toad (cat. no. 69) show more evidence of his powers of invention, which are further confirmed by perusing the numerous illustrations of his work that have appeared regularly in the catalogues of Chinese porcelain auctions over the past half century.

Xu Youyi's standing Buddha (cat. no. 72) seems just as closely based on late Ming models, but there is a richness and complexity in the modeling of his Buddhist Guardians (cat. nos. 73, 74) that is decidedly engaging and would have appealed widely to international taste in the age of their production; although our final exhibit, the amazing "dream boat" of the goddess Xiwangmu (cat. no. 77), will no doubt be regarded by many viewers today as "over the top." It is certainly far from being a work of devotion. Many unmarked figures exist, such as the reclining immortal Li Tieguai from the Virginia Museum of Art (cat. no. 76), which display a degree of artistic freedom not often on view in earlier Chinese devotional sculpture, and many such adventurous models no doubt await publication in collections around the world where *blanc-de-Chine* figures are treasured not only for their classic perfection of form but also for the rare quality of artistic invention expressed, as always, through the magical appeal of the porcelain material.

Notes

1. As cited by Hobson 1915, vol. 2, p. 109; see also translation by Geoffrey R. Sayer, ed. and trans., *Jingdezhen taolu*, by Lan Pu and Zheng Tinggui ([London]: Routledge & K. Paul, 1951), p. 68.
2. Contrary to some opinion, it is interesting to note that the use of the term in France was mentioned as early as 1876 by A.W. Franks in his *Catalogue of a Collection of Oriental Porcelain and Pottery Lent for Exhibition at the Bethnal Green Museum* (London, 1876).
3. Hobson 1915, vol. 2, chap. 7.
4. Hobson 1915, vol. 2, pp. 113–14; Brinkley 1903, vol. 9, p. 273.
5. Freedman 1985; Ayers 1986.
6. While this catalogue was in preparation there arrived Heidi Tan's informative and forward-looking catalogue of the Hickley Collection in Singapore. Surprisingly on account of the title page, it must be referred to as Kerr and Ayers 2002, although these two individuals are responsible only for some introductory pages. At the same time comes the announcement of the imminent publication of Robert H. Blumenfield's *Blanc de Chine: The Great Porcelain of Dehua* (Berkeley, 2002), from which further enlightenment is to be expected.
7. For example, Pamela Hickley, as cited by Heidi Tan in Kerr and Ayers 2002, p. 17.
8. Rose Kerr, in Kerr and Ayers 2002, p. 10, provides a list of families and the districts with which they are connected.
9. Xu Yixing 1993.
10. Kwok 1993 and 2002, pp. 47–48; Zeng 1990, p. 25. The same point was in fact made in an exhibition arranged by Anne Farrer at the British Museum in 1986, for which there was unfortunately no catalogue.
11. Donnelly 1969, p. 286.
12. Honey 1945, pl. 144.
13. Donnelly 1969, p. 285; for another just-published example, see the seated Guanyin in the Hickley Collection, Kerr and Ayers 2002, no. 2.
14. For a general survey from the Chinese viewpoint, see Ye and Xu 1980, and more specifically for Southeast Asia, Sullivan 1962, and for the Philippines, Locsin 1967, 1976.
15. Wood 1995.
16. Aga-Oglu 1975, p. 4 and figs. 78–96; see also Locsin 1968.
17. Sullivan 1957.
18. See Ho Chuimei 2002, p. 36. Rather confusing accounts are provided by a variety of other reports, see also Southeast Asia Ceramic Society, *Chinese Translations,* no. 2 (Singapore, 1980); and Ye and Xu 1980, which embraces the wider aspect of the overseas trade.
19. Donnelly 1969, p. 49, pl. 6A; Harrison-Hall 2001, no. 17:1, p. 508.
20. Xu and Chen 1996, pp. 20–21, figs. 2 and 3.
21. Locsin 1976, p. 6.
22. Donnelly 1969, pl. 6b and c.
23. Note for example the absence of Ming Dehua wares at Ardebil in Iran and their limited appearance in the great assemblage of porcelain at Istanbul: Pope 1956; Krahl 1986.
24. Donnelly 1969, pp. 61–62.
25. E.g., see R. Kilburn, "Chinese Porcelain in late 17th Century Inventories," in Hinton and Impey 1998, pp. 69–78.
26. Christie's Amsterdam 1984 and 1985.
27. Freedman 1985; Ayers 1986, reprinted in Kerr and Ayers 2002.
28. Xu Yixing 1993. It has been suggested by Derek Gillman that the expansion of porcelain production at Dehua in late Ming times was encouraged by the success of the ivory carvings produced in neighboring Zhangzhou, where production was spurred by the patronage of Spanish visitors to this port in the late 16th century (see Oriental Ceramic Society 1984, p. 50).
29. Donnelly 1969, pp. 273, 286.
30. Zeng 1995, p. 26.
31. Donnelly 1969, p. 132.
32. Hobson, R.L., "Descriptions of Specimens Exhibited," *Transactions of the Oriental Ceramic Society 1930–31*, p. 12; Donnelly 1969, pl. 71A; Ayers 1986, figs. 12–13; Harrison-Hall 2001, no. 17:8, pp. 511–12.
33. For the others see Ayers 1985, pl. 147, and Blumenfield 2002, p. 130, pls. A and B.
34. Blumenfield 2002, pp. 163–65, pls. A and B.
35. Donnelly 1969, p. 356, no. F.1.x.
36. Little 2000, p. 98.
37. Reidemeister 1932.
38. For another example of the same model reversed in the Fuzhou Provincial Museum, see Hong Kong 1990, no. 103.
39. Chinese Porcelain Company 2000, no. 70.
40. Donnelly 1969, pl. 140D.
41. Donnelly 1969, pls. 138 and 139.
42. Donnelly 1969, pl. 138D.
43. Donnelly 1969, pl. 149B.
44. Wilson 1998, p. 98, discusses a Guanyin figure apparently inscribed to record the commission for it issued by one Liu Menglong, an inhabitant of Jiangxi province early in the eighteenth century; no other instance of such an order is known.
45. Freedman 1985; Ayers 1986.
46. Donnelly 1969, p. 144.
47. Donnelly 1969, pl. 74A.
48. Lang 1983.
49. Kilburn 1998.
50. Donnelly 1969, pl. 71B.
51. Ayers 1986, p. 29.
52. Lisbon 2001, no. 88.
53. Godden 1979, pp. 266–72.
54. Fichtner 1937.
55. Godden 1979, pp. 264–68.
56. Christie's Amsterdam 1992.
57. The sheer volume and variety of later Dehua blue-and-white ware are illustrated in a recent survey, Chen 1999, which is based on the study of kiln-site material.
58. Freedman 2000.
59. Xu Yixing 1993.
60. Zeng 1995, pp. 25–27.
61. Xu Yixing 1993.
62. At the same time the recipients were given a similar box containing a pair of enameled figures of birds, typical Jingdezhen work of the same period. Perhaps all had been boxed up in Hong Kong, where it is said the Dehua potters took their wares for the international market.

Dehua White Ceramics and their Cultural Significance

Yuan Bingling

Minnan (Southern Fujian) in Historical Perspective

The district of Dehua is situated on the eastern slopes of the Daiyun Mountains of southern Fujian, some 50 miles inland at an altitude of fifteen hundred feet. The name Dehua, which means "Virtuous Cultivation," was bestowed by Taizu of Min (909–925), a monarch who established Fujian as an independent kingdom.[1] His dynasty did not reign for long, but it gained everlasting fame in ballads and local lore. During the next few centuries, the poor, hilly, and, in those times, still densely forested region of Dehua became the hinterland of the rich port of Quanzhou on the Fujian coast (fig. 7).

Dehua has always been closely linked to Quanzhou, which formerly could be reached, first by road to Yongchun and then by boat over the river Taoxi, in about two days of travel. Like the citizens of Quanzhou, the inhabitants of Dehua speak the Hokkien (Minnan) tongue. Their main link to the larger religious and commercial networks of southern Fujian is the worship of the regional saint Baosheng dadi, to whom the largest temple in the market town of Dehua is dedicated.[2] The founding temple of the Baosheng dadi cult is situated in the village of Baijiao on the shore of the Jiulong River. This is in Quanzhou territory, but also near Zhangzhou and Xiamen. Here were situated the great ports of Yuegang, Anpinggang, and other harbors that became the trading centers of Fujian after the port of Quanzhou had silted up (see below).

Quanzhou, known by Marco Polo as Zayton and viewed by him as the richest city on earth, had become at that time, thanks to the farsighted policy of the abovementioned king of Min, the gateway of China.[3] He sponsored the building of seaworthy sailing vessels and sent his envoys to Southeast Asia and the Ryûkyû Islands. The tribute paid by these states to the throne of China, and later to his own kingdom, came in through Quanzhou. Exports, mostly luxury goods like silk, lacquer, and stoneware (the famous celadon wares), were sent abroad in return, making the city the starting point of the so-called maritime silk road. Even when the Song dynasty unified China in 960 and subjected the fledgling Fujian kingdom of Min to its rule, Quanzhou remained the main trading center of the empire, a place it maintained right until the end of the fourteenth century. The silting up of the bay and the bloody wars that marked the end of the Mongol dynasty (Yuan, 1277–1367) put an end to Quanzhou's greatness.

The succeeding Ming dynasty maintained a strong nationalist and anti-foreign policy, inspired by the threats of the Mongols on the northern frontier and all kinds of pirates in the southern seas. All sea trade was forbidden, and government troops were stationed permanently in Fujian to guard the coast. After some time, the port of Quanzhou was reopened to again allow the Ryûkyû Islands to present tribute. This measure, however, did not result in increased trade. The tradition of shipbuilding and high-sea navigation that had become the specialties of southern Fujian now found no other outlet than illegal trade, at times with the active participation of Japanese and other foreign merchants. New harbors appeared on the coast around the estuary of the Jiulong River, away from Quanzhou and even farther away from Fuzhou, the seat of the provincial authority. These were the ports of Yuegang (near present-day Haicheng, the port city of Zhangzhou) and Anpinggang (present-day Anhai), at the southern end of Nan'an County, twenty-five miles south of Quanzhou. In these new places, small vessels could hide in creeks near the harbors, in order to escape whatever official scrutiny there was.

In spite of its illegal nature, trade developed on a massive scale, spurred on by Chinese commercial expansion in Southeast Asia. Trading posts on the routes between Fujian and India were manned with emigrants from southern Fujian joined later by their ethnic cousins from Chaozhou (Swatow), Putian, and Fuzhou. The volume and diversity of trade increased. No longer were precious products from overseas matched with Chinese luxury goods. Trade in bulk freight developed, including all kinds of foodstuff. Spices, timber, and minerals were imported, while a thriving local economy produced silks and cotton cloth, ceramics, tea, sugar, dyes, and also paper and printed books for

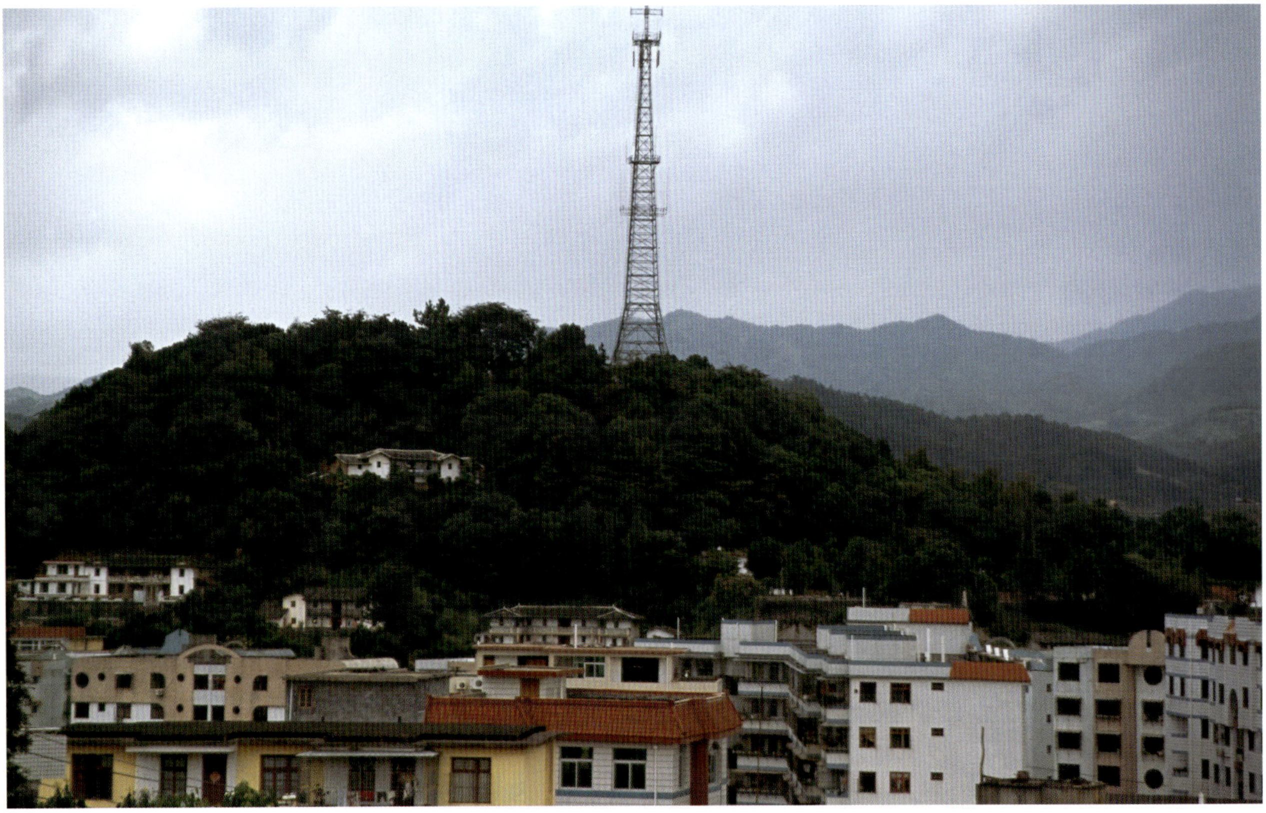

Fig. 7. A view of Dehua. Photo courtesy of Yuan Bingling.

the export market. Such was the scope and importance of this trade that historians nowadays tend to think that the maritime expansion of European nations (Spain and Portugal, and later England and the Netherlands) linked up in the Far East with what was essentially an already existing Minnan trading network.

The Golden Century (1563–1664)

Two hundred years after the founding of the Ming dynasty, the strain of the costly upkeep of coastal garrisons in Fujian in the face of the enormous gains made through illegal trading and contraband became so critical as to make the government yield. In 1563 the port of Yuegang became a legal place for trading with foreigners. A form of maritime customs was installed that soon yielded vast sums of money for the Fujian treasury. Other ports, such as Anpinggang were also opened. Traders from Spain and Portugal, and later from other Western European countries, joined Japanese and Malay traders on the Fujian coast. A golden period in maritime trade began and was to last until 1664, when the new Qing dynasty installed another total embargo.

Fujian overseas expansion during this period and the resulting prosperity had far-reaching results at home. One of the major impacts was of a religious nature. The government had always tried to finance its expenditures for maritime defense in the province through taxes imposed largely on the rural population. Arable land in Fujian, however, has always been at a premium, as the province is largely composed of mountainous regions. Moreover, much valuable acreage had long ago become the property of Buddhist monasteries, which were exempt from paying taxes. The insufficient tax yields created a trend to take this land away from the clerics and make it yield income for the government and its representatives; the Confucian elite took, therefore, an ever stronger anti-Buddhist stance. When the new merchant bourgeoisie emerged, it generally turned away from supporting the traditional Buddhist monastic institutions in order to pursue more personal and private forms of religion.[4] Lay Buddhist associations developed rapidly, checked only by the threat of being considered by the government as heterodox sectarian movements.

Another marked development was the rise in local temple organizations for the worship of popular saints and deities generally incorporated into the Daoist pantheon. These temple associations often functioned as guilds and merchant corporations. They were run by the lay members themselves and were independent and democratic in nature. Temples were mutually linked through networks of affiliations, insuring cooperation and mutual protection. The adoption of Mazu as the patron saint of Fujian merchants, for instance, spread the cult throughout the coastal region with the founding or restoring of temples in her honor by Minnan merchant-guilds in the large commercial centers where they operated.[5] Temple committees were never directed by priests, but were wont to hire secular Daoist and Buddhist ritual specialists whenever the need for their services arose. In the great port cities of Fujian, there was an ever-increasing number of temples and related organizations.[6]

We find during the golden century of Fujian a society that was very different from the Chinese stereotype. It was not the imperial government and its bureaucracy of scholar-officials that yielded the greatest authority and set the standards for religion and culture; instead, rich merchants and artisans, such as the famous Zheng family, were the leading elite. Foremost among the merchants was Zheng Zhilong (1604–1661), who built a trading empire that stretched from Malakka to Japan.[7] In the religious sphere, Buddhist lay associations and local temple networks had largely replaced large monasteries and officially recognized institutions. The search for a new society with greater individual freedom is best exemplified through the works of the anti-conformist philosopher Li Zhi (1527–1602) of Quanzhou, who attacked the authoritarian and hypocritical society created by the reactionary Confucians of his time and advocated absolute equality before the law for all.[8]

The refined culture of those times can still be appreciated. It is evident, for instance, in the exquisite temple architecture of southern Fujian. Nowadays only a few buildings of that era survive in the Minnan region itself, but many of those built by the Fujian merchants in Southeast Asia, especially in Indonesia, still exist. Another great cultural treasure is the highly refined and universally beautiful Nanyin music of Quanzhou and Zhangzhou, the only form of Asiatic music that has developed a precise musical scoring system and which requires a conductor to be performed.[9] The temple associations established special conservatories for the transmission of this art; it was only taught to respected and wealthy citizens, male as well as female, who performed strictly as amateurs. And finally, this refined culture can be seen in the *blanc-de-Chine* porcelain of Dehua, which attained its true artistic expression during this very period.

WHITENESS AND PURITY

Religious objects figured prominently in the *blanc-de-Chine* art of the Ming period. This means that the white porcelain incense burners, candlesticks, flower vases, and, most of all, the small and large statuettes representing a variety of deities and saints were intended to be used in worship.[10] We can see from their size as well as from current usage that they were not made for temples or monasteries, but for the home altars of Fujian families and the private prayer halls of lay Buddhist associations.

But before we say more about these issues, we should perhaps address the general question of the emergence of this particular art form. It may seem surprising indeed that this kind of religious art appeared in a culture where white is related to rituals of death and mourning and is therefore generally considered to be inauspicious. In fact, white statuettes of saints and deities, as well as ritual utensils, appeared during the Ming dynasty not only in Dehua but also earlier in Jingdezhen.

One of the reasons may well be an imperial decree of 1370, at the very beginning of the Ming dynasty, concerning the vessels to be used for state rituals. It stipulated that henceforward all ritual vessels should be made of porcelain and imitate archaic forms. As stated in the *Mingshi* (History of the Ming):

> In the third year of the Hongwu era, a report from the Ministry of Rites said: "According to the 'Jiaotesheng' (Chapter on the Special Sacrifice on the Altar of Heaven) in the *Liji* (Records on the Rites) it is said, 'For the sacrifice in the Southern Suburb, ceramic vessels should be used, as it is the most plain [material].' In the 'Bianren' (Chapter on the Attendants of the Sacrificial Vases) of the *Zhouli* (Rites of the Zhou) it is said, 'There are the [different species] of the sacrificial grains and viands to be offered'; and the (canonical) commentary adds, 'in all cases when offerings are made to the gods, ceramic vessels should be used.'
>
> "That nowadays for the sacrifices we use porcelain (*ci*) is therefore in accordance with the ancient rules. The only [problem] is that the forms of the plates and water bowls are different from the *fu, gui, deng,* and *xing* of ancient times. We now recommend that all sacrificial vessels be made of porcelain, and that their forms imitate those used in ancient times. Only the *bian* should continue to be made of bamboo." An imperial decree was issued in conformity to this proposal.[11]

Another decree, issued by the Xuande emperor (1426–1435), reminds those concerned that this porcelain should be white. Officials were sent to the kilns at Raozhou (Jingdezhen) to supervise their fabrication. Again we quote the *Mingshi*:

> Beginning with the reign of Xuanzong, the eunuch Zhang Shan was sent to Raozhou for the making of sacrificial vessels in white porcelain with dragon and phoenix decoration for the ceremonies in the ancestor hall.[12]

This is confirmed by the *Mingshilu* (Veritable Records of the Ming dynasty), which notes that in the year 1429 the emperor ordered the Ministry of Public Works to see to it that in Raozhou the white porcelain sacrificial vessels were made for the ceremonies in the ancestor hall for the former emperors Taizong (Yongle) and Renzong (Hongxi).[13] Again, for the reign of the Zhengtong emperor, it is stated that: "All the different kinds of vessels in white porcelain were made in Raozhou."[14] Although this is not expressly specified, we may assume that again this refers to sacrificial ware.

The preference of the Yongle emperor (1403–1424) for white porcelain is well known. Many examples of pure white Jingdezhen ceramics from the early Ming period have been preserved at the Palace Museum, as well as excavated from the imperial kiln site itself.[15] In later times, however, the ritual vessels of the Ming dynasty were also made in blue or red.

Scholars have, as far as I know, not yet addressed the question as to what may have been the reason behind all this. According to the dynastic annals, the choice of white was inspired by a wish for classical simplicity and thrift. But this is not entirely convincing. It does not explain why ritual vessels formerly made of wood should now be made of porcelain, which is admittedly more expensive.[16] It does even less to clarify the choice of pure white. Colored or white glazes must have been more or less equally expensive, although making pure white objects may well have been more difficult from the technical point of view. All through the Song and Yuan periods, kilns, especially in northern China, had been producing high quality white and ivory-colored porcelain for private use, but this again does not explain why the Ming dynasty opted for white ceramics in its state rituals.

The true reason must reside elsewhere. We should recall here how tremendously important matters of symbolism were for the state sacrifices. These ceremonies took place not only on certain dates during the year, but also on each day in the palace on a smaller scale as part of the court protocol; they were nothing less than the expression and implementation of the legitimacy of the dynasty. Therefore, at the beginning of the Ming, white must have been chosen for a particular ideological reason, and likewise the switch to other ritual colors must also have been dictated by certain theories pertaining to the "virtue" of the dynasty. In the absence of any other arguments, one may perhaps feel free to speculate that the initial choice of white may be related to the name the dynasty chose for itself: *ming*, that is "light" and especially "white luminosity." As recorded in the *Mingshi* (History of the Ming), the founder of the dynasty Zhu Yuanzhang (r. 1368–1398) had close ties to a messianic sectarian movement which historians have included under the general name of "White Lotus" (Bailian). Toward the end of the Yuan dynasty, the movement attempted to establish a new dynasty and set up a ruler who called himself the Little King of Light (Xiao Mingwang).[17] The White Lotus sect itself is also often called the Religion of Light (*mingjiao*) or the Doctrine of Light (*mingzong*). All these names refer in fact to Manicheaism.

Manicheaism had an important foothold in Fujian.[18] A Manichean shrine survives in the Quanzhou area, and archeological evidence confirms the vivacity of this faith in the region.[19] Religious manuscripts dating from the Qing period but copying original Ming texts link the establishment of the Ming dynasty with the religion of Mani and, as a third protagonist, the sectarian White Lotus movement.[20] These sources also show that at that time Manicheaism was already fully integrated into Chinese Buddhism, with its founder, Mani, transformed into Buddha Lord Mani (Manigong fo) and its worship of the Buddha of Light or the White Lotus Buddha (Bailian fo) a form of lay Buddhist devotion. All this suggests that pure white may have been chosen for religious objects as an expression of ritual purity, a consideration that is still alive today whenever discussions about the choice between wooden images and white Dehua statuettes arise. The latter has always been considered made of a purer material, sublimated through the fire of the kiln and therefore less prone to be eventually infested by demon spirits. Porcelain statuettes are equivalent in almost all respects to those of wood, stone, bronze, or lacquer. Although the ritual of consecration through the "opening of the eyes" (*kaiguang*) is the same, Dehua statuettes do not have an opening (cache) in their backs for sealing written documents with spells, talismans, or bundles of medicinal herbs meant to give the images spiritual power. These caches are found universally in wooden images, as well as in ceramic statuettes from Jingdezhen, but never in those from Dehua.

That Dehua devotional art is unlike that produced in other places and by other techniques during the Ming and Qing periods is certain. Its very special character is moreover confirmed in the writings of at least one contemporary Confucian polemist, a certain Wen Zhengheng (1585–1645). Born in present-day Suzhou, Wen was a renowned and influential scholar who committed suicide out of loyalty to the Ming dynasty when the latter was toppled by the Manchu invaders. His handbook on art and architecture, entitled *Changwu zhi*, was first published during his lifetime and has been re-edited several times since. In several places in his book Wen mentions the Dehua ceramics produced in his time and absolutely rejects them as religiously improper. Writing on the subject of the household altar, he states:

> For making cupboards or tables for [the worship of] the Buddhas (this term includes all saints and deities), one can make use of black as well as red lacquered wood... Also the Japanese [style], which consists of leaving the wood in its natural untreated state, is most suitable and elegant... As to the recent eight-cornered tables with curved feet, and also those religious images from the Fujian [Dehua] kilns, they are absolutely not to be used![21]

Elsewhere, Wen writes on the subject of incense burners, stating:

> Incense burners dating from antiquity or tripods from Han times, or those made in Guan, Ding, Longquan, or Xuan[de] ware are all so highly valued that they should not be employed for daily use. Only the larger bronze censers from the Xuande period are really fit for this...Among those censers the use of which should be especially forbidden are those recently made in the kilns of Fujian (Dehua).[22]

Finally, the same judgment is meted out to Dehua flower vases: "New-fangled bronze vases, as well as vases from the Fujian kilns are all improper to be used in worship."[23] Perhaps at the root of his rejection of Dehua ware for the altar is the possible sectarian background of the almost puritanically stark white religious art.

All the preceding is still speculative, and the hypothesis is aimed solely at initiating a discussion on the question of how this very particular art form of Dehua came into being. We will see below how the figure of the white Guanyin, which is so prevalent in the Dehua potters' repertoire, again raises the issue of sectarian, that is, White Lotus, influence. Not to take into account sectarian religion and the possible influence of Manicheaism in late Ming Fujian is comparable to neglecting the Christian roots of much the art of the sixteenth and seventeenth centuries in Italy. Hence the question will not go away. It must be addressed, even though, given the present state of our knowledge, everything connected with it remains highly conjectural.

Devotional Art for Domestic Worship

As we have seen, ritual objects from Dehua, such as incense burners, oil lamps, candle sticks, wine cups, and offering dishes, do conform to the official stipulations of the early Ming period, not only in their whiteness but also by imitating the shapes of archaic ritual vessels.[24] Each object rarely exceeds twenty inches and is often much smaller. It follows that these vases and incense burners were not made for large rituals, but were made instead for the family altar or for small community temples. The same holds true for the many different kinds of statuettes of deities and saints.

In traditional China every family used to have its domestic shrine (fig. 8). Depending on region, religious traditions, and economic status, these were of course different in form and size, varying from small wall niches in the poor regions of northern China to the elaborate cupboard shrines with double doors of Beijing and the even more lavish high open altars of Fujian. These consist of two tables: one high, narrow praying table (*anqi zhuo*) or incense table (*xiang zhuo*) and one lower, square Eight Immortals table (*baxian zhuo*). The latter is in fact a dining table. The two tables are positioned against a wall, normally the wall opposite the entrance of the main room; this is the so-called reception hall (*keting*) of the house and its ritual center. Above the tables hangs a painting with a religious subject, often showing the three star deities of Fortune, Blessings, and Longevity (*fu, lu, shou*). The high table holds the ritual objects of worship. First, there are the five offerings (*wugong*): incense-burner, two candlesticks, and two flower vases. Behind these are displayed the statues of the patron deities and saints. These figures vary according to the religious orientation of the household. In Dehua itself, always a stronghold of lay Buddhist and sectarian movements, the image of Guanyin is *de rigueur*. Next to her, in a lower position, stands the Lord of the Earth (Tudi gong), who presides over the family's worldly fortunes.

In other parts of southern Fujian, other patterns and traditions of worship prevail. The different districts of the Quanzhou region all have their important local saints: Baosheng dadi in Tongan, Qingshui zushi in Anxi, Guo Shengwang in Yongchun and Nan'an, and so on. Holy Mother Mazu from Putian, the patroness of seafaring people, is worshipped everywhere along the coast. The great monkey saint Qitian dasheng (Sun Wukong) has his devotees in the mountainous regions of southern and central Fujian. It should be noted that the Dehua potter's repertoire of local saints is limited to these areas. Other important Fujian patron saints, like Lady Chen (Chen Jinggu), the Holy Mother of Fuzhou, have apparently never been portrayed in Dehua white porcelain. Needless to say, great deities from northern China, like the Princess of the Morning Clouds (Bixia yuanjun), who enjoys the eternal devotion of the inhabitants of Beijing, or those from the Guangdong area are entirely absent.

The vocational saints make up another group, whose foremost member is Lord Guan, or Guandi, the legendary hero of China's Three Kingdoms period (220–316) who was later deified as a divine protector of trade.[25] Next in importance is the celestial protector of scholars, Wenchang; he is often associated with other saints of literature, such as Kuixing. Also very popular is Tiandu yuanshuai, who was especially venerated in Quanzhou as patron saint of the performing arts and as an exorcising spirit. Equally remarkable is Dongfang Shuo, the famous court jester of Emperor Wu of the Han dynasty (157–87 B.C.), who became the protector of goldsmiths. Xuantian shangdi (Supreme Divine Ancestor of the Dark Heaven), historically related to the Song deity Zhenwu (True Warrior), was a great Daoist god who personifies the powerful exorcising energies of the North; he was also the divine protector of the Ming dynasty and therefore universally worshipped. Similarly, the Qing dynasty placed itself under the protection of Lord Guan. Last but not least we find the domestic deities, such as the already mentioned Tudi gong.[26]

Lay Buddhist organizations were of course also very numerous outside Dehua, and the demand for the White-Robed Guanyin, who was also the embodiment of the Ancestral Mother (Wusheng laomu) in many sectarian movements, was universal.[27] This may explain why statuettes of Guanyin in particular have found devotees all over China. There is, moreover, a great iconographical variety among these images. The most prevalent variation is Guanyin on Mount Putuo (Potalaka), often accompanied by her acolytes Shancai and Longnü as well as her faithful parrot. Next in popularity we find Guanyin crossing the seas (of sorrow) or walking over the lotus pond (picking flowers). She is variously shown with the water bottle, with the Lotus Sutra, with the fish basket, and in the act of bestowing children. All these forms of the White-Robed Guanyin derive, as Chün-fang Yü has shown, from the Water Moon Guanyin, the archetype female manifestation of the bodhisattva Avalokiteśvara.[28]

For the shrines and temples of lay associations and sects, images of other bodhisattvas, such as Maitreya, were also produced in great quantities. Maitreya (Mile fo), as a giver of happiness and fortune, was very popular, and his statuettes are almost as numerous as those of Guanyin. Among the arhats (luohan), Bodhidharma occupies an important place for reasons as yet not entirely clear. Sets of the Eighteen Arhats are also known.

Purely Daoist icons were less prevalent. The abovementioned Xuantian shangdi and the Mother of the Dipper Stars (Doumu), a deity who governs human life and destiny, are the most popular. Dehua potters pushed religious eclecticism so far that they also made devotional art for non-Chinese religions, for example holy water bottles for Hindus and statuettes of the Holy Virgin for the already important Roman Catholic communities of Fujian during the Qing period.[29]

Most of the deities and saints whose statuettes were manufactured in Dehua were not regularly worshipped there, but were intended for sale outside the district. We are not well informed about the market network for Dehua products, and thus can only say with certainty that the distribution area for most of them, as we have seen, did not go beyond the Minnan region, because the repertoire of saints and deities is absolutely limited to this area. Nowadays, devotional statuettes for worship outside Dehua are produced on demand. Usually a potter is approached by a representative of a temple or a local community who brings a model, either in porcelain or in wood, of the holy image to be reproduced in a specified number of copies. A mold is then made, and when a first trial product is approved, production can begin. It rarely exceeds the required number. The Dehua potters are perfectly familiar with this kind of catering or working to order.

The Potters Of Dehua: Artisans And Artists

The artisans and their temple

The Dehua kilns are not concentrated in the Dehua Township, but are distributed throughout the surrounding countryside. The raw materials of clay, minerals, and firewood used to be available locally and could be obtained at many locations. The particular quality of Dehua clay which allows the pure whiteness of its ceramic products will certainly be mentioned elsewhere in this catalogue. Here we may stress that although Dehua can boast of this natural resource, the clay has to undergo a long process of purification before it can be used. Although it lacks plasticity and is unfit for the potter's wheel, it can generally be molded. Even so, the unfired products sag easily. They also often crack in the oven. All this makes *blanc-de-Chine* wares expensive to produce.

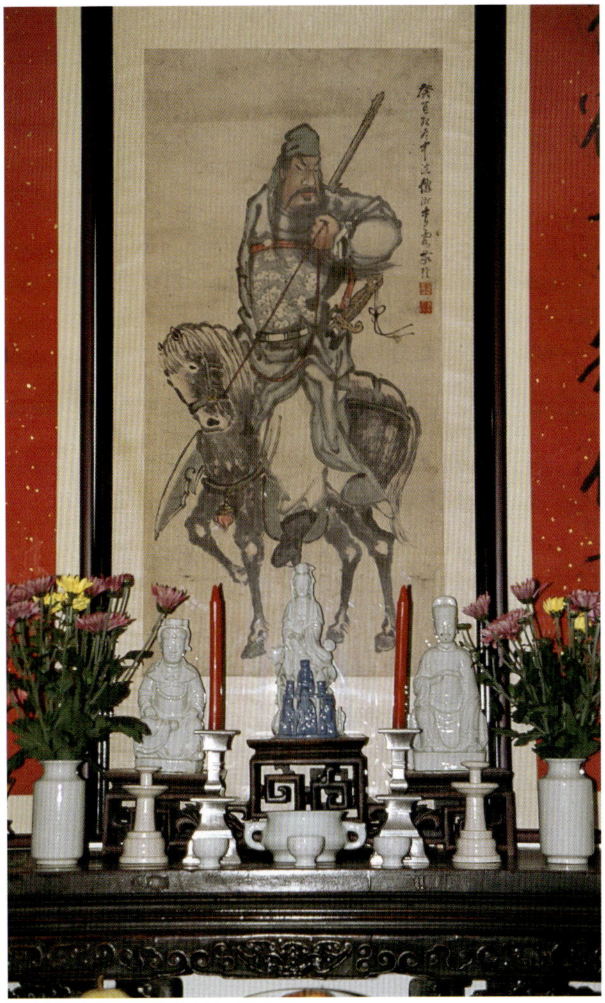

Fig. 8. A home altar with *blanc de Chine*. Photo courtesy of Yuan Bingling.

It appears that all the kilns were, and as a matter of fact still are, family enterprises. Among these families, the Lin and Su lineages are considered to be the most prominent nowadays. They both live in and near the central market town of Dehua and share the management of the Zulong gong temple, about which more will be said. Many famous artists came from these lineages, the most well remembered today being Su Xuejin (1869–1919), active in the late Qing period. He signed his works with the seal *Boji yuren*, "The Vastly Accomplished Fisherman,"[30] and *Yunyu* (see below), but his successors in the Su family continued to use his seal for several generations, so that figurines with the mark of Boji yuren are nowadays quite numerous. The Lin family proudly points to not only a great number of famous artists, such as Lin Chaojing and Lin Xiaozong, but also to the very first among them, the patron saint Lin Bing (see below).

Other illustrious families can be found in the villages. The He family of Housuo, potters since time immemorial, claims the great He Chaozong and He Chaochun among its ancestors (see below). But little else remains of these artists apart from their names and the works attributed to them; their mention in the lineage genealogy have yet to be verified. He Chaozong, who is no doubt the most famous Dehua artist to the outside world, is also considered in his place of origin to be a great artist but also an outsider. One reason may be the fact that he did not come from one of the dominant lineages; another reason may be that, according to local oral tradition, he became a Buddhist monk (*heshang*) in the later part of his life and had no progeny. The more educated members of the Dehua community tend to attribute He Chaozong's celebrity to the fact that, of all the potters, only his name can be found in one of the local gazetteers, and he was therefore familiar to scholars.

All Dehua potters, either from the market town of Dehua itself or from the surrounding countryside, are joined into a kind of guild organized around the veneration of a founding figure and patron saint named Lin Bing together with his divine spouse, the Woman of Mystery (Xuannü), from whom he obtained his skills. Both are enshrined in the small temple that is nowadays called the Palace of the Ancestor Dragon (Zulong gong). It is situated in the outskirts of the market town of Dehua near the hills where most of the kaolin clay, the main ingredient of porcelain, is dug out. There, at the yearly festival held on the sixteenth day of the fifth lunar month, all the potters and their families convened and exhibited their newest and finest products as homage to their divine founders and protectors.[31]

Lin Bing, the patron saint of the Dehua potters is said to have lived a long time ago, in the beginning of the Song period. He was a potter by vocation, working with a small furnace, square and flat, which demanded much firewood for rather meager results. He longed to make a larger furnace, which would enable him to produce more for a market that demanded ever more. But in spite of his endeavors, all the new furnaces he built did not work properly or caved in. One day, exhausted by his exertions, he fell asleep in front of his furnace. In his sleep, he saw a divine woman standing naked before him. He could see her large breasts and round belly. From her throat came wisps of smoke. This goddess was no other than Lady Jin (Gold). One of the seven daughters of the Lord of Heaven, she had already chosen to come to Dehua and reside there.[32] For this purpose she had someone set up her incense burner on the shores of the Dragon Gate Stream; the inhabitants understood her wish and built a temple for her. Lady Jin loved the youth of Dehua and their rites of spring that took place on the shores of the stream. She very much wished to help them. She was also greatly moved by the beauty and character of young Lin Bing, and decided to reveal herself to him in this way. The young potter, inspired by this lovely vision, built a new furnace in the shape of the divine body. It had a large dome in the middle (the belly) and two smaller domes on each side (the breasts). Built this way, it could fire many pieces at the same time. This first great furnace was built in the year 1094. After that, all the potters of Dehua built similar furnaces. As for Lin Bing, he was asked by the potters of Jiangxi to come over and help them, which he did. He never returned. In order to commemorate his great contribution, the families of Dehua built a shrine, where he is worshipped alongside his divine female companion, Lady Jin.[33]

Similar stories can be found elsewhere, notably in Jingdezhen. There a young potter called Tong Bin (instead of Lin Bing) inspired by a deity, sacrifices himself in the burning fire of the kiln, assuring the eternal success of the workmanship.[34] All these stories have their antecedent in the myths concerning the metal artisans, bronze casters, and sword makers of ancient China, like the story of Gan Jiang and his wife Mo Ye, in which hierogamy and self-sacrifice are leading themes.[35]

The ritual and religious unity of the potters of Dehua allowed them to maintain a true corporate structure. A kiln from the fourteenth century, the vestiges of which have been unearthed and researched, measured 57 meters in length and had more than ten rooms. From the shards discovered on the site it can be seen that different families of potters used this kiln at the same time. According to modern estimates such large kilns could fire four hundred tons (*dan*) of ceramics at the same time, a ton being equivalent to one hundred Chinese pounds (*jin*). This shows the extent of corporate exploitation. Of course, it must noted here that these large quantities of ceramics had nothing to do with the high grade *blanc-de-Chine* wares shown in this exhibition, but rather pertain to the mass production of bowls and other objects for everyday use that were in early times a specialty of Dehua. The tradition of yearly exhibits of new and outstanding products in honor of their patron saints resulted in mutual emulation and inspiration, enabling the potters to keep up their standards and their inventiveness, and also to renew their techniques. As in other great centers of Chinese ceramics, the guildlike activities of liturgical organizations did more for the quality and continuity of Chinese art than imperial patronage or foreign demand. The function of these organizations in the areas of investment, the exchange of information, and the production process, as well in the marketing of finished products, should therefore not be overlooked.

The artists

It may seem strange that an article about the splendor of Dehua ware does not begin with what has always been the greatest jewels in her crown: artists such as He Chaozong, whose fame has become almost proverbial, and the many other masters who left their names on the splendid pieces they created. By showing the general context of the Dehua kilns first, I hope that the exceptional nature of the artists might be better understood.

In China, sculpture representing human figures is largely of Buddhist origin, something that can be observed by the fact that any devotional image is still called a bodhisattva (*pusa*) in the vernacular. Throughout the later periods, Chinese sculpture remained essentially religious. It also had its great artists, some of whose names are known to us. During the Yuan period, Chinese art received fresh influences from India and Central Asia, and in 1262, the great Buddhist patriarch 'Phags pa (1235–1280) introduced one of his disciples, the Nepalese prince and sculptor Anige, at the court of Kublai Khan. Anige remained in China and during his long life produced many works of art and had many disciples. One of these was the Daoist disciple Liu Yuan (Liu Bingyuan; second half of the 13th and beginning of the 14th centuries), who later became famous all over China for his dry lacquer sculptures in a temple dedicated to the Lord of the Eastern Peak (Dongyue miao) in Beijing. Both Anige and Liu Yuan became high officials, but their work was considered a religious accomplishment.[36] From the sources that describe the works of these artists and their followers it becomes clear that Daoist iconography was not just a question of canonical rules, but also personal inspiration and vision. Although the Ming court did not honor its artists in the same way as the Yuan, sculptors of religious statues in later times remained highly esteemed. This can be seen from the inscriptions on certain bronze statuettes,[37] each of which was obviously a unique work of art—first sculpted in clay and then cast from molds—made especially for a given patron.

The *Quanzhou fuzhi* (Quanzhou Gazetteer) of 1763 contains a short chapter on various Minnan artists of the Ming period, which fortunately also mentions He Chaozong. He's biographical note is attached to that of a certain Wang Bi from Jinjiang,[38] whose nickname was Shengshi. This Wang was "skilled in writing poetry and prose, as well as in calligraphy and painting. He was especially gifted in modeling clay and making portraits as well as figures of Daoist and Buddhist deities.[39] In this no one was his equal and even the hollowed out [statues] in dry lacquer[40] by Anige and Liu Bingyuan could not rival his [art]."[41] The text then continues:

> During the same period there was also a certain He Chaozong. His place of origin is not known, but some say he was a native of Dehua, and [later] came to live in the city of Quanzhou. He was a most expert modeler of ceramic figures, and [the statues of] the Great Worthy of the Sangha (i.e., Guanyin) he made are transmitted and treasured [everywhere] in the empire.[42]

This may seem a very short and laconic text, but in fact this section on biographies of specialists and craftsmen (*yishu*) in the Quanzhou gazetteer contains only about thirty entries, of which only five or so are painters, sculptors, and calligraphers, the others being mainly medical specialists. Seen from this viewpoint, it is remarkable enough that He Chaozong is mentioned at all. Wang Bi, who made "portraits," was apparently also a scholar, and this may have also been true for He Chaozong.

He Chaozong signed his works, but as far as I know he did not date them.[43] From his inclusion in the section on Ming artists in the Quanzhou gazetteer we may safely deduce that he worked during the Ming dynasty. No doubt he belonged to the later part of that period, which, as we have seen, coincides with Minnan's golden century. There are three other artists who signed their *blanc-de-Chine* creations: Lin Chaojin, Chen Wei, and Zhang Shoushan.[44] Again, none of these signatures is accompanied by a date. On the other hand, we do have a number of dated pieces.[45] Those claiming to be Ming should be treated with caution, as some of them are of a later period. Dated pieces have no signatures. Thus we may distinguish between signed pieces and dated pieces.

Among the dateable *blanc-de-Chine* pieces we find a number of statuettes of saints and deities, such as the Wenchang in the British Museum.[46] These statuettes, although of a fine quality, are very traditional, formal, and hieratic renderings of the divine beings in question. In fact they are closely similar to devotional statuettes made of wood or bronze.

Those who have signed their names on the *blanc-de-Chine* statuettes of the late Ming period, no matter whether small or large, can be termed true artists. This can be seen in the quality of their work, but also more objectively in the great freedom with which they treated their religious subjects. The signed statuettes—that is, those which stand a chance of being authentic or copies of authentic works—are not formal and rigid. Instead, we find great freedom and unconventionality. The Guanyin signed by He Chaozong in the Ashmolean Museum is a most personal and visionary rendering of the hallowed theme of Guanyin with the Lotus Sutra.[47] This manifestation of the Bodhisattva of Mercy is shown as a very young girl clad in a simple robe and almost completely without ornaments or jewelry. Immersed in thought after having read a passage in the sacred text of the Buddha, she is pondering her resolve to devote herself to the salvation of all creatures.

We may say with some certitude that all these artists—He Chaozong, Lin Chaojin, Chen Wei, and Zhang Shoushan—worked during the late Ming, that is, during the above-mentioned golden age of southern Fujian. Works of the Qing period that carry personal signatures are those by He Chaochun, Lin Xiaozong, Lin Xizong, Lin Zixin, Lin Jiesheng, etc. During the very last years of that dynasty we encounter The Vastly Accomplished Fisherman (Boji yuren), or Su Xuejin; his work belongs, however, to the modern development of Dehua art.

Later Developments

Only in 1664, a full twenty years after the founding of the Qing dynasty in Beijing, did the Manchu rulers finally impose their rule on southern Fujian. The retaliation was severe. With the remainder of the army of the Ming hero

Zheng Chenggong (Coxinga) and the last loyal servants of the Ming dynasty still holding out on Taiwan, the Qing government spared no effort to seal off the coast and enforce a rigorous embargo on all sea trade. Once more, southern Fujian was sealed off from the world, but this strict embargo could not go on forever. Already towards the end of the seventeenth century, illegal trade and emigration, contraband, pirating, and other unsanctioned practices flourished anew. In the meantime, Fujian had become severely impoverished and was condemned to remain poor for a very long time. Together with the severe losses caused by the dismantling of the overseas trading houses and the embargo, there was the loss of their trade routes to the Western powers. Also, many former export goods, like sugar, were now produced in other places. Fujian's economic situation was exacerbated by the galloping increase in population that marked the early years of Manchu rule.

With the decline of the local market, *blanc-de-Chine* production in the early seventeenth century began to depend on markets in other regions of China and also outside the country. Some of the Dehua wares imitating European shapes and models were made to order. Whether the potters made others to attract Western buyers is not quite known, because foreign subjects were of interest in China.[48]

The perception of the Dehua artists about the final purpose of their art gradually changed too. During the Qing period, the influence of Confucianism became pervasive, and the importance of lay Buddhist and of Daoist worship declined. The culture of the Confucian literati became dominant. Instead of a religious attitude towards Buddhism and Daoism, the literati developed an antiquarian and sentimental sensibility. They collected bibelots, *objets d'art*, and curios. In their studios appeared elaborate stands especially made for exhibiting all kinds of "treasures." Partly by imitation, partly through innovation, Dehua started to produce *blanc-de-Chine* collectibles and bibelots on a grand scale. Figures were no longer confined to purely religious art, although that always remained in production, but were now also derived from folklore, literature, or theater, giving us such subjects as the Eight Immortals; the mad monk Jigong; the two jester monks Hanshan and Shide; Xiwangmu, Royal Mother of the West; the fairy Magu, or Hemp Lady; Shouxing, the Star of Longevity; and the like. Objects for the scholar's studio, especially brushwashers and water droppers in all kinds of animal forms, also became fashionable.

Su Xuejin is the great Dehua name of the late Qing period. He used the signature "Boji yuren," a strange and perhaps somewhat ridiculous appellation meaning "the vastly accomplished fisherman." A rather immodest fisher in the high mountains! According to his own descendants, Su Xuejin liked to put his poetic "Fisherman" name or his literary style "Yunyu" on the works he himself considered the best. He also molded and imitated a great number of Ming statuettes, on which he put a gourd-shaped seal mark which reads *Dehua* and another seal with the message "made in the Wanli era of the Great Ming dynasty." Occasionally he would sign his creations by engraving them with the message "handmade by Su Xuejin." His commercially successful folkloristic figurines became the stock in trade of Dehua, and his seals were used during several successive generations.[49]

With the advent of the Republic in 1912, the Dehua repertoire changed again. Historical figures became popular. Great poets like Qu Yuan and statesmen from former times, as well as popular heroes like Lady Mulan, made their appearance in white porcelain. After 1949, Dehua was put to work on the propaganda of the proletarian revolution. Henceforward, it produced a vast line of portraits of great Communist leaders and heroes. It also began imitating Meissen porcelain and other types of "romantic" Western art, not just for export to the Soviet Union, but also to a Westernized Chinese market. During the Cultural Revolution, Dehua artisans applied their very best technical skills and prime materials in order to produce the most immaculate statuettes of the Great Leader and the heroes of the revolution. Portraits of the stars of the new proletarian opera in their most famous roles were produced on a truly massive scale.

In recent years, Dehua boasts several hundred workshops and factories. Most are industrialized with electric kilns and produce cheap white cups and saucers for a national and increasingly international market.[50] Pious images, especially of Guanyin with a vase (dripping true water if one cares to fill the reservoir) and folkloristic subjects continue to be turned out on a grand scale. This industry has brought a relative affluence to Dehua, which is visible in the building boom that has completely done away with the ancient Chinese architecture and replaced it with multi-storied concrete housing blocks. Only some descendants of the great families continue to work as before, using kilns fired with charcoal, making molds, and finishing their products by hand. Their main line of business consists of replicas and pastiches of antiques.

Notes

1. On the Min kingdom, see Edward Shafer, *The Empire of Min* (Rutland, 1954).
2. On the worship of Baosheng dadi, see Kenneth Dean, *Taoist Ritual and Popular Cults of Southeast China* (Princeton, 1993), pp. 61–98.
3. For the description of Marco Polo's Zayton, see *The Book of Ser Marco Polo, the Venetian, concerning the Kingdoms and Marvels of the East,* trans. and ed. Henry Yule, 3rd ed. rev. Henri Cordier, vol. 2 (London: John Murray, 1903), p. 242; Marco Polo also mentions the city Tiunguy as a production center for ceramics. Could this be Dehua?
4. See Tian Rukang, "The Decadence of Buddhist Temples in Fukien in Late Ming and Early Ch'ing," in *Development and Decline of Fukien Province in the 17th and 18th Centuries*, ed. E.B. Vermeer (Leiden: Brill, 1990), pp. 83–100.
5. See Baren J. Ter Haar, "The Genesis and Spread of Temple Cults in Fukien," in *Development and Decline in Fukien Province in the 17th and 18th Centuries*, ed. E.B. Vermeer (Leiden: Brill, 1990), pp. 374–75.
6. See Kristofer Schipper, "Neighborhood Cult Associations in Traditional Tainan," in *The City in Late Imperial China*, ed. G.W. Skinner (Stanford: Stanford University Press, 1977) and "The Cult of Pao-sheng ta-ti and its Spreading to Taiwan—A Case Study of Fen-hsiang," in *Development and Decline in Fukien Province in the 17th and 18th Centuries*, ed. E.B. Vermeer (Leiden: Brill, 1990), pp. 397–416. Compare, for similar facts concerning old Beijing, the recent book by Susan Naquin, *Peking: Temples and City Life, 1400–1900* (San Francisco: University of California Press, 2000).
7. In his later years, Zheng Zhilong agreed to cooperate with the already very weakened imperial power in order to defend China against foreigners. He was given a peerage, as was his son, Zheng Chenggong, who was given the title Grandee of the Imperial Clan (Guoxing ye, or, according to the Dutch rendering of the Hokkien prononciation of this title, Coxinga). The latter ultimately led the Ming resistance against the Manchus and held his last stand on Taiwan (after having first ousted the Dutch) in 1662.
8. See the extensive biography of Li by K.C. Hsiao in *Dictionary of Ming Biography* (New York: Columbia University Press, 1976), pp. 807–818.
9. See Piet van der Loon, *The Classical Theatre and Art Song of South Fukien* (Taipei, 1992). Sound recordings of Nanyin music are available as compact discs: *Chine: Nan-kouan*, vols. 1–6, Ocora C559004, C560037–41 (distributed by Harmonia Mundi).
10. We may perhaps extend this claim to many of the more refined white porcelain tea and wine cups of this period. These were also not intended for everyday use, but for the offerings on the home altar and for ceremonial banquets. Miniatures of musical instruments may also have been intended for votive use.
11. *Mingshi* (History of the Ming), ed. Zhang Tingyu et al. (1739; reprint, Beijing: Zhonghua shuju, 1974), *juan* 47, p. 1237. The *bian* is a receptacle made of woven bamboo.
12. *Mingshi, juan* 82, p. 1998. A similar passage can be found in *Mingshi, juan* 82, p. 1989, and in *Mingshilu* (Veritable Records of the Ming) (reprint ed., Taipei: Academia Sinica, 1962), *Xuanzong, juan* 9, p. 231.
13. *Mingshilu, Xuanzong, juan* 9, p. 231.
14. *Mingshi, juan* 82, p. 1989.
15. See *Yanseyou: Monochrome Porcelain*, vol. 37 of *Gugong bowuyuan cang wenwu zhenpin quanji* (Hong Kong: Shangwu, 1999), pl. 99–105; see also Nigel Wood, *Chinese Glazes: their origins, chemistry, and recreation* (London: A & C Black; Philadelphia, Pa.: University of Pennylvania Press, 1999), p. 68, for an example from the Victoria and Albert Museum. For white wares excavated in Jingdezhen, see Liu Xinyuan, *Jingdezhen chutu Wudai zhi Qingchu cichan / Ceramic Finds from the Jingdezhen Kilns (10th– 17th Century)* (Hong Kong: The Fung Ping Shan Museum, 1992), nos. 211–215.
16. For instance, it was decreed that the sacrificial vessels for the worship of Confucius, which used to be made in wood, would henceforward also be made in porcelain. See *Mingshi, juan* 50, p. 1295.
17. *Mingshi, juan* 122, Biography of Han Liner.
18. See Edouard Chavannes and Paul Pelliot, ed. and trans., *Un traité manichéen retrouvé en Chine* (Paris: Imprimerie nationale, 1912).
19. See *Quanzhou lidai zongjiao shike* (Fuzhou, Fujian: Renmin chuban she, 1992).
20. For example, *Daojiao yuanliu*, a manuscript from southern Fujian recovered from Tainan, Taiwan, and now in the collection of the Yimen Foundation, Fuzhou University, Fujian.
21. In the modern edition of Wen Zhengheng's work, *Changwu zhi jiao zhu*, annotated by Chen Zhi (Nanjing: Jiangsu kexue jishu chubanshe, 1984), pp. 140–41. That the reference here is to Dehua ware is confirmed by Chen's commentary.
22. Ibid., p. 247. Here again, the context indicates clearly that the ceramics of Dehua are meant.
23. Ibid., p. 283.
24. See *Yanseyou*, pl. 106–110.
25. His full name is Guan Yu, but out of respect his personal name (Yu) is never pronounced. Instead he is called Lord Guan (Guan gong) or more ceremoniously the Imperial Sovereign Saint Guan (Guansheng dijun).
26. In contrast there appears to be no Dehua statuettes of the Kitchen God, Zaojun.
27. On this very important issue, see the book by Chün-fang Yü, *Kuan-yin: The Chinese Transformation of Avalokiteśvara* (New York: Columbia University Press, 2001).
28. See the many relevant discussions in the above-mentioned work by Chün-fang Yü.
29. Roman Catholicism, first introduced in the sixteenth century by Dominican friars from Spain, experienced a kind of breakthrough with the missionary efforts of the Jesuit Giulio Aleni, a companion of Matteo Ricci. The church founded by Aleni in Dingtou, a village on the coast of eastern Fujian (Fuan, Mindong), is still active today. The antagonism between the Dominicans and the Jesuits in Fujian is at the origin of the infamous "rites controversy," which has so enduringly influenced Western perception of China.
30. This strange epithet also sounds awkward in Chinese. Its exact meaning remains obscure. Mountainous Dehua is not a place known for fishing!
31. This remarkable custom appears to be quite old and unique to Dehua. When asked, the oldest living potters in Dehua assured me

that in their youth they had seen the exhibition take place, and they were told by their parents that this had been the custom since time immemorial.

32. This means that she already had a temple cult in Dehua, probably as a saintly protector of potters.
33. This account is given in a booklet distributed by the Dehua temple committee: Guo Shaoqing and Lin Muzhu, *Yaotai taoyuan* (Beijing, 1999), pp. 14–20.
34. See Ma Shutian, *Huaxia zhushen, Sushen juan*, (Taipei 1993), p. 182.
35. See Marcel Granet, *Danses et légendes de la Chine ancienne* (Paris,1926), pp. 496–503.
36. On these two artists, see Wang Gang, *Beijing tongshi*, vol. 5 (Beijing: Beijing shehui kexueyuan, 1989), pp. 293–296.
37. See Stephen Little, ed., *Taoism and the Arts of China* (Chicago: Art Institute of Chicago; [Berkeley]: University of California Press, 2000), p. 294, for the inscription on a bronze figure of Zhenwu. It names the artist, Chen Yanqing from Hangzhou, and gives a date equivalent to 1439.
38. A county situated to the south of the city of Quanzhou.
39. Literally, "immortals and bodhisattvas."
40. The text reads "lacquered cloth and extractable [mold]," an expression referring to a kind of hollow "dry lacquer" technique.
41. In a rather obscure article published in *Fujian gongyi meishu* 1981 (2), the author, Lin Zuliang, ascertains that the statue of Mazu (Tianfei) in her famous temple in Quanzhou was made by Wang Bi. This statue and that of her two demon helpers, Qianliyan and Xunfenger, were destroyed during the Cultural Revolution, but the ivory court tablet which Mazu kept in her hands was preserved. It carries a Wanli date.
42. *Quanzhou fuzhi* (1763), *juan* 63, pp. 6b–7a. Contrary to what has been written by some Chinese specialists, this note, or for that matter any other information about He Chaozong, does not appear in the *Quanzhou fuzhi* of the Wanli period, published in 1612.
43. Mr. Robert H. Blumenfield, in his recent book *Blanc de Chine, The Great Porcelain of Dehua* (Berkeley: Ten Speed Press, 2002), p. 164, claims to possess a statuette of Guanyin by He Chaozong that carries an inscription in ink on her aureole that can be made legible through x-ray photography, revealing a date corresponding to 1618. The author does not transcribe or translate the inscription in question, and this makes it impossible for us to verify his claim. Mr. Blumenfield moreover considers Dehua to be the capital of Fujian province (p. 1) and does not provide us with information about the provenances of most of the pieces shown in his book. All this inevitably does cast some doubts as to the scholarly value of his work.
44. For Lin Chaojin, see P.J. Donnelly, *Blanc de Chine: the Porcelain of Tehua in Fukien* (London: Faber and Faber, 1969), pl. 140C and D; for Chen Wei, see Donnelly, pl. 82B; and for Zhang Shoushan, Donnelly, pl. 138 and 139.
45. See for example, a figure of a saint (usually identified as Caishen, but who is more probably a Wangye) dated to 1610 (Donnelly, pl. 71A) and a figure of Guanyin dated to 1629 (Donnelly, pl. 71B).
46. See Rose Kerr and John Ayers, *Blanc de Chine: porcelain from Dehua* (Chicago: Art Media Resources, 2002), p. 28, fig. 14.
47. The figure is published in Daisy Lion-Goldschmidt, *La Porcelaine des Ming* (Fribourg, Switzerland: Office de Livre, 1978), p. 236, pl. 270.
48 The author wishes to thank Mr. John Ayers for his help in writing this passage.
49. See Guo and Lin, *Yaotai taoyuan*, pp. 40–42.
50. The figure given for the commercial value of exports of Dehua ware for the year 2001 is about three billion Chinese yuan, equivalent to some three hundred fifty million U.S. dollars.

CATALOGUE

EARLY WARES

1. Circular Box and Cover

圓盒
Yuan dynasty, 14th century
Porcelaneous stoneware with white glaze
H. 3 ½ in., D. 6 ⅛ in.
The Metropolitan Museum of Art, New York.
Gift of Mrs. Stanley Herzman, 1984
(1984.483.2ab)

The box and cover is decorated with an overall molded scrollwork design and covered with a greenish-tinged glaze. Many boxes of this kind, perhaps used for cosmetics, were exported to Southeast Asia under the Song and Yuan dynasties and later. They have also been found at old Dehua kiln sites such as Qudougong (see Hong Kong 1990, no. 10 ff.). For the relationship between this type of scrollwork design, as found on a comparable box in the Hickley Collection, and the form of carved lacquerwork known as *tixi*, see Kerr and Ayers 2002, no. 150.

Published: Valenstein 1989, fig. 124, pp. 126, 130.

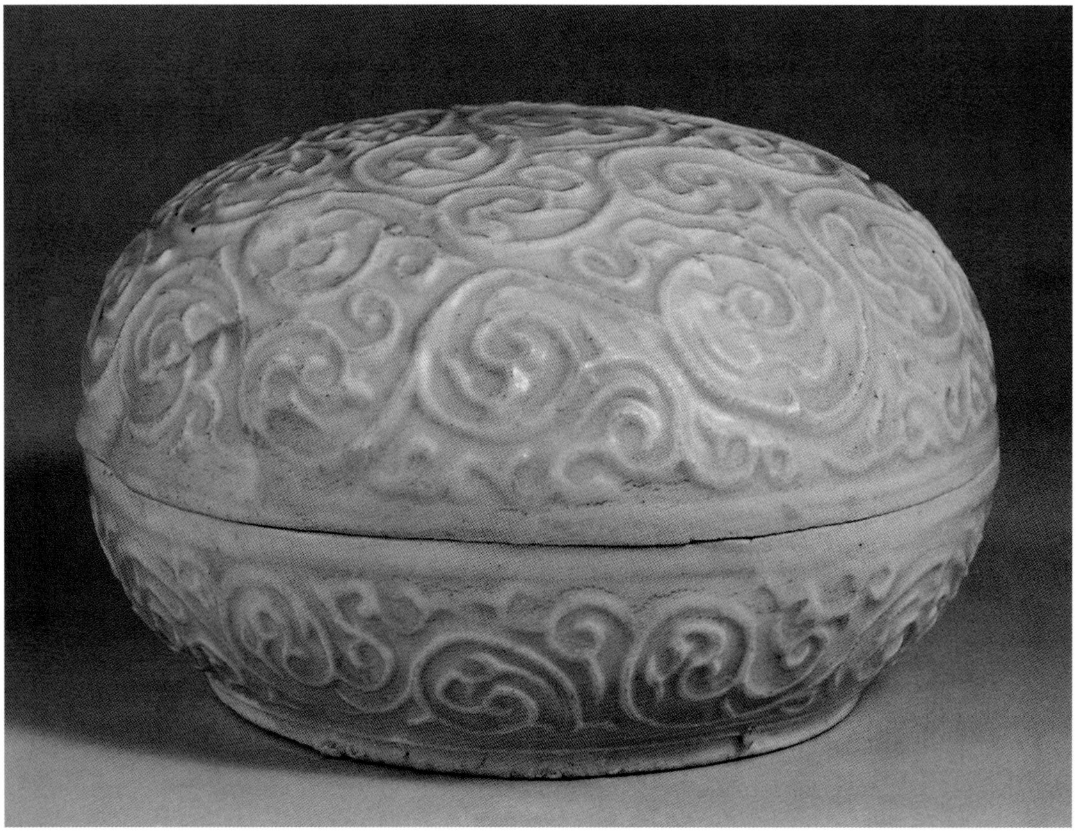

2. Pouring Vessel, *Kendi*

軍持

Yuan dynasty, 14th century
Porcelaneous stoneware with white glaze
H. 4 3/8 in., W. 6 1/4 in. with spout, D. 5 1/8 in.
The Detroit Institute of Arts, Gift of the Honorable & Mrs. G. Mennen Williams (72.569)

The *kendi* has molded scrollwork decoration and a cream-toned glaze. Vessels of this un-Chinese form with a projecting spout, probably made originally in metal, were used for pouring pure water in Muslim rituals which were already being practiced in Southeast Asia about this period (see Sullivan 1957). Other *kendi* from the same collection made in the Philippines are reproduced by Aga-Oglu 1975, no. 95.

Published: Aga-Oglu 1985, no. 94.

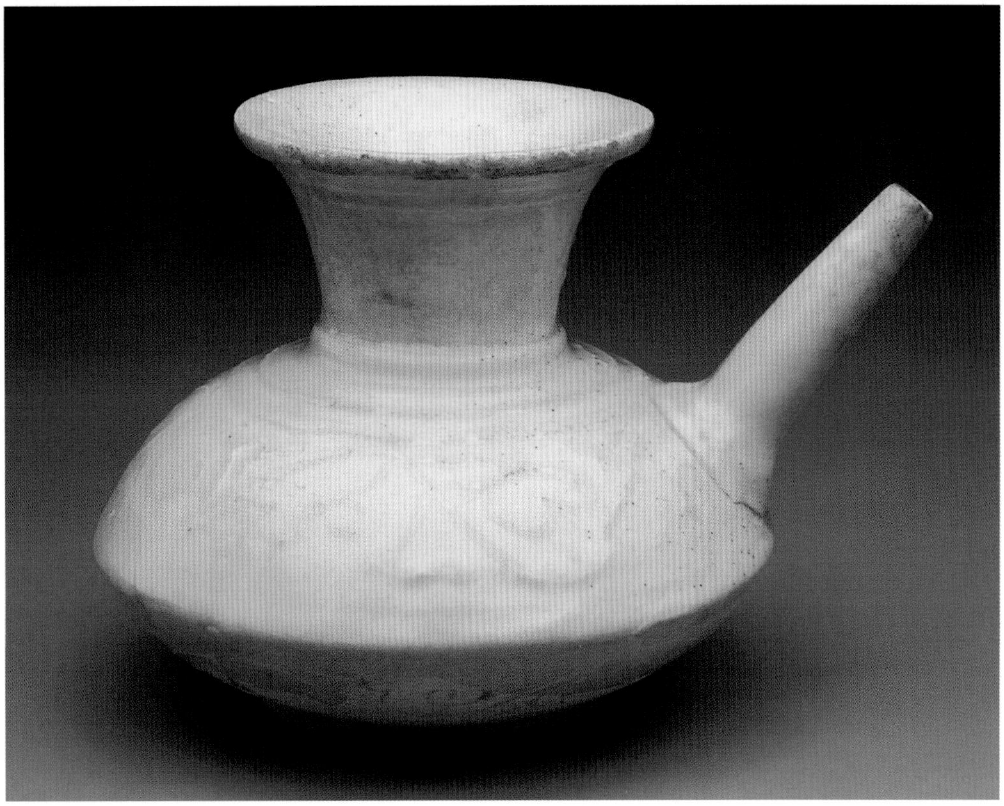

3. Dish with Cut, Foliated Rim

花口盤

Ming dynasty, 16th or early 17th century

H. 1 in., W. 4½ in., D. 4½ in.

The Koger Collection, The John and Mable Ringling Museum of Art, the State Art Museum of Florida (33.222)

This dish comes from a collection formed in the East Indies. The sides are molded in eight bracket-shaped lobes. An identical dish in an English private collection, probably from the same source, bears the ghost of an enameled floral design which would have worn off during a long burial.

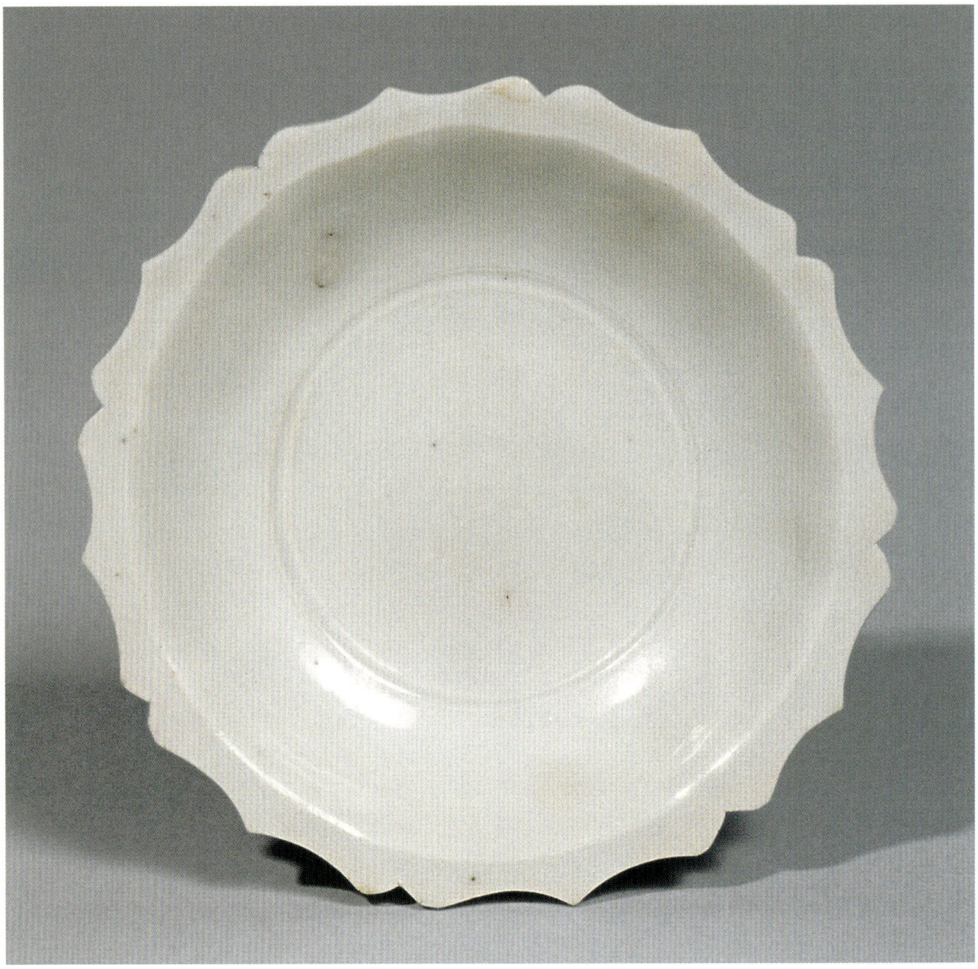

4. Altar Vase with a Pair of Lion-mask Handles

铺首供瓶

Ming dynasty, late 16th or early 17th century

H. 6 ¾ in., W. 4 in., D. 4 in.

The Koger Collection, The John and Mable Ringling Museum of Art, the State Art Museum of Florida (33.217)

In Ming times pairs of vases like these were made in metal and ceramics for use on temple or domestic altars; *blanc-de-Chine* examples are illustrated in Donnelly 1969, pls. 6B and C. Vases from dated sixteenth-century tombs at Dehua are published by Xu and Chen 1996, figs. 2 and 3; for one of these buried groups, dated 1519, see fig. 3 in the Introduction of this catalogue.

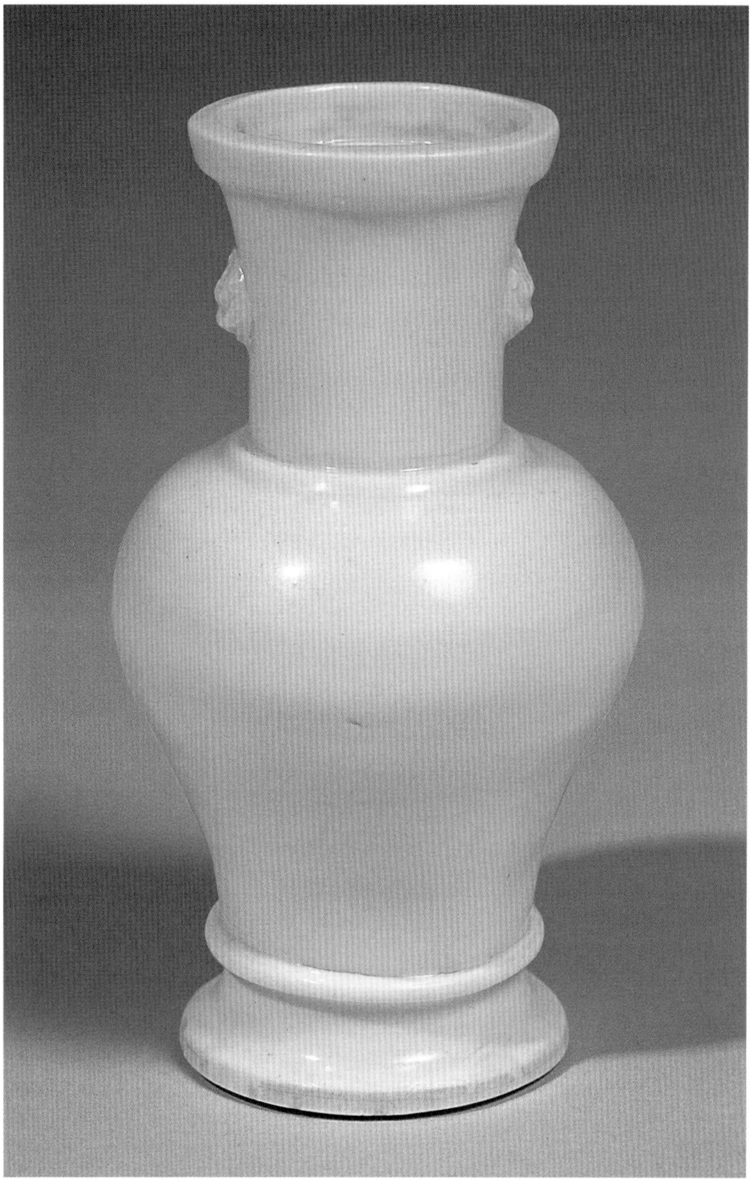

5. Brushpot with Openwork Sides Cut with a Swastika Pattern

透雕筆筒

Ming dynasty, 17th century

H. 6 in., W. 3 ⅞ in.

Robert H. Blumenfield Collection

In late Ming times a range of fine vessels were made in *blanc-de-Chine* porcelain for scholars' use, including brush holders and a variety of water pots for writing and painting. A brushpot almost identical to this one but inscribed on the base with the incised reign mark of Tianqi (1621–28) and the name of the Lin family is illustrated by Donnelly 1969, pl. 9A, who considered it, however, to be of later date. The piece, believed to have been sold by Christie's in London, had a European ormolu mount of around 1700. In the light of our improved knowledge of late Ming *blanc de Chine* it seems less certain that this inscription must be regarded as a forgery.

Published: Blumenfield 2002, p. 30, pl. C.

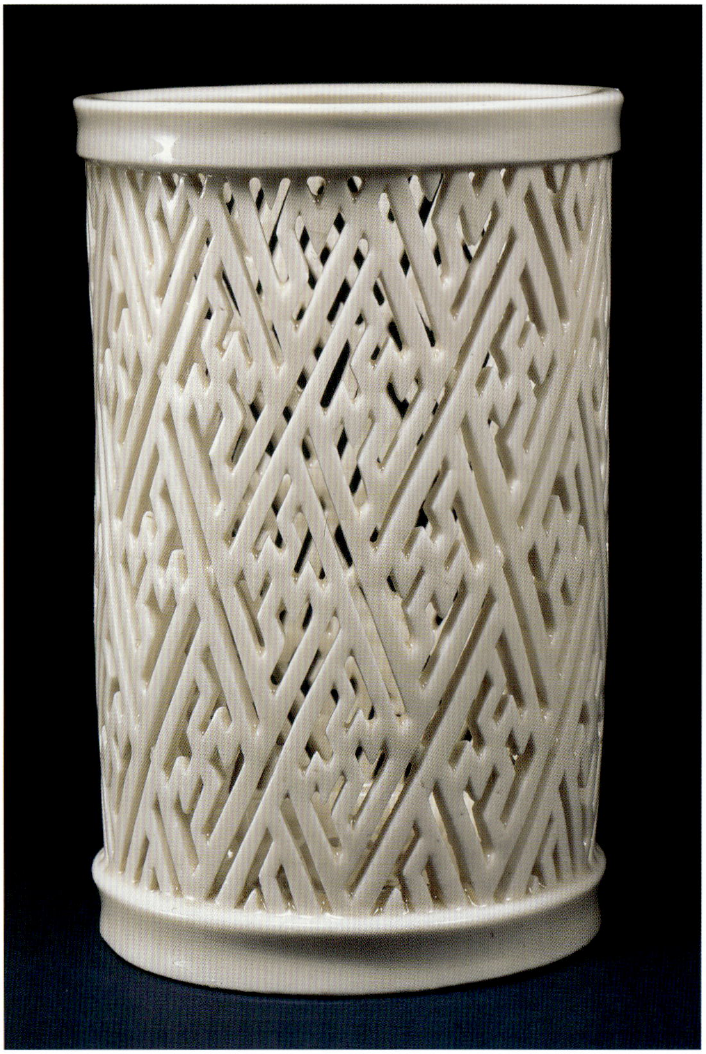

6. Brushwasher in the Form of a Lotus Leaf

蓮葉形筆洗

Ming dynasty, first half 17th century

H. 1 ½ in., W. 4 ½ in., D. 3 ¼ in.

The Koger Collection, The John and Mable Ringling Museum of Art, the State Art Museum of Florida (28.179)

This is a typically charming instance of the adaptation of a natural form to grace the scholar's table. It has a stem attached to the center and joining a flower bud at one side.

Published: Marchant 1985, no. 35.

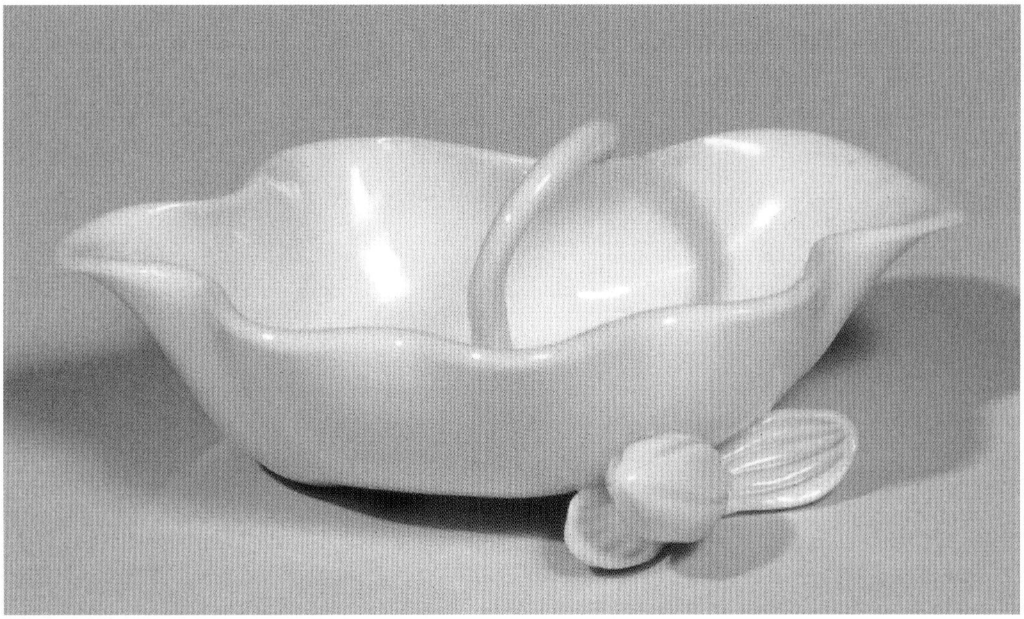

7. Water Dropper in the Form of a Crab Resting on a Dish

蟹形水注

Ming or early Qing dynasty, 17th century

H. 4 ¾ in., W. 5 ¾ in.

Richard Lehman Gray Collection

Another example of such a water dropper was in Augustus the Strong's collection at Dresden by 1721 (Donnelly 1969, p. 105; see also Marchant 1985, no. 33).

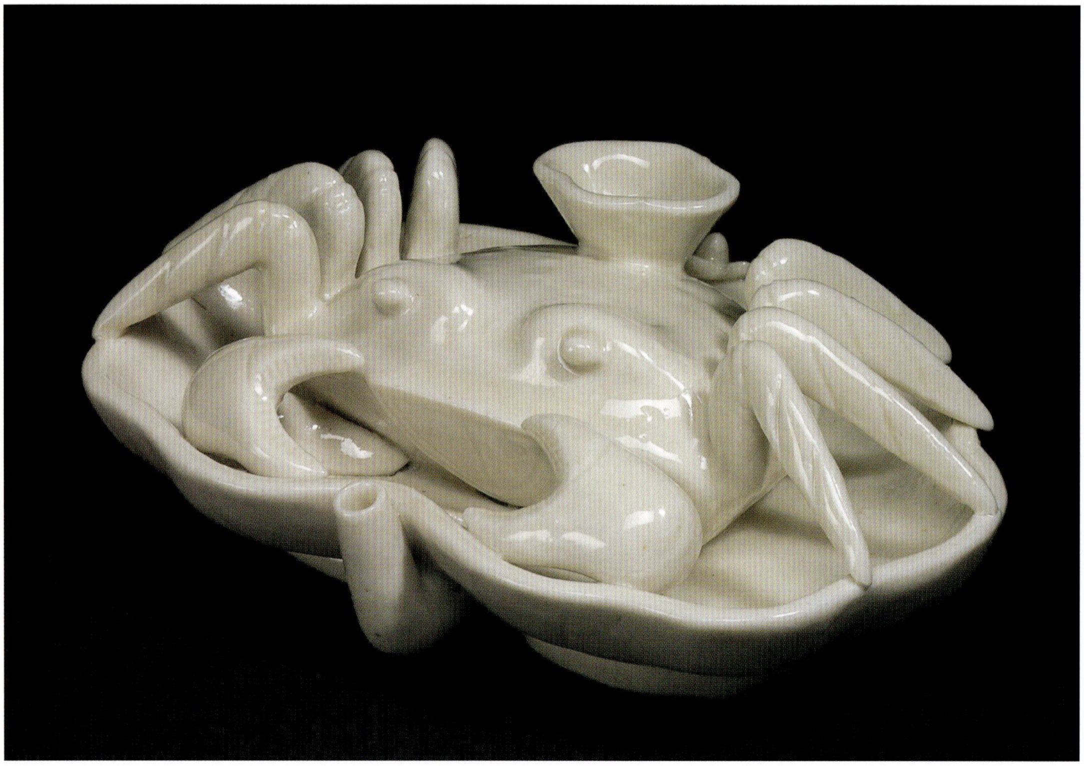

8. Brushwasher in the Form of a Three-legged Archaic Bronze *Ding*

鼎形筆洗

Ming dynasty, early 17th century

H. 3 ⅓ in., W. 3 ⅜ in., D. 3 ⅜ in.

The Koger Collection, The John and Mable Ringling Museum of Art, the State Art Museum of Florida (28.176)

The washer has a pair of upright handles on the rim. Archaistic, as well as naturalistic forms were adopted for these vessels, which were often also made in metal.

Published: Marchant 1985, no. 31.
Ex coll.: Edward T. Chow.

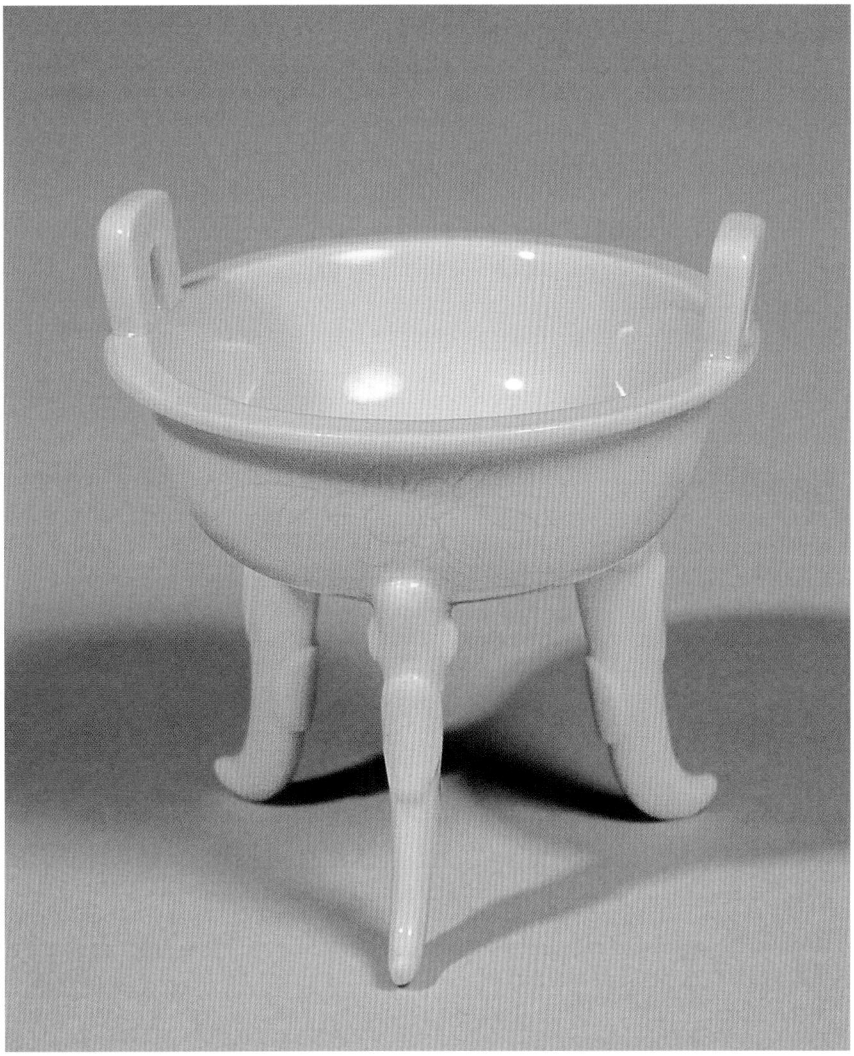

9. Water Dropper in the Form of a Pomegranate Spray

石榴形水注
Ming dynasty, early 17th century
H. 2 ⅕ in., W. 4 ¼ in., D. 4 ¼ in.
Virginia Museum of Fine Arts, Richmond, Bequest of Forrest R. Brauer (85.1493)

The vessel is shaped as two fruit, the stem forming a handle. Note also the teapot in pomegranate form below (cat. no. 16).

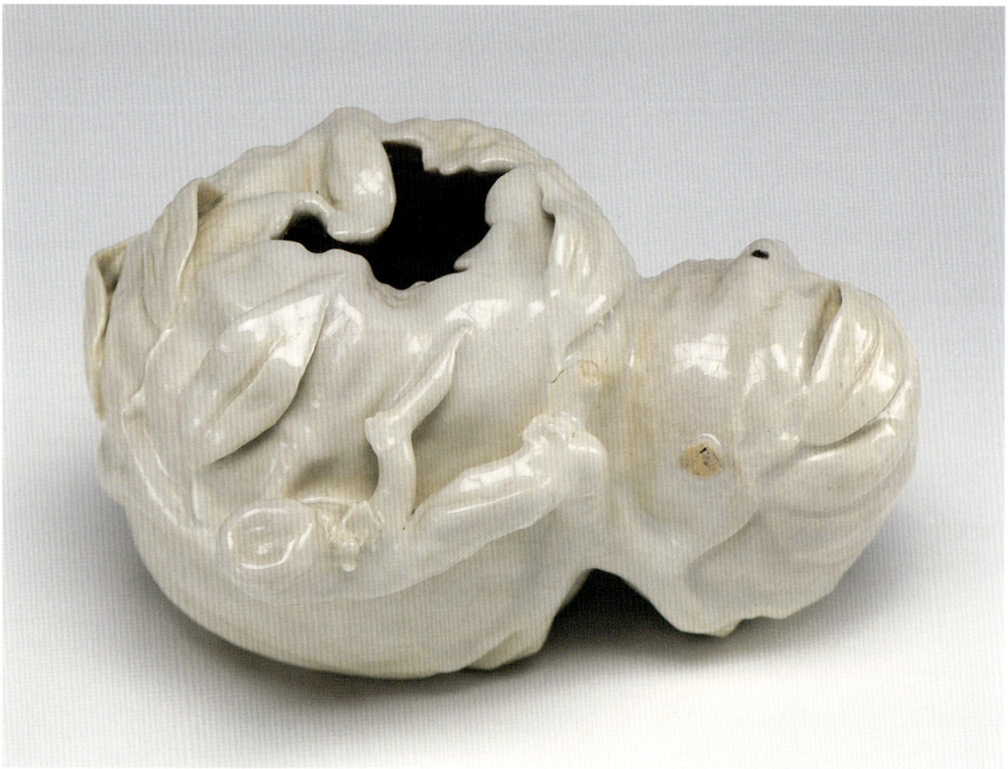

10. Waterpot in the Form of a Rocky Landscape

山形水器
Ming dynasty, early 17th century
H. 7 ½ in., W. 7 ½ in., D. 2 ¾ in.
Robert H. Blumenfield Collection

This waterpot displays the scholar's devotion to mountain scenery and to the shapely rocks that were employed in the making of gardens. The landscape includes a figure, a bridge over a torrent, and a pagoda.

Published: Blumenfield 2002, p. 30, pl. B.

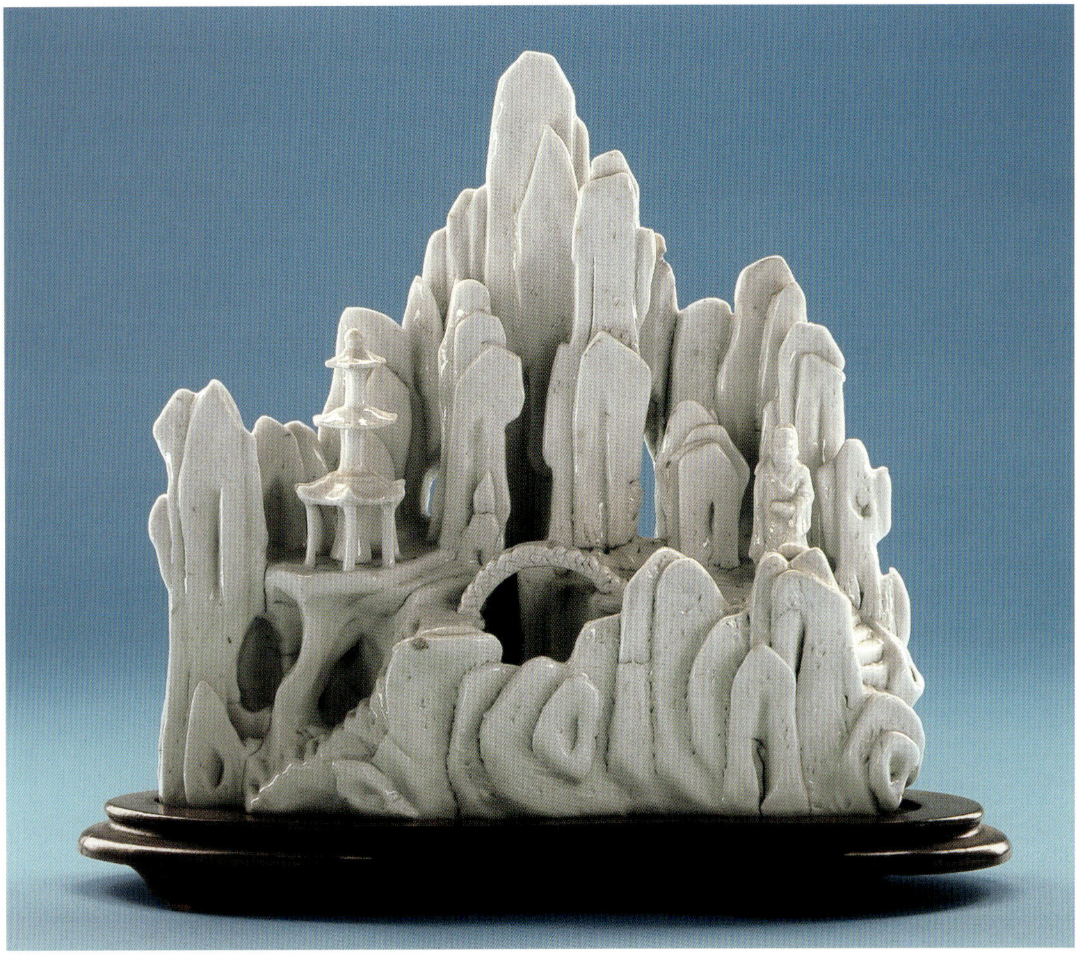

11. Box with Lid in the Form of Three Lichee Fruit

荔枝形盒
Ming dynasty, first half 17th century
H. 2 ⅝ in., W. 5 in.
Richard Lehman Gray Collection

The three fruit are joined by a leafy stalk which forms a handle to the cover. A vessel in the form of two halves of a lichee is illustrated by Donnelly 1969, pl. 44B.

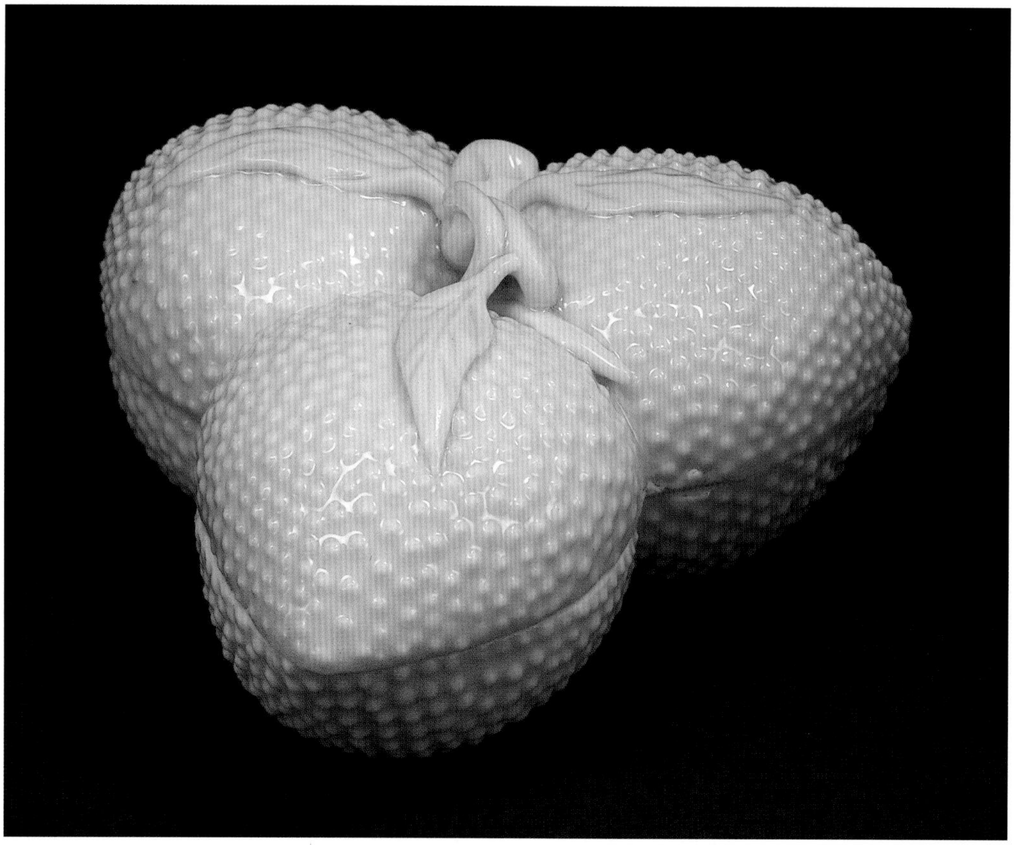

12. Vase of *Gu* Beaker Form

觚形壺

Ming dynasty, first half 17th century

H. 8 ¾ in., W. 5 ½ in., D. 5 ½ in.

The Koger Collection, The John and Mable Ringling Museum of Art, the State Art Museum of Florida (33.223)

The central bulb of the vase is encircled by pairs of ribs in relief. A *gu* vase broadly comparable to this one was found in the tomb of the Wanli emperor (d. 1619); see the illustration in James Watt's Introduction to Hong Kong 1975. The form is of course derived from that of an archaic ritual bronze. For another example, see Marchant 1985, no. 21.

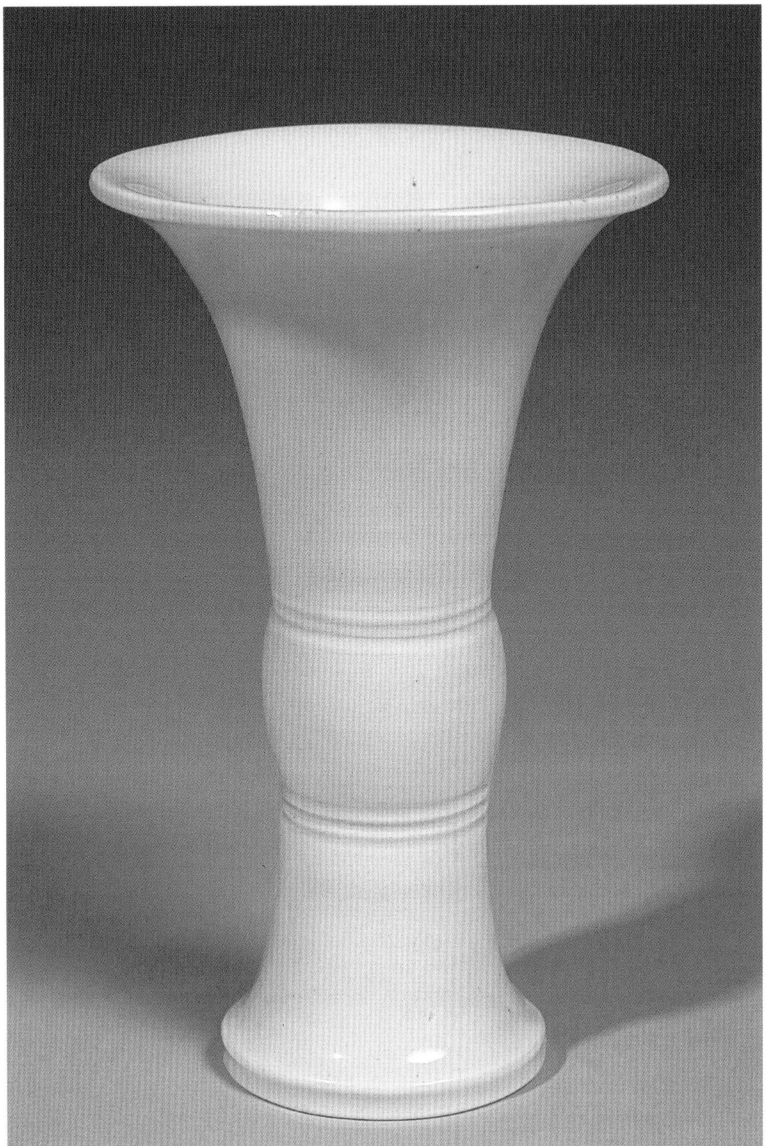

13. Incense Burner in the Form of a Bronze *Gui*

簋形香爐

Ming dynasty, first half 17th century

H. 3 ¾ in., W. 9 ½ in., D. 6 ⅞ in.

The Koger Collection, The John and Mable Ringling Museum of Art, the State Art Museum of Florida (28.168)

This incense burner is embellished with molded bronze-style decoration, a pair of animal-mask handles, and tiger feet. The ceremonial burning of incense was customary among the scholar class as well as in religious rituals. A wide variety of differently-shaped incense burners were made at Dehua, in this case echoing the current vogue for archaic bronze vessels. Here, the adaptation includes suitably modified animal-style decoration. See Hong Kong 1975, no. 43, for another example.

Published: Ayers 1985, no. 150

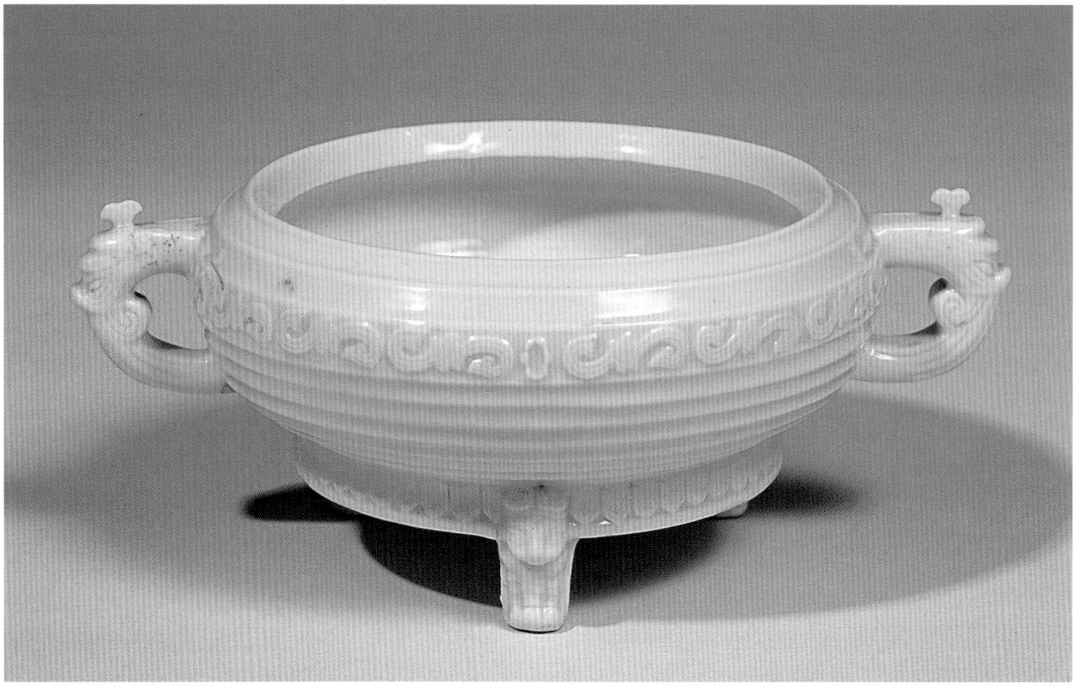

14. Bottle and Tripod Stand

三足座龍瓶

Ming or early Qing dynasty, mid-17th century

H. 4 ¾ in., W. 3 in., D. 3 in.

The Koger Collection, The John and Mable Ringling Museum of Art, the State Art Museum of Florida (28.183)

An applied dragon encircles the tapering neck. Bottles similarly decorated with dragons were made also in bronze at this time. Whether they were intended to hold water or plant sprays is not clear.

Published: Ayers 1985, no. 148.

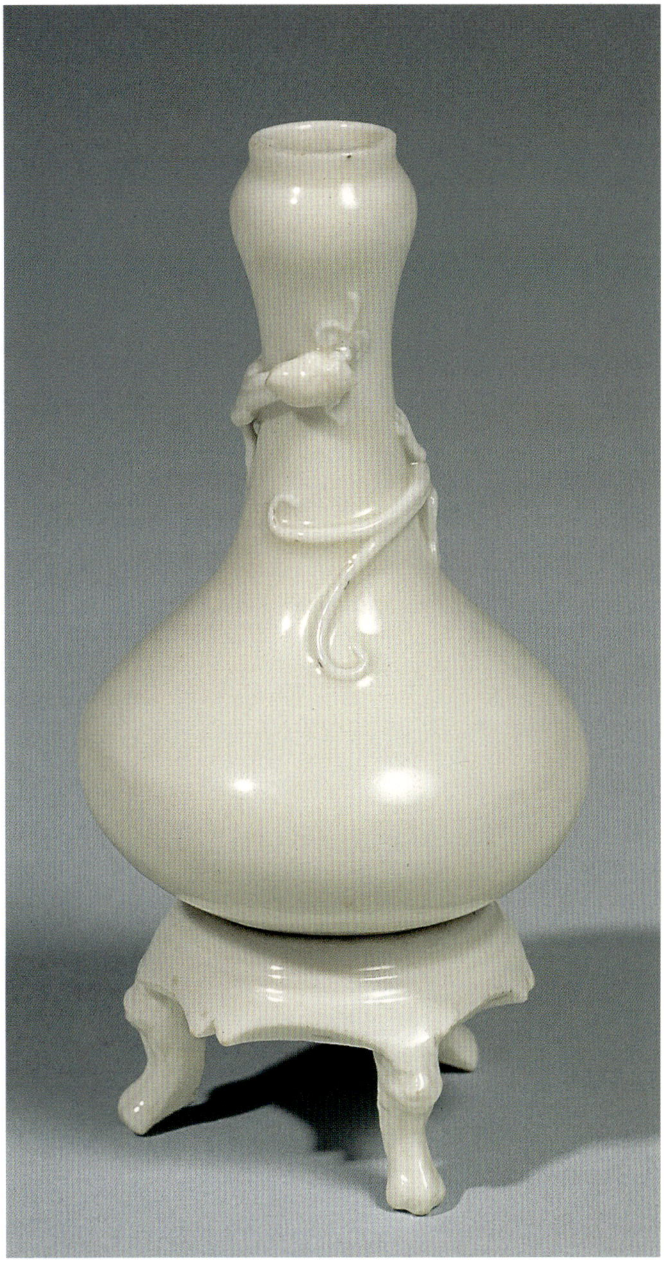

15. Globular Lamp with Wick Holder and Stand

鏤空圈足瓷燈

Ming or early Qing dynasty, mid-17th century

H. 3 in., W. 5 ¼ in., D. 5 ¼ in.

The Koger Collection, The John and Mable Ringling Museum of Art, the State Art Museum of Florida (28.184)

These lamps may have been used in the shrines where devotional images were placed. (Cf. Donnelly 1969, pl. 40A and p. 99.)

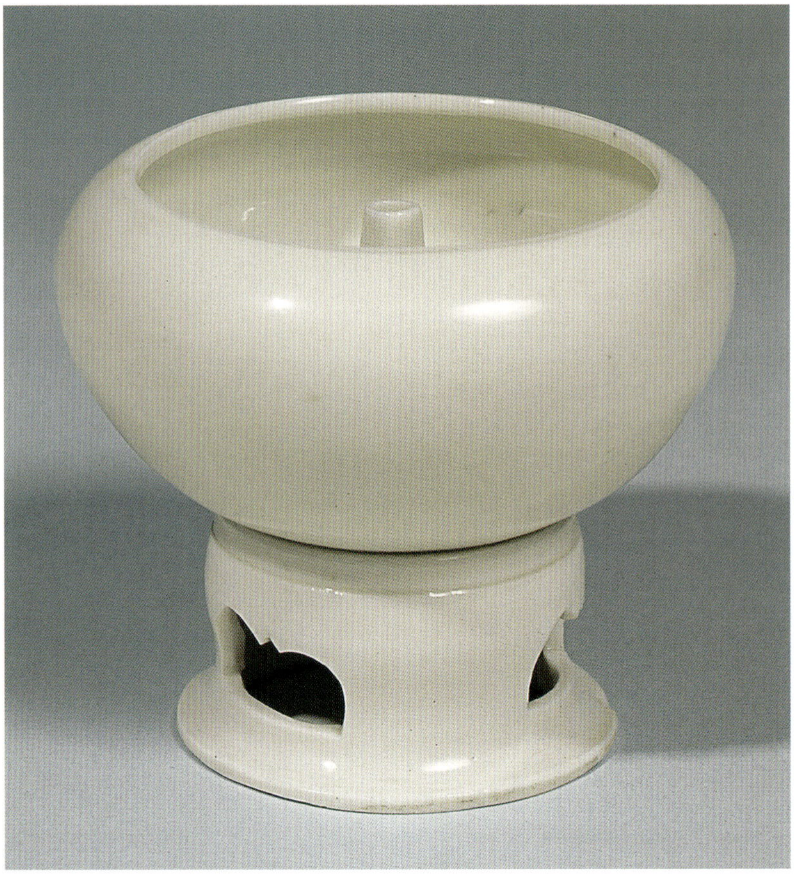

16. Teapot in the Form of a Pomegranate

石榴形茶壺

Ming dynasty, first half 17th century

H. 4 ⅝ in., W. 6 in., D. 4 in.

The Koger Collection, The John and Mable Ringling Museum of Art, the State Art Museum of Florida (26.155)

The handle and lid of this pot takes the form of a branch and leaf; the foot is shaped like a six-pointed star. A virtually identical pot in the Museum of Fine Arts, Boston, has an incised inscription relating to tea. Imports of tea into Europe from China began about this time. Early in the eighteenth century this form was reproduced in "soft-paste" porcelain at the St. Cloud factory near Paris (Beurdeley and Raindre 1987, fig. 344, possibly illustrating this piece).

Published: Ayers 1985, no. 152.

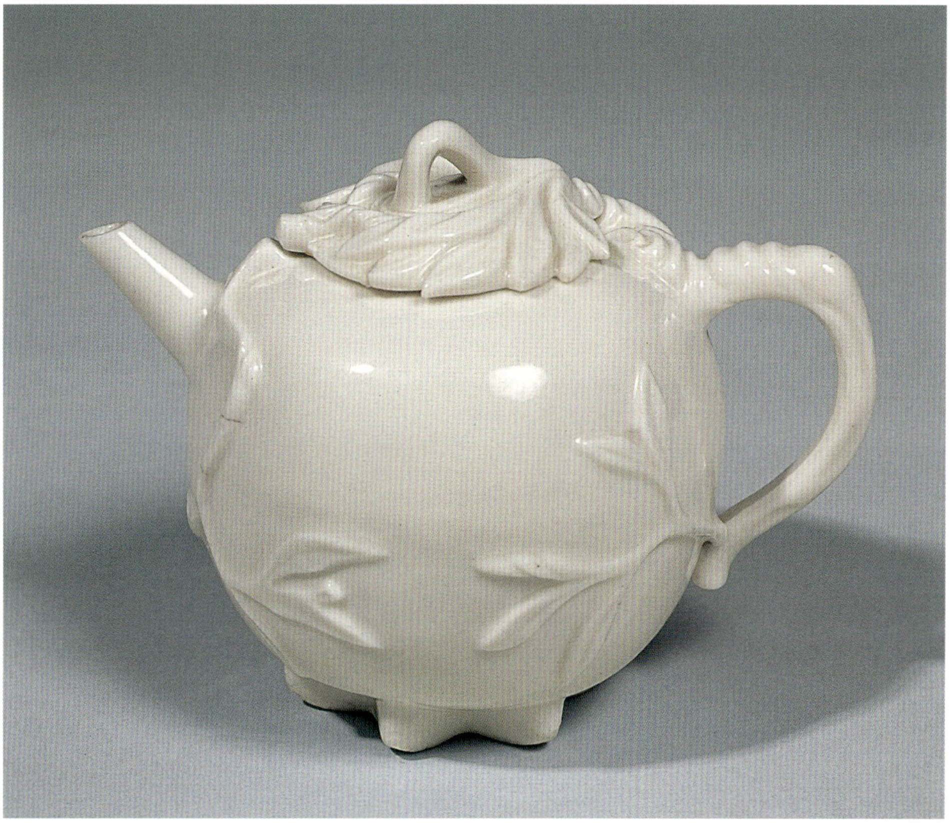

17. Teapot with Flat Lid and a Ball Knob

茶壶

Ming dynasty, first half 17th century

H. 4 in., W. 5 ¾ in., D. 3 ½ in.

The Koger Collection, The John and Mable Ringling Museum of Art, the State Art Museum of Florida (33.226)

The teapot was recovered by Captain M. Hatcher from a trading vessel that sank in the South China Sea in about 1643. This must have been among the earliest shipments of teapots from Dehua. It was in 1639 that the Dutch East India Company in Batavia submitted an order for teapots, apparently for the first time, to the Chinese merchant Jousit. Blue-and-white teapots from the Jingdezhen factories were recovered from the same sunken cargo (Volker 1954, p. 43). See Christie's Amsterdam, *Sale Catalogue* (March 1984), no. 296, and (February 1985), no 13.

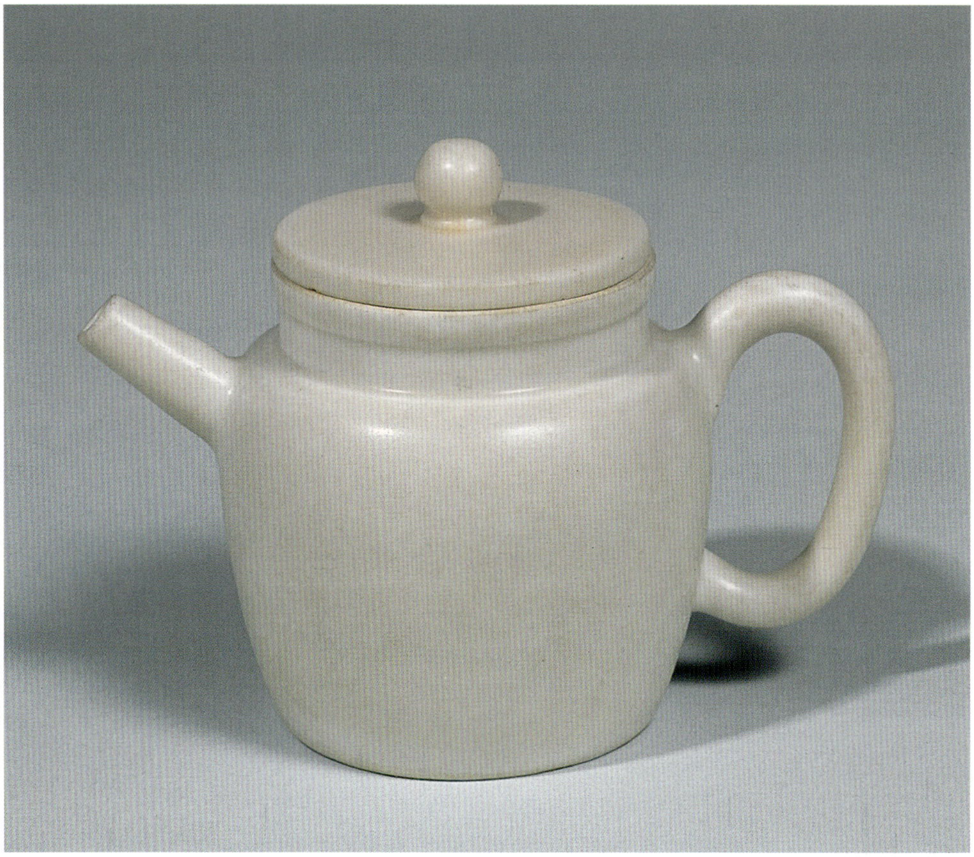

18. Wine Cup in the Form of a Magnolia Flower

玉蘭花形酒杯
Ming dynasty, first half 17th century
H. 2 ¼ in., W. 3 ½ in., D. 3 in.
The Koger Collection, The John and Mable Ringling Museum of Art, the State Art Museum of Florida (26.151)

Blanc-de-Chine wine cups were produced in great variety and many have floral or plant-inspired forms. Here, the cup stands on three vestigial feet, and it is embellished with incised decoration of a crane and a *qin*, and a three-character inscription on the other side. Cranes were a symbol of long life and of the independence of the scholar, while the *qin* zither was a mark of his closeness to the harmonies of nature. (Cf. Donnelly 1969, pl. 28A and p. 92, where their combination is interpreted as an allusion to a Daoist legend; also see Kerr and Ayers 2002, no. 119, for a similar cup in the Hickley Collection.)

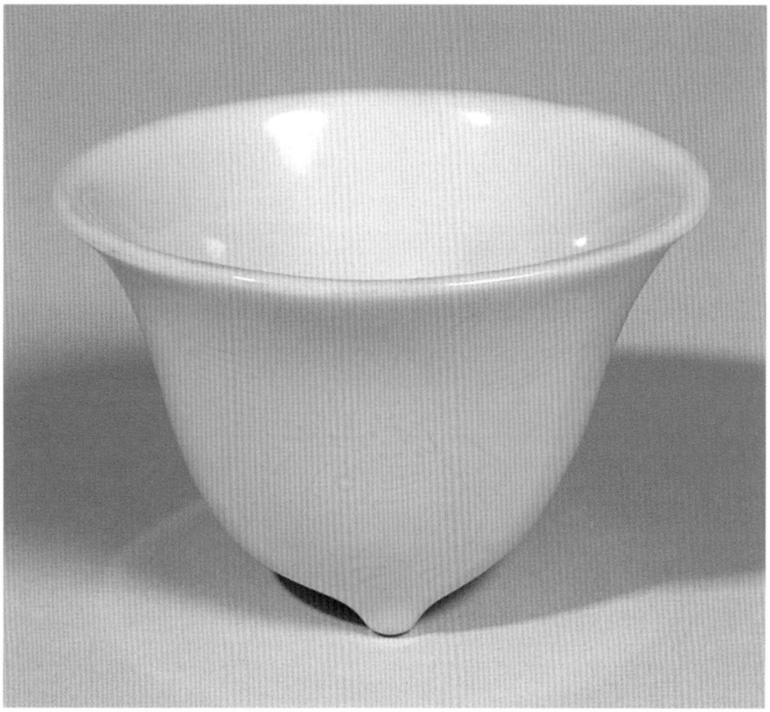

19. Wine Cup in Rhinoceros Horn Form with Supporting Metal Stand

犀牛角形酒杯

Ming dynasty, first half 17th century

H. 3¾ in., W. 4⅞ in.

Richard Lehman Gray Collection

Resembling the tip of a horn, the cup is embellished in molded relief with scenes of a scholar seated by a tree and rock on one side and two more playing checkers on the other. Donnelly identifies cups of this form as wedding cups (see Donnelly 1969, p. 83, pl. 24A). Their description in older books as "libation cups" is probably mistaken, libations being in the ancient world of the West poured offerings made to a god. There is an evident relationship between the work of the Dehua porcelain modelers and that of the carvers of rhinoceros horn who worked in Fujian province (see Chapman 1999). (Also, cf. Kerr and Ayers 2002, no. 127.)

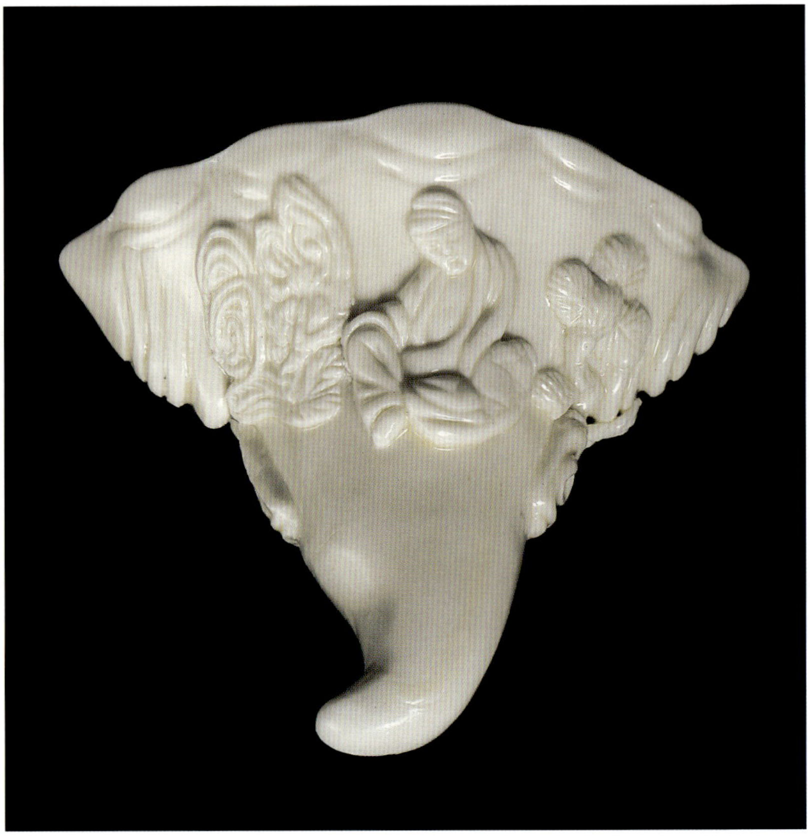

20. Hexagonal Winepot and Lid

六角形茶壺
Ming or early Qing dynasty, 17th century
H. 8 ¼ in., W. 6 ⅞ in.
Richard Lehman Gray Collection

This winepot has an overhead handle, and the side panels are decorated with molded relief scenes depicting scholars enjoying the landscape. An identical winepot at Hampton Court Palace near London, evidently part of the collection formed by Queen Mary II before her death in 1694, is illustrated by Lane 1949, pl. 8c. Donnelly remarks that in Augustus the Strong's collection at Dresden another such pot was inventoried before 1721 as "No. 1" in his list of "tea things" (Donnelly 1969, p. 121); the introduction of the drink into Europe was still quite recent at this time, but most teapots were rather small.

Published: Cooper-Hewitt Museum 1988, no. 205.

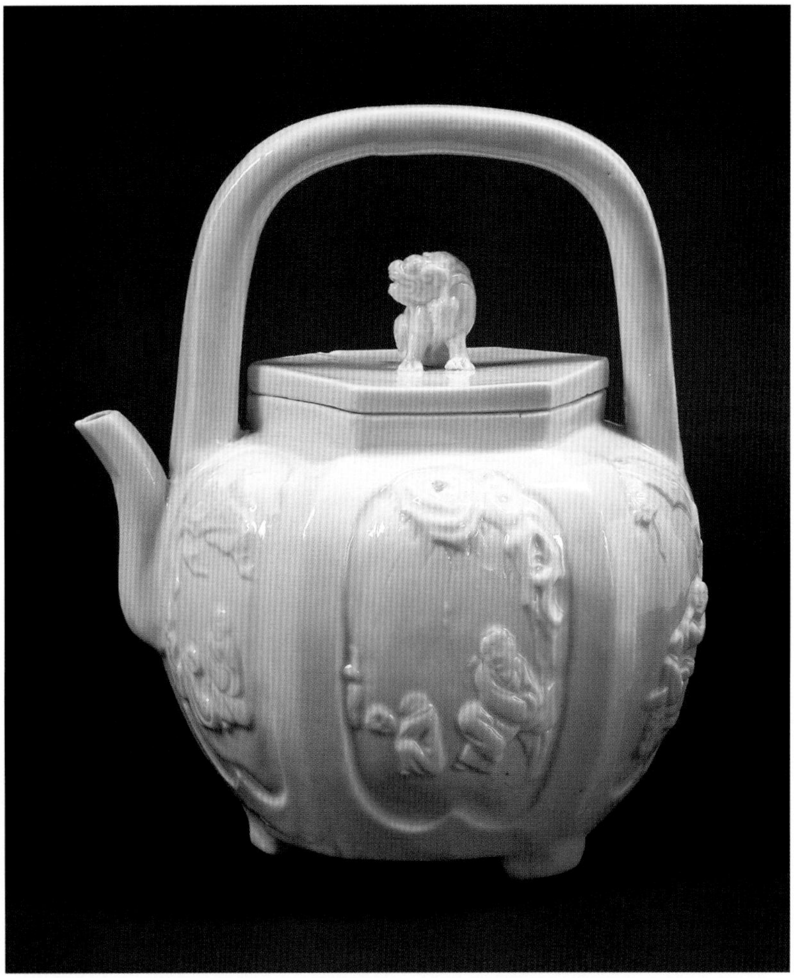

21. Cylindrical Winepot

筒形酒壺

Ming or early Qing dynasty, mid-17th century

H. 5 ½ in., D. 3 ⅜ in.

Virginia Museum of Fine Arts, Richmond,
Bequest of Forrest R. Brauer (85.1490)

This winepot is furnished with a dragon-shaped handle and spout, and an infitting lid with a dragon knob. A comparable winepot was in the cargo of the Chinese trading ship wrecked in the South China Sea in about 1643 and recovered by Captain M. Hatcher (see Ayers 1986, fig. 7 and p. 20). The type is also identified as appearing in the Dresden inventory (Donnelly 1969, p. 122).

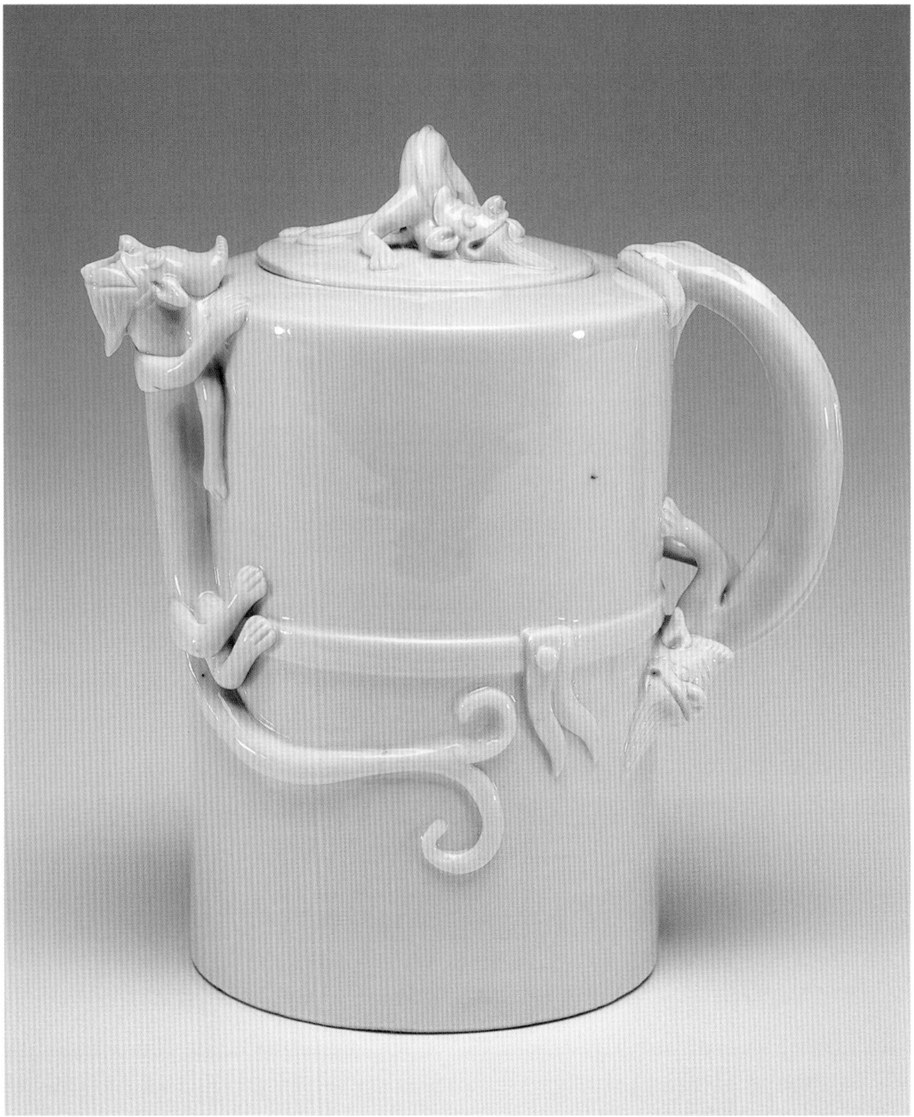

22. Model of a Stringed Instrument, *Qin*

模型琴

Probably late Ming or early Qing dynasty, 17th century

H. 2 in., W. 4 in.

Robert H. Blumenfield Collection

This is an unique model, probably not intended to be played on account of its small size. For a discussion of the *qin* and its place in Chinese life and art, see Stephen Addiss, *The Resonance of the Qin in East Asian Art* (New York: China Institute, 1999).

Published: Blumenfield 2002, p. 32, pl. C.

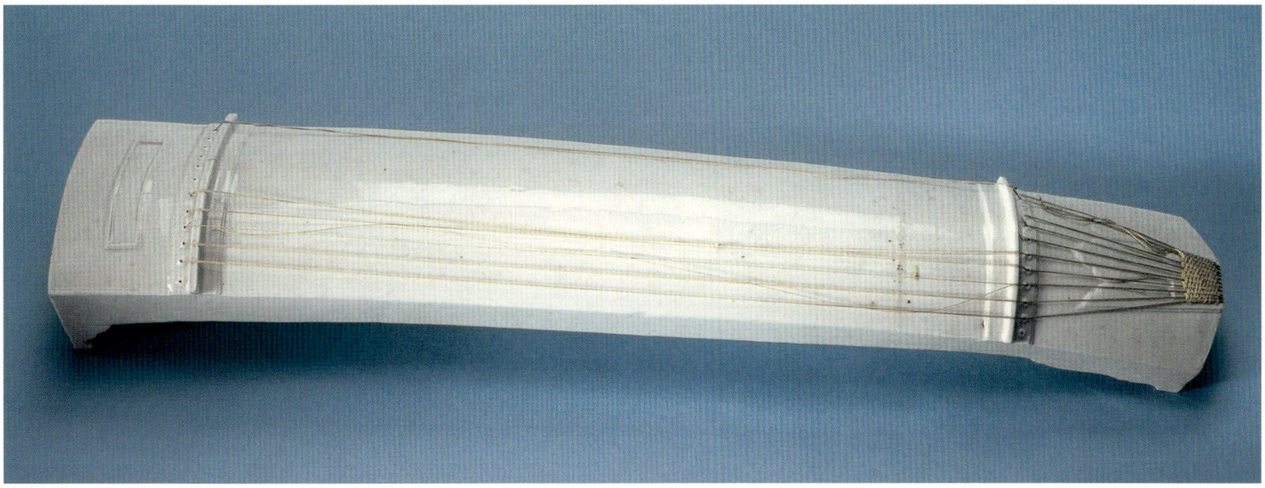

23. Vertical Flute (*Xiao*) with Incised Phoenix Design

白瓷簫

Probably late Ming or early Qing dynasty, 17th century

H. 1 ¼ in., W. 1 ¼ in., D. 23 ½ in.

The Koger Collection, The John and Mable Ringling Museum of Art, the State Art Museum of Florida (25.137)

The instrument is molded in sections like a bamboo flute; it is incised towards the top with a phoenix design and below with the formalized characters *ming feng* (the call of the phoenix). Donnelly discusses two flutes from the collection of the late Professor Cheng Te-k'un, which are said to be tuned to the pitch of d´: a value found only in late Ming-period instruments (Donnelly 1969, pl. 68A and p. 126). Chinese musical literature reports that such porcelain flutes have a particularly pure tone, and a mid-seventeenth-century work is cited that speaks of their excellence. The tonal quality of this flute has been proved in recent performance.

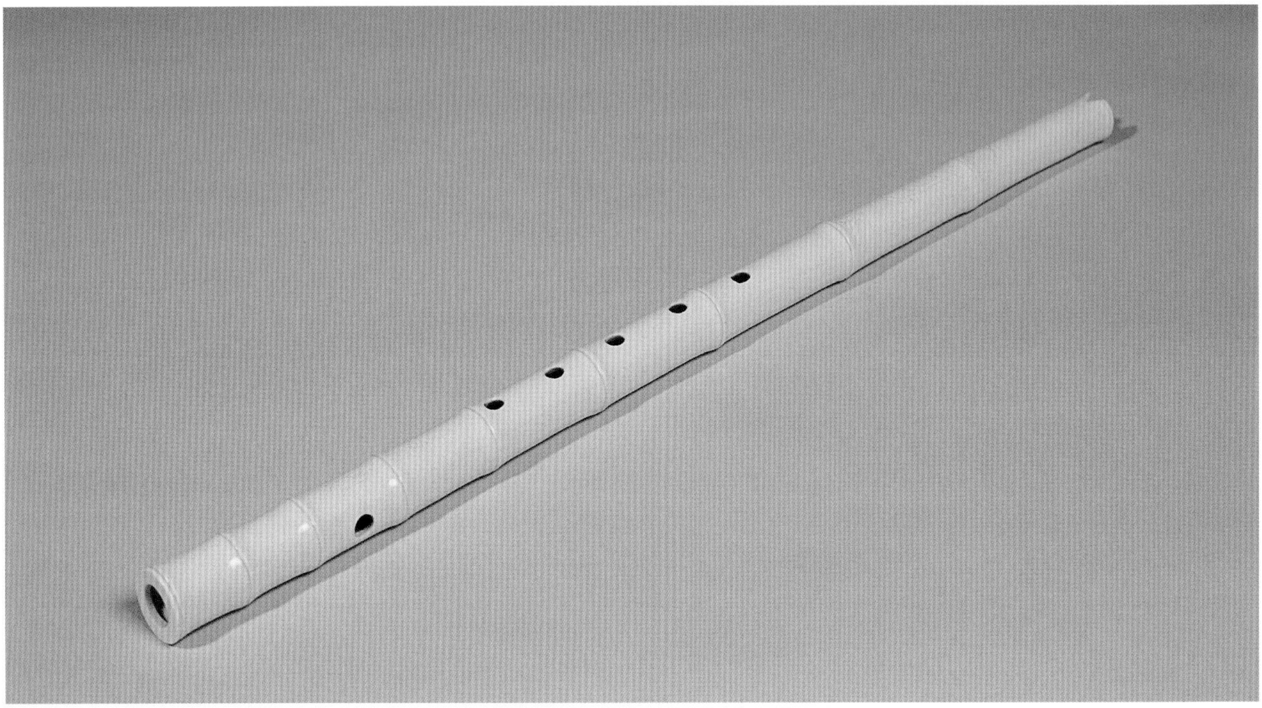

24. Cylindrical Vase

透雕筒形瓶

Probably late Ming or early Qing dynasty,
17th century

H. 15 in., W. 7 ½ in., D. 6 ¾ in.

Robert H. Blumenfield Collection

The sides of this vase are cut with an openwork design of the "Three Friends of Winter"—bamboo, pine, and prunus flowers—growing by rocks, and with a lotus scroll border on the shoulder.

Published: Blumenfield 2002, p. 37 with illustration.

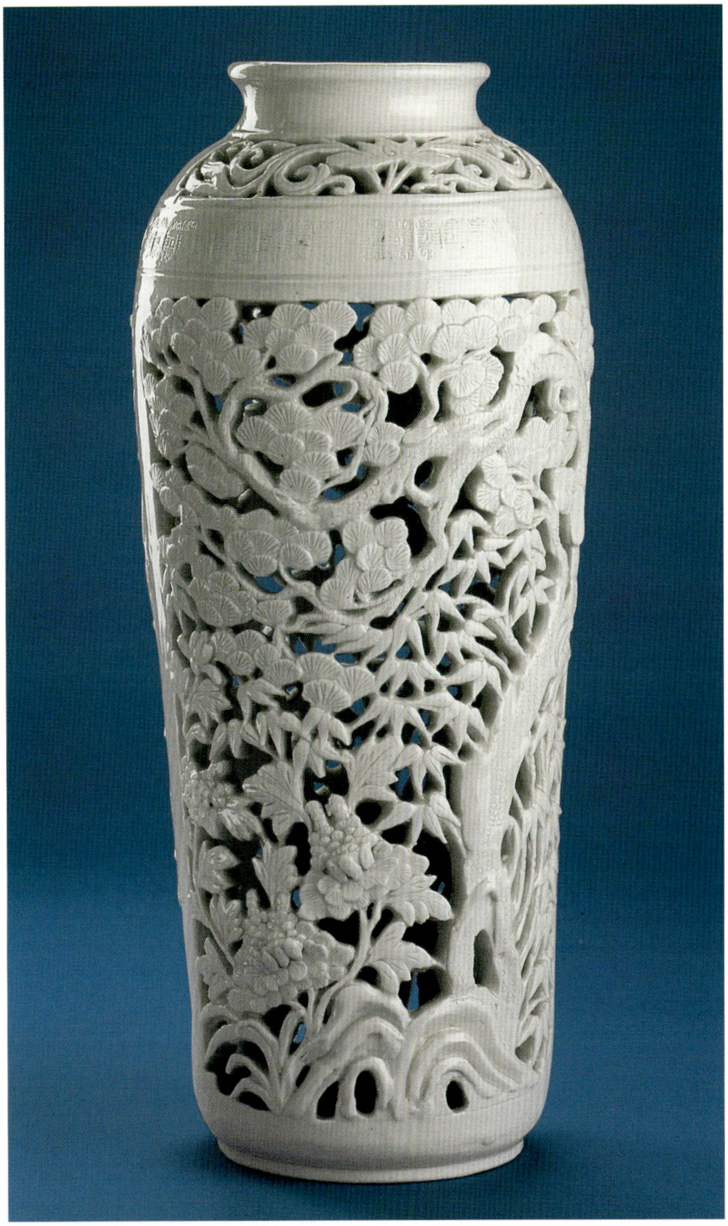

DEVOTIONAL FIGURE MODELS MAINLY OF THE LATE MING PERIOD

25. He Chaozong (early 17th century) Guanyin (Goddess of Mercy) Seated in Contemplation

何朝宗 坐觀音像

Late Ming dynasty, 1619
H. 17 in., W. 8 ¼ in., D. 6 ¼ in.
Square seal: *He Chaozong yin*
Inscribed: *jiwei nian* (corresponding to 1619)
Private Collection, New York

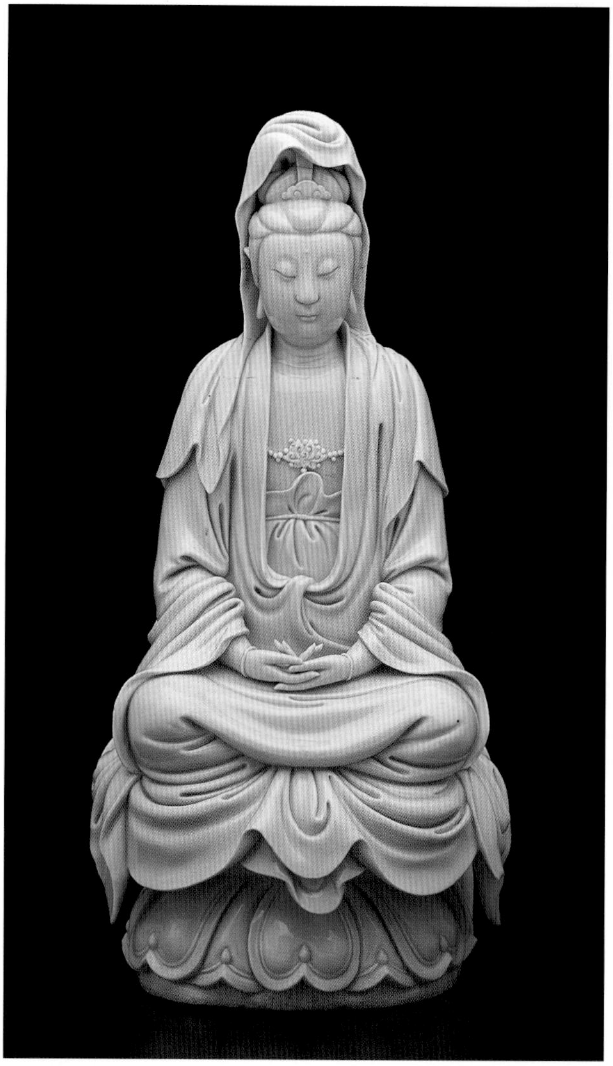

The deity is enthroned on a base modeled with conventional lotus petals; she sits with legs folded and hands resting on her lap in the mudra of meditation. She is dressed in voluminous white robes, with a mantle covering her head and falling to her shoulders, and she wears a diadem containing the image of Amida Buddha, a jeweled necklace, and pearl bracelets on her wrists. Her eyes are lowered and the expression is contemplative.

The square seal of the modeler He Chaozong, *He Chaozong yin*, is stamped on the back, and at the foot of the throne in front are incised the characters *jiwei nian*, representing a year in the sixty-year cycle that corresponds to 1559, 1619, or 1679.

This distinguished and important figure is one of three known similar versions of the model by He Chaozong, all in the United States: the others being in the Koger (Ayers 1985, no. 147) and Blumenfield Collections (Blumenfield 2002, p. 130, pls. A, B). In combination with the 1763 Quanzhou gazetteer cited in the Introduction, it appeared to provide the only known written evidence for dating the work of Dehua's greatest figure modeler. Further evidence is provided however by a different Guanyin figure in the Blumenfield Collection (just announced in Blumenfield 2002, pp. 163–65, pls. A, B), which is backed by a mandorla bearing an inscription reported to record that it was made by He Chaozong in the year of Wanli's reign corresponding to 1618, i.e., in the year before this figure.

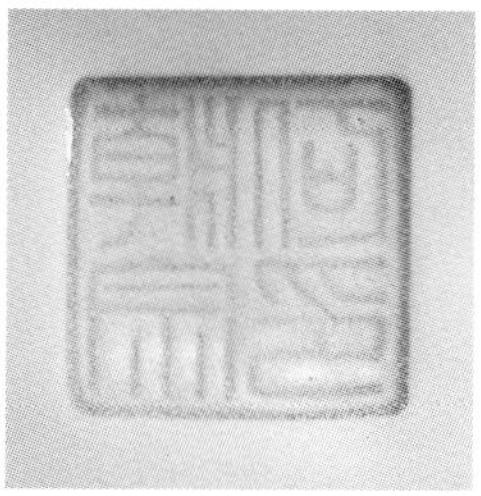

Published: Chinese Porcelain Company 1999, p. 17.

26. He Chaozong (early 17th century) Guanyin, the Protector of Fishermen

何朝宗 立觀音像

Ming dynasty, early 17th century

H. 20 in., W. 6 ½ in., D. 5 ½ in.

Square seal: *He Chaozong yin*

The Koger Collection, The John and Mable Ringling Museum of Art, the State Art Museum of Florida (20.98)

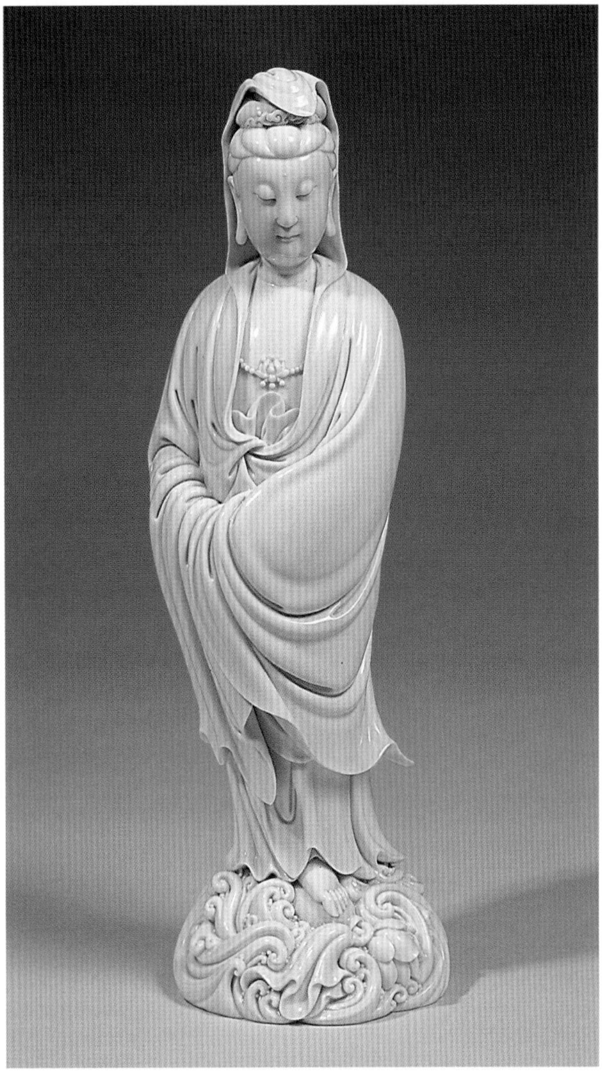

The deity stands on a low base lapped by waves, her extended left foot resting on a vase from which project a lotus flower and leaf. Her body is turned slightly to the right; her hands are clasped beneath her outer robe, which appears gently agitated by the breeze; and her high-piled hair is covered by a mantle that falls to her shoulders. There is an *urna* mark on her forehead, and her eyelids are lowered; a jeweled necklace adorns her breast. The square seal of the modeler He Chaozong, *He Chaozong yin*, is stamped on the back.

Apart from this remarkably elegant model of Guanyin by the sea, He Chaozong also produced a characteristically fine figure of the deity standing on clouds (for an example in the Victoria and Albert Museum, see Donnelly 1969, pl. 145A).

Published: Marchant 1985, no. 1; Beurdeley and Raindre 1987, pl. 333.
Ex coll.: Edward T. Chow

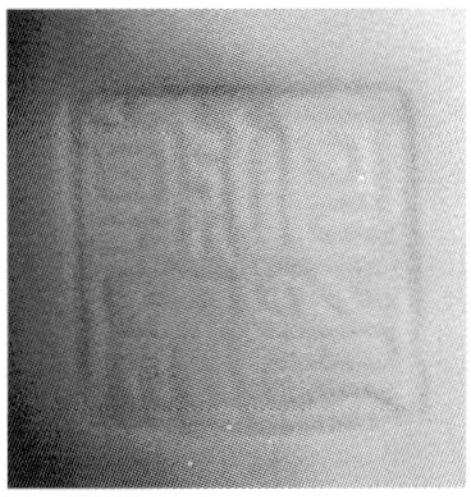

27. He Chaozong (early 17th century) Damo (Bodhidharma) Crossing the Yangzi on a Reed

何朝宗 達摩一葦渡江

Ming dynasty, early 17th century
H. 17 ⅛ in., W. 5 in.
Square seal: *He Chaozong yin*
Wang Xing Lou Collection

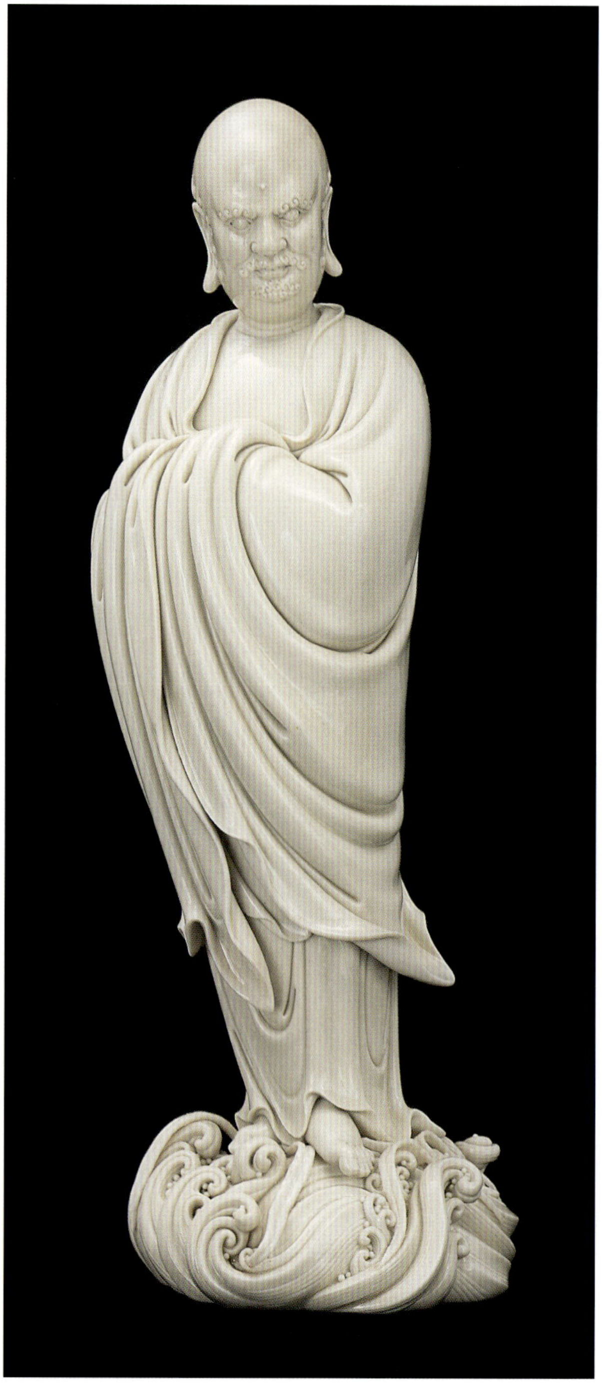

The figure stands barefoot on a low domed base ornamented with swirling waves. He wears full-length robes concealing his hands, which are clasped at the chest. The largely bald head leans slightly forward and to the left, showing somewhat protruding eyes, bushy eyebrows, a broad nose, slightly parted lips revealing the teeth, and a curled beard and moustache, as well as curling sideburns; the ears have characteristically long lobes and there is an *urna* mark on the forehead. The square seal of the modeler He Chaozong, *He Chaozong yin*, is stamped on the back.

Damo is the Indian monk who traveled to China early in the sixth century, bringing the precepts of the Buddhist faith to the northern state of Wei. More particularly, he is a patriarch of the meditative cult known as Chan Buddhism (Japanese: Zen), which appealed strongly to the scholar class.

A similar model in the Palace Museum, Beijing, is published in *Zhongguo meishu quanji, Gongyi meishu bian 3: Taoci* (Shanghai, 1993).

Published: Priestley and Ferraro 1996, no. 50.

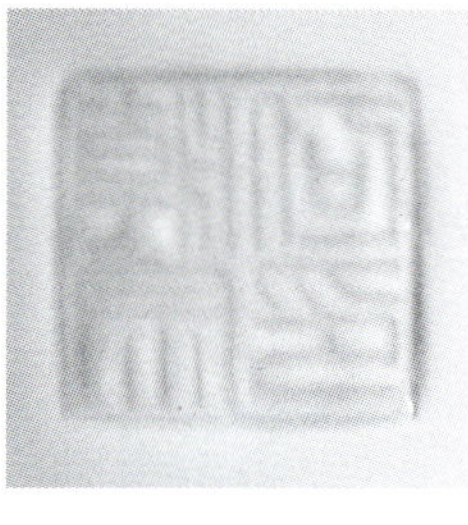

28. Chen Shixin (early 17th century)
Damo Seated in Meditation

陳氏信　坐禪達摩
Ming dynasty, early 17th century
H. 10 ⅝ in., W. 6 ¼ in., D. 4 ½ in.
Square seal: *Chen shixin yin*
Private Collection, New York

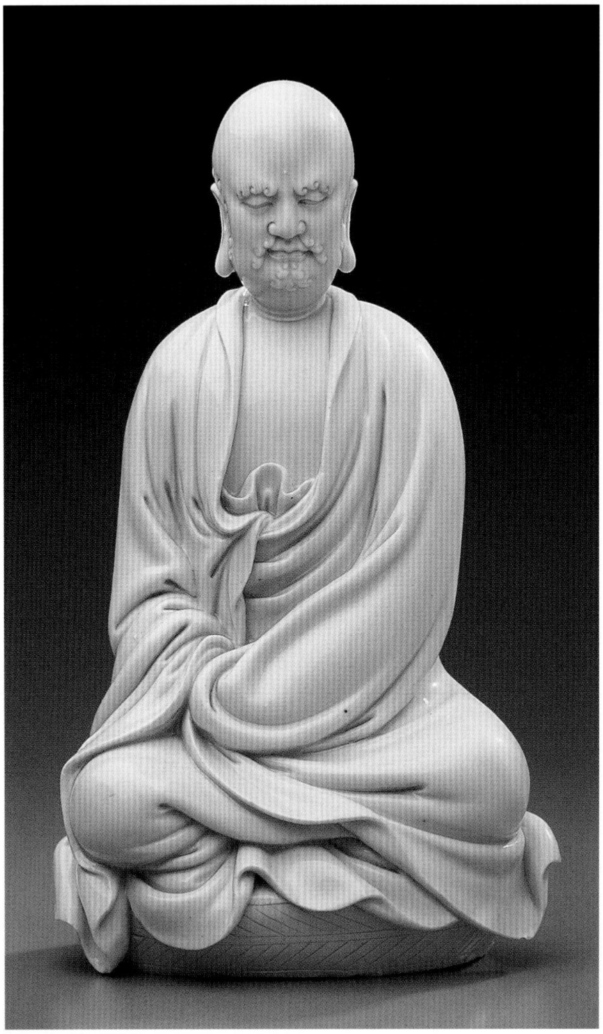

The patriarch is seated on a reed mat, his hands concealed above the lap in his long robes which lie open at the chest. He has a largely bald head with large ears, bushy eyebrows, eyes with lowered lids, a broad nose, and curling moustache and beard around the closed mouth. The square seal *Chen shixin yin,* apparently that of an otherwise unknown modeler, is stamped on the back.

The style of this admirable figure is close to that of He Chaozong's standing model (see cat. no. 27), and it is unlikely that they differ much in date. This Damo comes from the collection of the leading Shanghai and Hong Kong dealer Edward T. Chow.

Published: Beurdeley and Raindre 1987, pl. 336 (right), Chinese Porcelain Company 2000, p. 22.
Ex coll.: Edward T. Chow

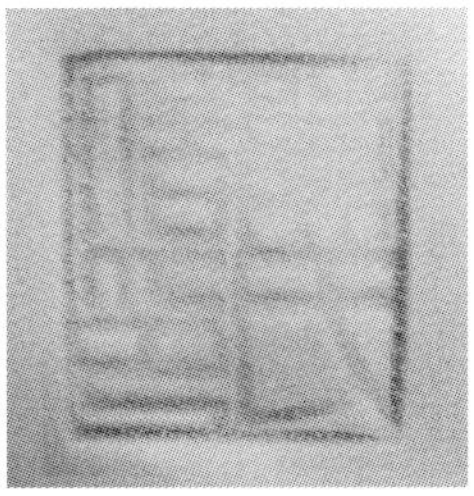

29. Lin Xiaozong (17th century) Guanyin Floating on a Lotus Leaf to the Isle of Putuoshan

林孝宗 渡海觀音

Ming dynasty, 17th century

H. 9 ¼ in., W. 4 ¾ in.

Square seal: *Lin Xiaozong yin*

Richard Lehman Gray Collection

The goddess sits with her hands clasped round her raised right leg. She wears long robes tied with a cord at the waist; the hair is swept back with coiled tresses falling to the mantle on her shoulders. Her expression is serene, and the *urna* mark of sanctity appears on her forehead. She wears a jeweled necklace and bracelets on her wrists.

The square seal of the modeler Lin Xiaozong, *Lin Xiaozong yin*, is stamped on the back.

Donnelly discusses the little-known work of Lin Xiaozong and illustrates other examples of figures ascribed to him (Donnelly 1969, pp. 279–80 and pl. 142).

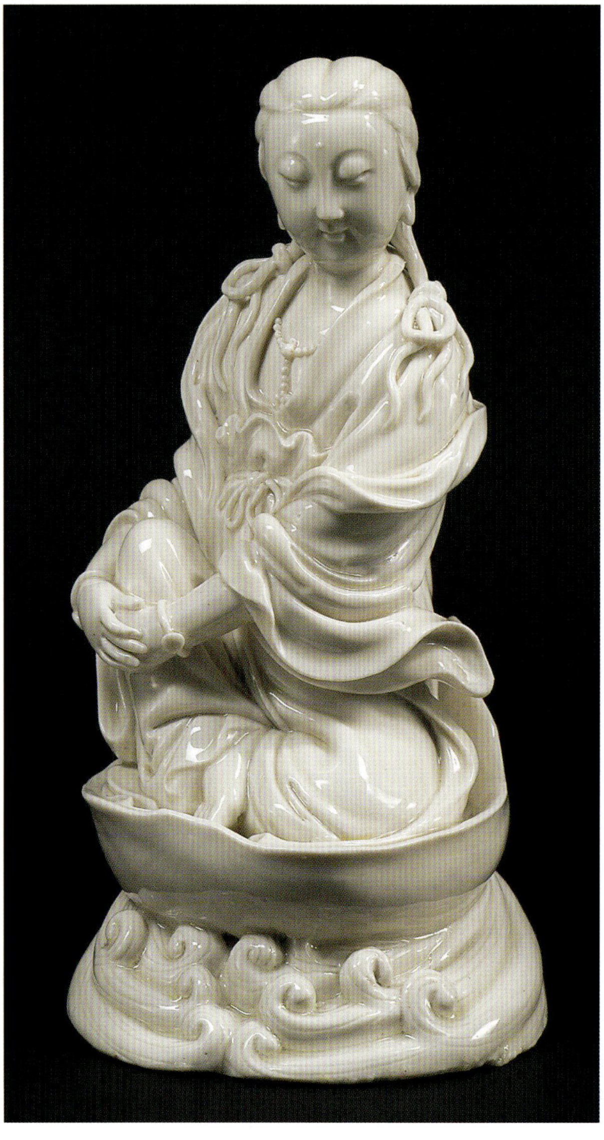

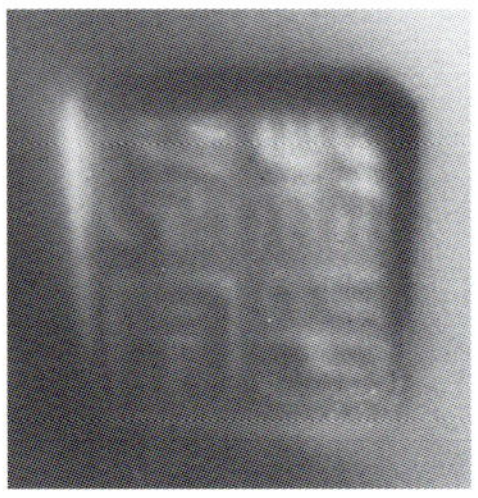

30. Damo Seated in Meditation

坐禪達摩

Ming dynasty, 17th century

H. 11 ¾ in., W. 7 ½ in., D. 5 ½ in.

The Metropolitan Museum of Art, New York. Gift of Mrs. Winthrop W. Aldrich, Mrs. Arnold Whitridge, and Mrs. Sheldon Whitehouse, 1963 (63.176)

The patriarch is seated cross-legged on a reed mat; his clasped hands lie on his lap beneath his long robes, which fall open to expose his chest.

In its pose, the modeling of the head, and the arrangement of the robes, this fine figure much resembles the version by Chen above (cat. no. 28), and it is surprising that it bears no modeler's mark. See also a model in the British Museum from the Franks Collection (Harrison-Hall 2001, no. 17:14, p. 514–15).

Published: Valenstein 1989, fig. 197.

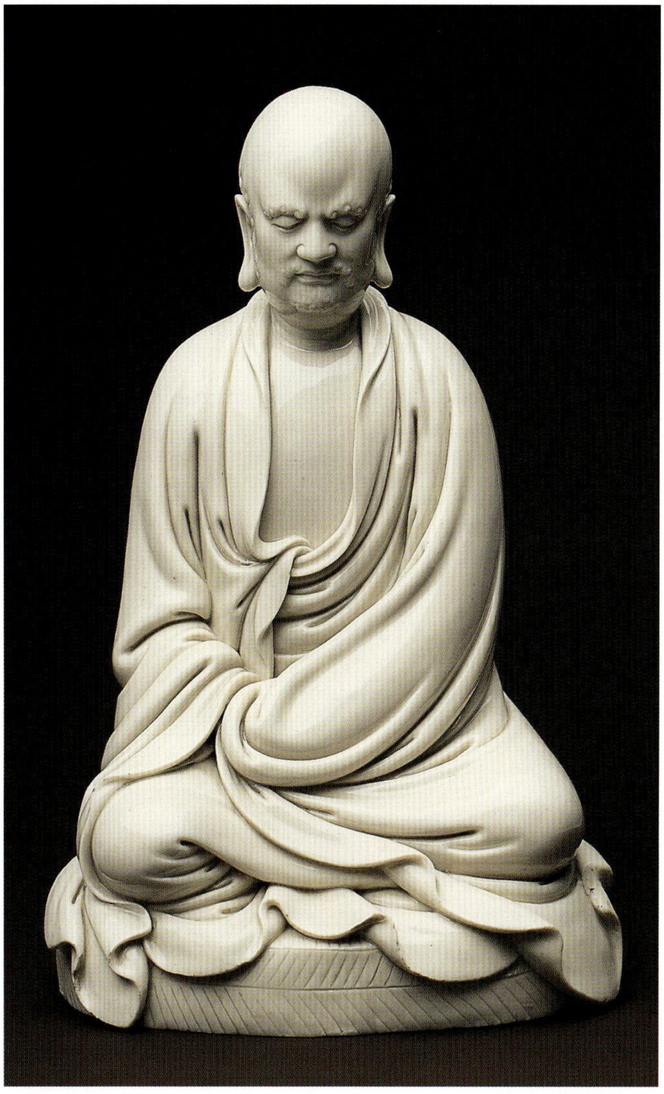

31. Guanyin Enthroned on a Lotus Base

蓮座觀音

Ming or early Qing dynasty, 17th century

H. 28 ¼ in., W. 11 ¼ in., D. 12 ¼ in.

Mr. and Mrs. Stanley F. Druckenmiller

The figure is massively potted and the pose highly formalized. It sits in an attitude of contemplation, with legs folded and hands lying in the lap in *dhyana* mudra. The long robes hang symmetrically, while the mantle frames the head where the hair is crowned by a diadem bearing an Amida figure. Its features are withdrawn and there is an *urna* mark on the forehead. The formal pose and large size of this image suggest that it was intended for a similarly imposing location.

Published: Chinese Porcelain Company 2000, no. 1.

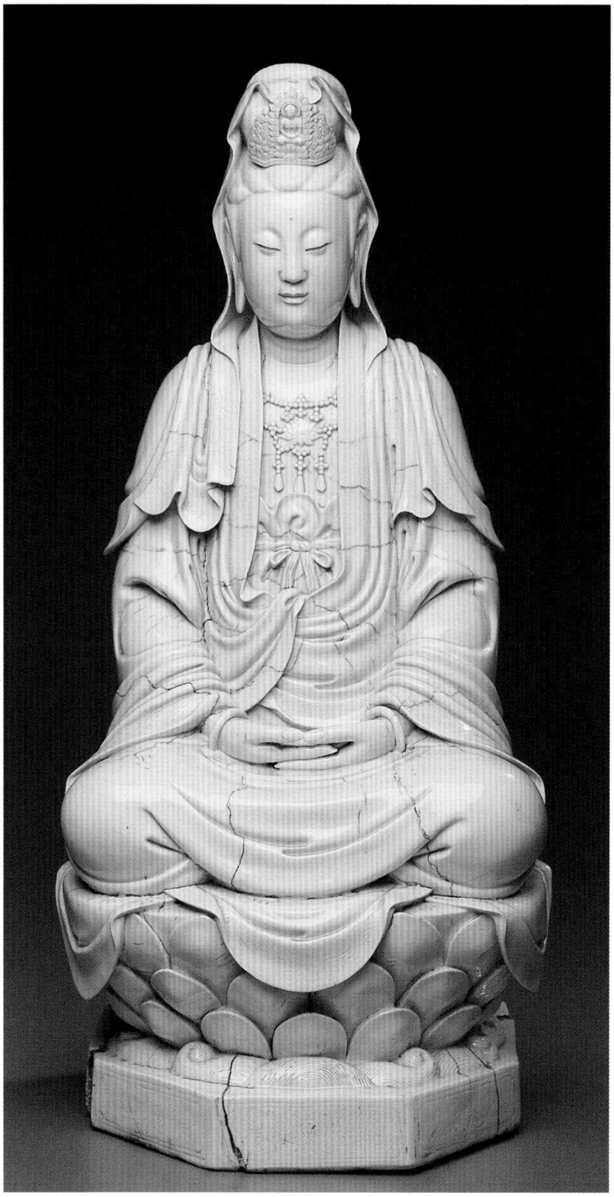

32. Buddha Seated in Meditation

禪定佛

Ming or early Qing dynasty, 17th century

H. 10 ¾ in., W. 7 ¾ in., D. 5 ½ in.

Private Collection, New York

This heavily potted figure is seated with his legs crossed in *padmasana*, the lotus posture, and his hands lying in the lap in *dhyana* mudra; his robe spreads over the base, the sides of which are molded with heavy lotus petals in relief. The robe is draped over the shoulders, leaving an expanse of bare chest above the dhoti. His placid face with downcast eyes is framed by the elongated earlobes and a mass of tight curls that cover the head. For a comparable model, see Marchant 1994, no. 4.

Published: Chinese Porcelain Company 2000, no. 2.

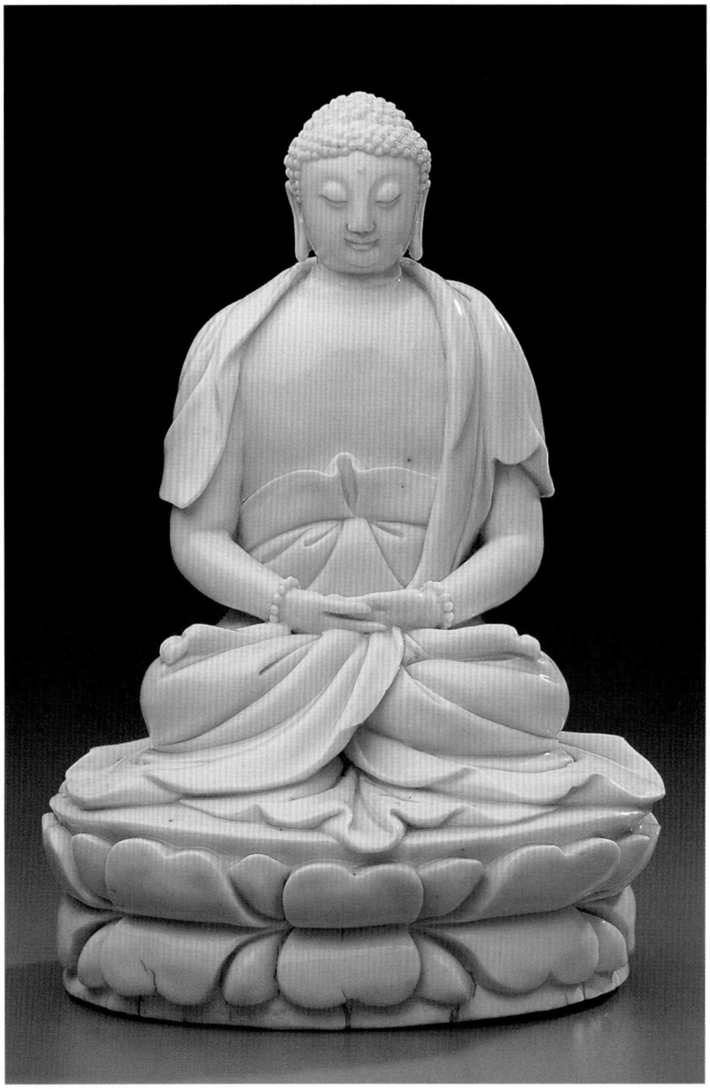

33. Doumu (Dipper Mother)

斗母像

Late Ming or early Qing dynasty,
mid-17th century

H. 9 ½ in., W. 4 ¾ in., D. 3 ¼ in.

The Koger Collection, The John and Mable Ringling Museum of Art, the State Art Museum of Florida (18.96)

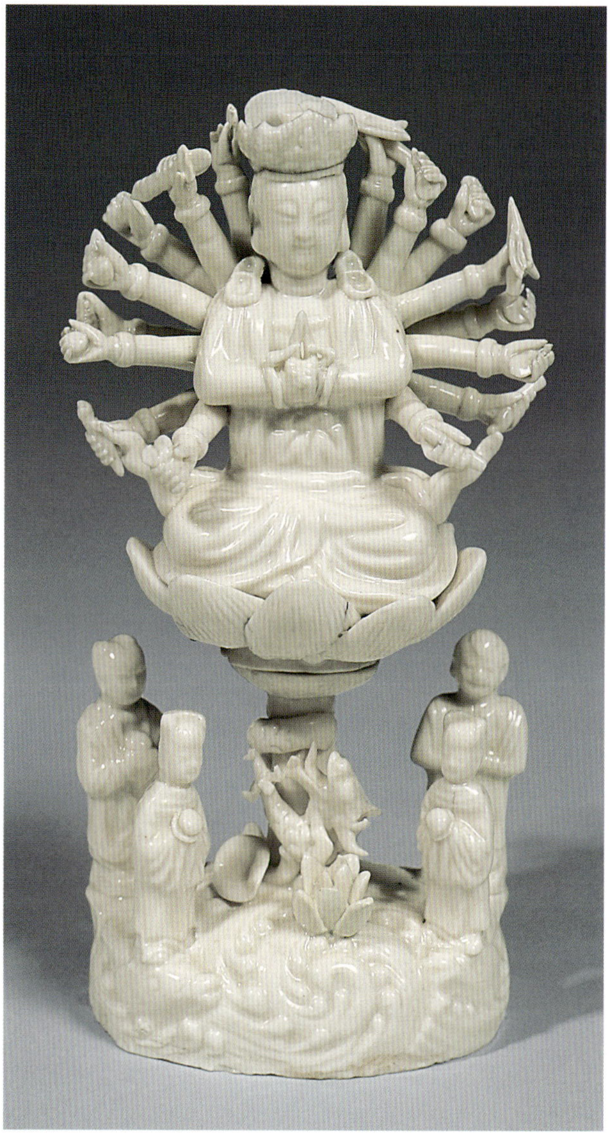

This model consists of two parts: the popular Daoist deity is seated on a lotus flower, which slots into a stem rising from an oval mound base on which are the figures of a dragon and four standing acolytes. She wears a diadem and a jeweled necklace, and has altogether eighteen arms, one pair of which are held across the chest in a gesture of greeting, while the rest hold a variety of precious objects and weapons.

Often described in the West as "the eighteen-armed Guanyin," Doumu is one of the most popular images of Daoism. She is, according to legend, the mother of the seven stars of the Northern Dipper (Ursa Major), her complex image being apparently derived from that of Marichi, one of the devas of Buddhism. For a discussion of her significance in the Daoist pantheon, see Little 2000, pp. 275–83.

Donnelly 1969, pl. 99A, illustrates an example of this model now in the British Museum. Another example in Hampton Court Palace is apparently from the collection formed by Queen Mary II before her death in 1694; while yet another one probably belonged to her close relative Princess Louise Henriette, Electress of Brandenburg (d. 1667), and was in the 1688 inventory of the Kunstkammer at Oranienburg (Reidemeister 1932, p. 175 ff.). A somewhat later version, apparently modeled in one piece, was inventoried in Augustus the Strong's collection at Dresden by 1721 (Stroeber 2002, fig. 3), and a late Qing dynasty version is illustrated by Donnelly 1969, pl. 99C.

Published: Marchant 1985, no. 59.

34. He Chaozong (early 17th century) Guanyin with the Scroll of Wisdom

何朝宗 持卷觀音

Ming dynasty, first half 17th century

H. 9 ⅜ in., W. 6 ⅛ in.

Gourd-shaped seal: *He Chaozong*

Private Collection

The goddess sits on a reed mat, wearing a voluminous robe from under which her right foot protrudes. Her left hand, held across her body, grasps a scroll and rests on her raised right knee. Her piled-up chignon is held in place by a hairpin. Her eyes are lowered, and her face expresses her state of contemplation. The gourd-shaped seal of the modeler He Chaozong, *He Chaozong*, is stamped on the back.

A comparable model formerly belonging to the great Chinese collector-dealer Edward T. Chow and marked *zhu jun fu ji* on the pin of her chignon is illustrated by Beurdeley and Raindre 1987, pl. 335 left.

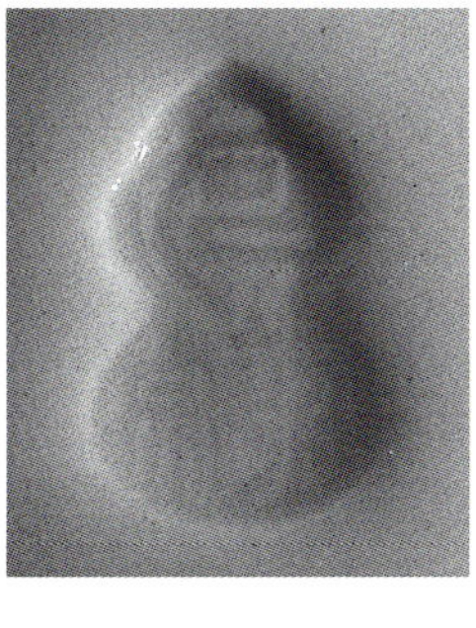

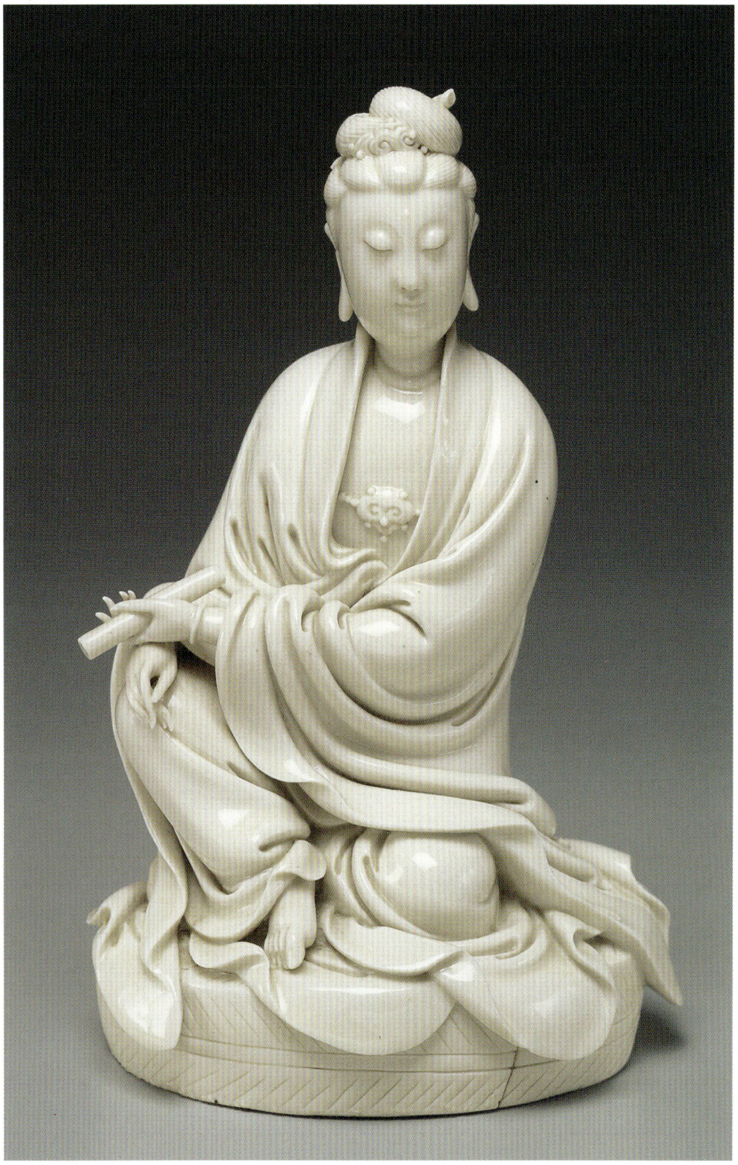

35. Standing Guanyin

立觀音像

Ming or Qing dynasty, 17th century or later

H. 20 in., W. 5 ½ in.

Commendation mark: *wan bang* (all nations)

Richard Lehman Gray Collection

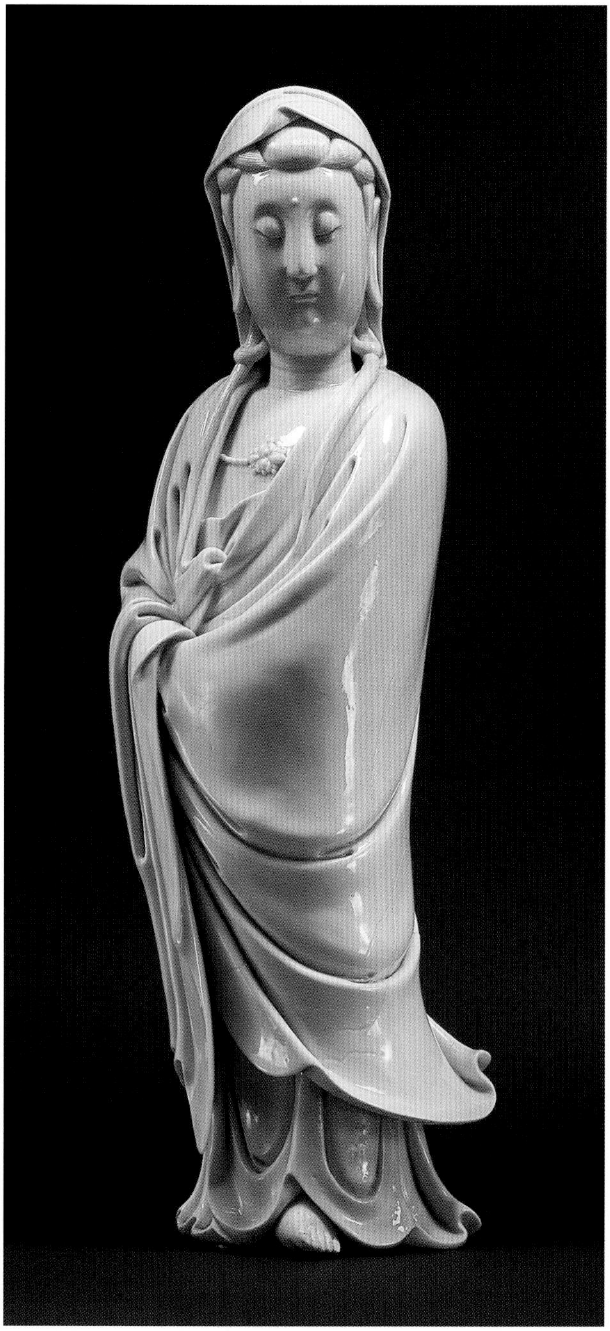

Her hands are clasped beneath the long, flowing robe that falls to the floor, leaving only her left foot protruding; her features are composed in the act of contemplation; and her head is covered by a mantle, while long tresses fall to the shoulders on either side. A mark of commendation, *wan bang* (all nations), is stamped on the back.

The mark, the purport of which is obscure, is noted by Donnelly 1969, p. 256 and p. 354, no. E. 13, and its use ascribed to the eighteenth century.

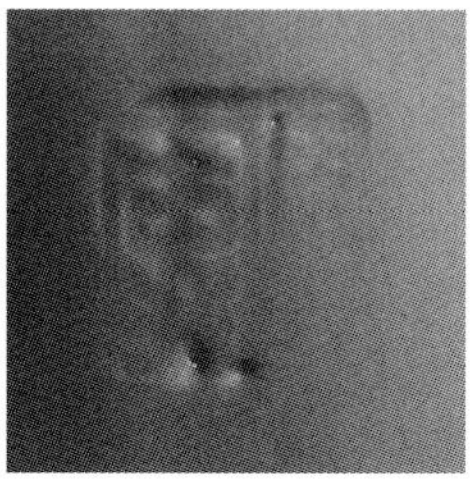

36. Guanyin Seated on a Rocky Throne

坐觀音像

Ming dynasty, first half 17th century

H. 9 ⅝ in., W. 5 in., D. 3 ½ in.

The Koger Collection, The John and Mable Ringling Museum of Art, the State Art Museum of Florida (22.100)

The goddess sits on a rough rocky prominence in *lalitasana,* the pose of royal ease, wearing long robes and with one hand resting on her raised right knee. To her right stands a flask of heavenly dew.

This model may be compared with the earliest known Dehua figure of Guanyin similarly posed on rocks; it is inscribed with a date corresponding to 1629 (Donnelly 1969, pl. 71B) and is said to be in a Hong Kong private collection.

Published: Ayers 1985, no. 146.

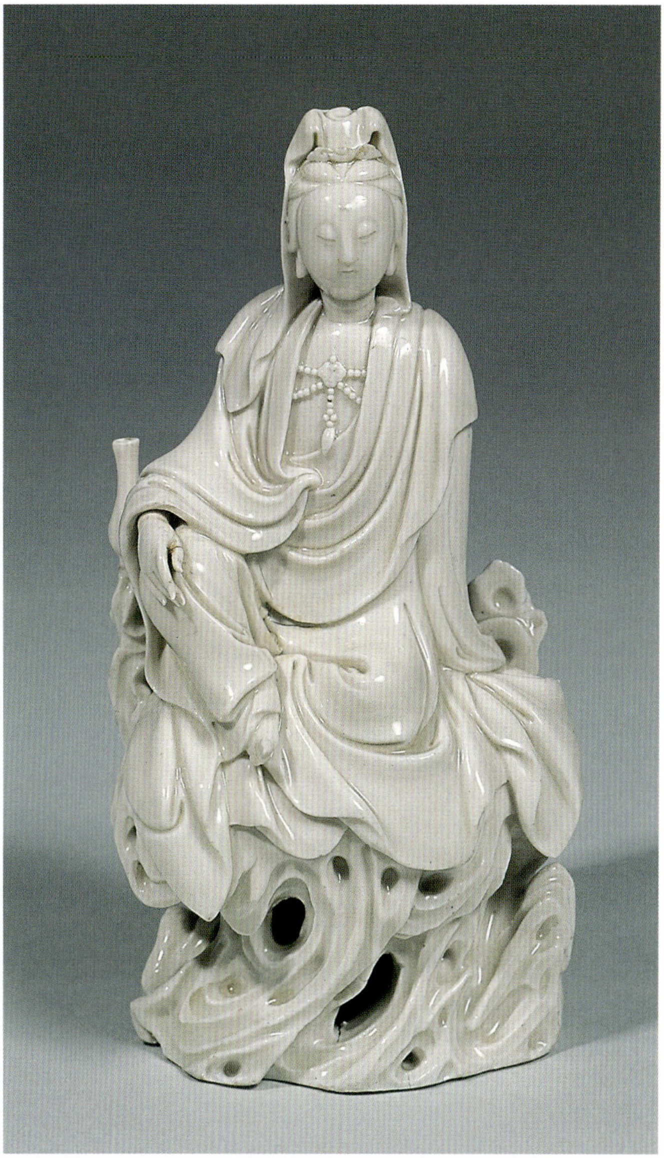

37. Grotto with Guanyin, Acolytes, and the Eighteen Lohan

觀音菩薩龕

Ming or early Qing dynasty, 17th century

H. 14 ½ in., W. 9 ½ in., D. 7 in.

Robert H. Blumenfield Collection

This group represents Guanyin's shrine on the island of Putuoshan. A comparable grotto model which bears a porcelain label with the inscription "Putuoshan" is illustrated by Donnelly 1969, pl. 92. The shrine was a noted place of pilgrimage for devotees of Guanyin.

Published: Blumenfield 2002, pl. on p. 63.

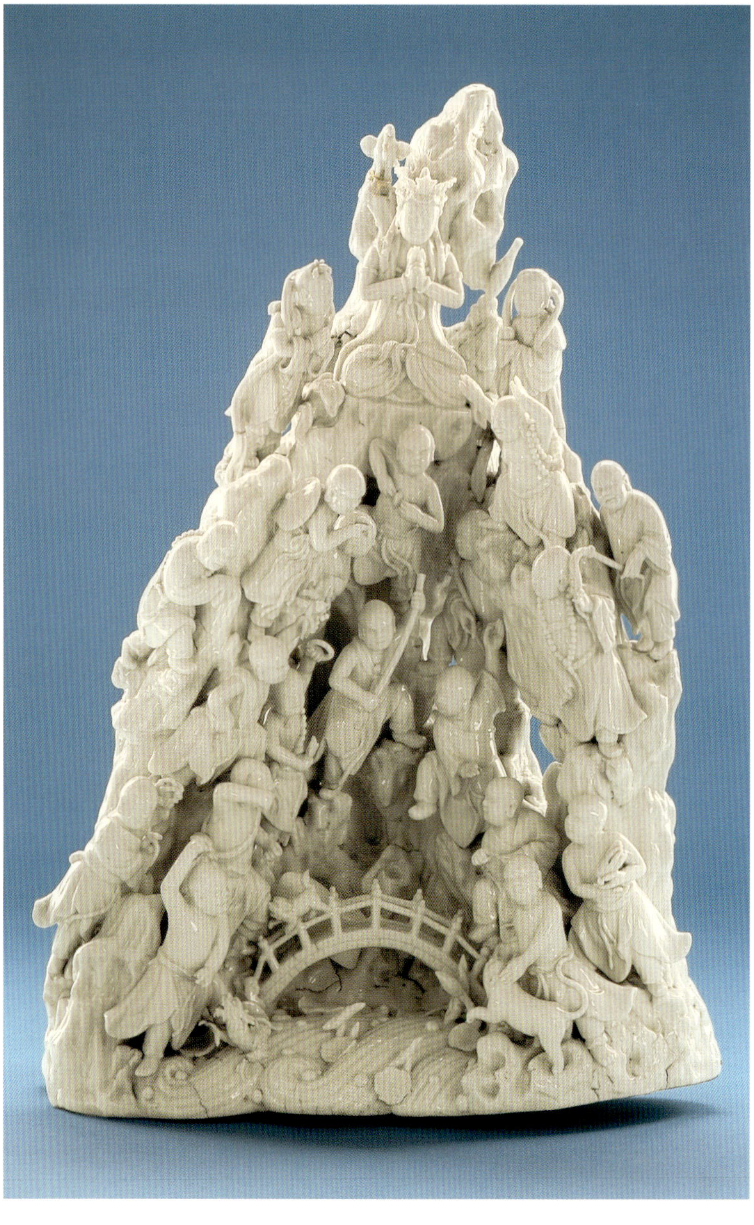

38. Guanyin with a Mythical Lion

倚獅觀音

Ming or early Qing dynasty, 17th century

H. 4 ½ in., W. 3 ¼ in., D. 3 in.

The Koger Collection, The John and Mable Ringling Museum of Art, the State Art Museum of Florida (15.92)

The goddess is seated on a rocky plateau, holding a scroll and resting her arms on a lion's head; the creature has a single horn and a divided mane on its back.

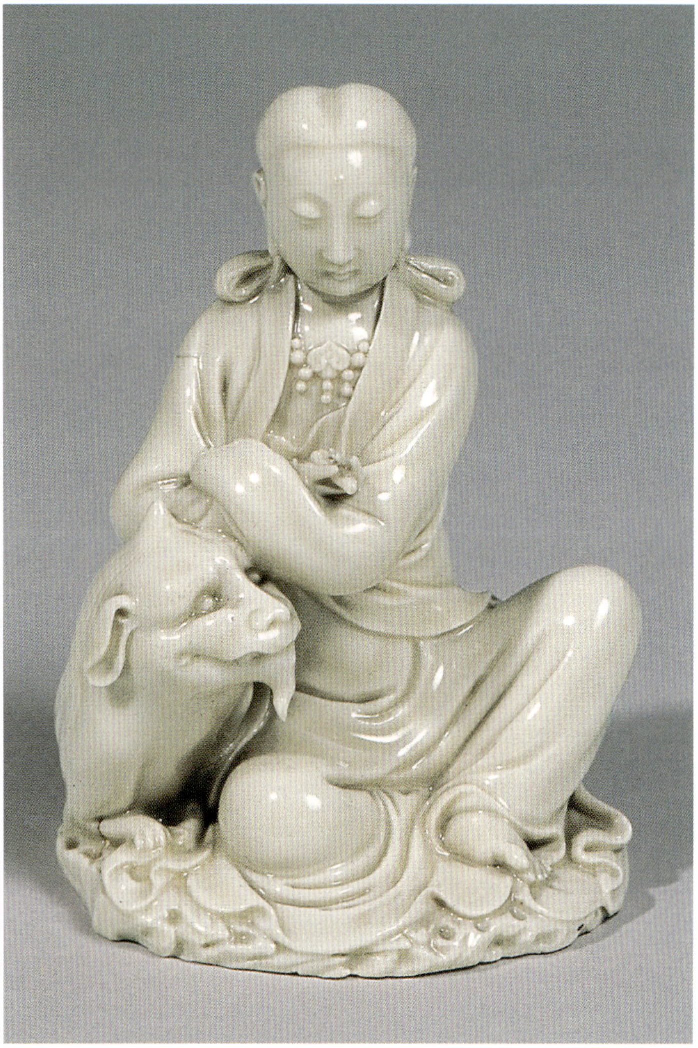

39. Budai with His Bag of Plenty

布袋和尚

Ming or Qing dynasty, 17th century or later

H. 9 ¼ in., W. 4 ¼ in., D. 3 ¾ in.

The Koger Collection, The John and Mable Ringling Museum of Art, the State Art Museum of Florida (15.84)

This Buddhist monk is bald-headed, bare to the waist, and wears a smiling expression; he holds a fly whisk and stands on his bag, which is lapped by waves. To one side is a covered basketwork box from which a creature, perhaps a bat, is attempting to escape.

Budai, who lived towards the end of the Five Dynasties period (618–906), was said to be the last incarnation of Maitreya Buddha. In later times his image was popularly believed to bestow good fortune (symbolized by the bat). For a seated figure of Budai, typical of many exported to the West, see fig. 6 in the Introduction; it was mounted in mid-eighteenth-century rococo-style ormolu in France, where such models were known as *magots*.

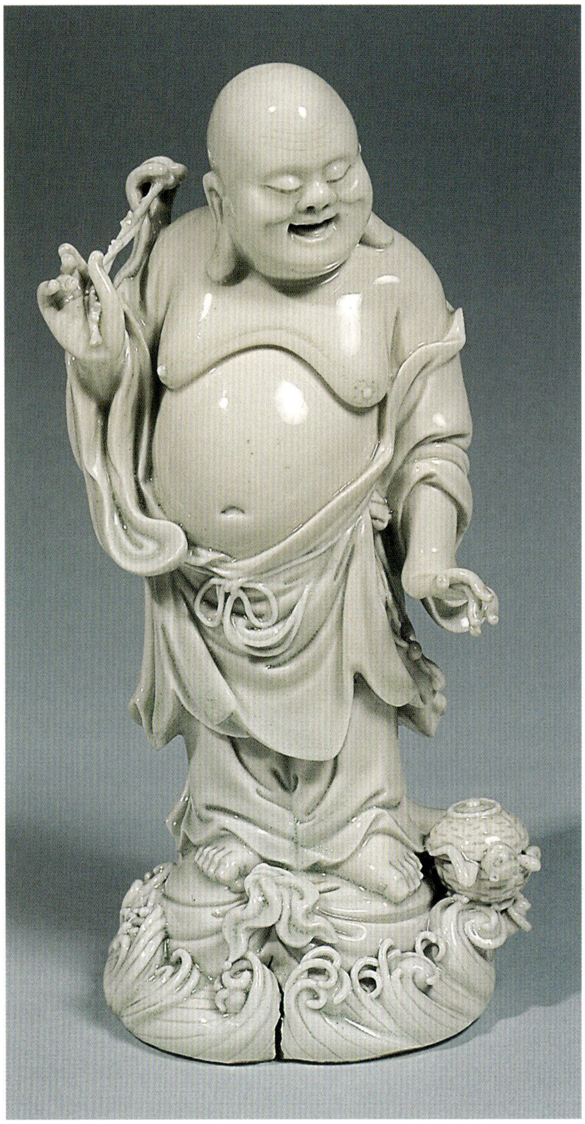

40. He Chaozong (early 17th century) Wenchang (Daoist God of Literature) Enthroned

何朝宗 文昌神像

Ming dynasty, early 17th century

H. 15 in., W. 6 ½ in., D. 5 ½ in.

Square seal: *He Chaozong yin*

The Koger Collection, The John and Mable Ringling Museum of Art, the State Art Museum of Florida (19.97)

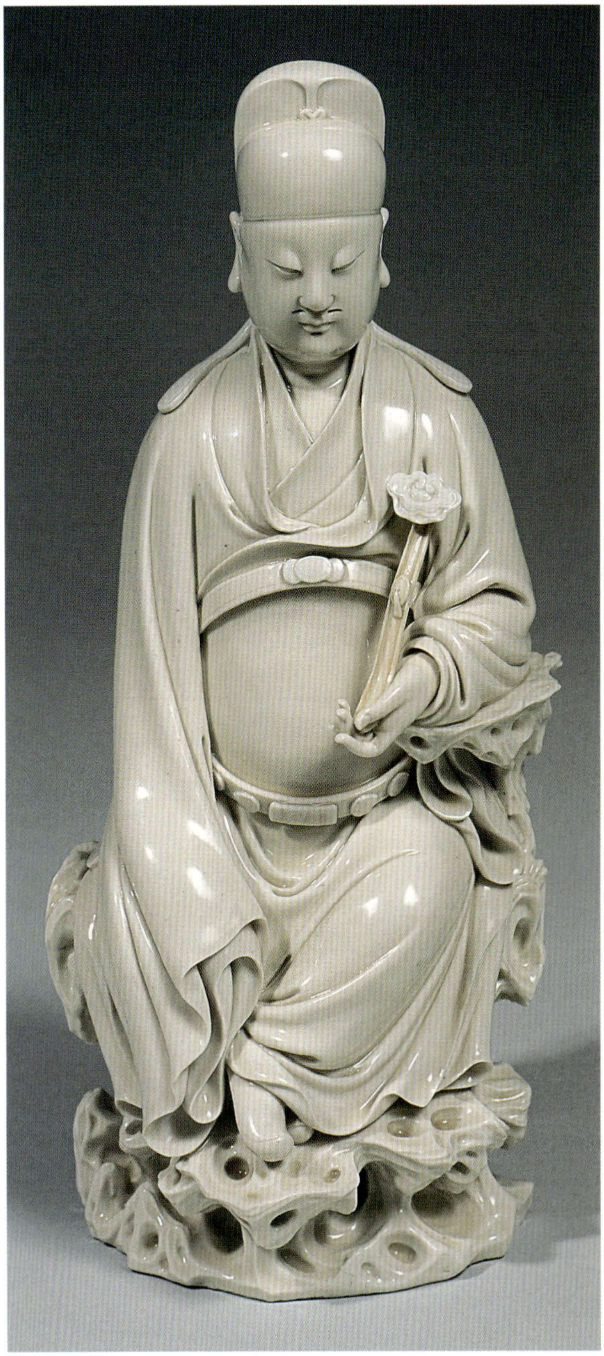

The divinity is seated on a rocky throne, his left arm supported on an outcrop and holding a *ruyi* "good wish" scepter. He is dressed in long, flowing robes that conceal his right arm but not his feet and are constricted across his body by two ornamented belts. He wears an official's hat and has a somewhat severe expression. There are piercings on his upper lip and chin for the insertion of real hair. The square seal *He Chaozong yin* of the modeler He Chaozong is stamped on the back.

Wenchang's image was widely revered in China, where he was regarded as bestowing success in the all-important literary examinations that were the path to official preferment (see Little 2000, p. 267).

Another example of this model is in the Meiyintang Collection (Krahl 1994, no. 1004). See also Hong Kong 1975, no. 103, for a similar model in the Fujian Provincial Museum, without throne and with the scepter in the right hand. Another reversed model, but once again with a rocky throne, is in the Hickley Collection (Kerr and Ayers 2002, no. 27).

Published: Marchant 1985, no. 3, and Donnelly 1969, pl. 145D.

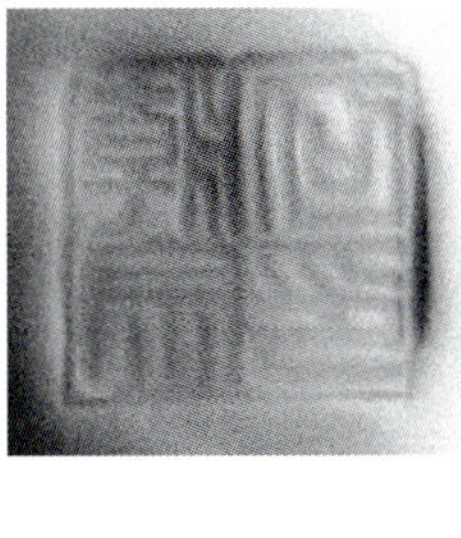

41. Zhenwu (Perfected Warrior, Dark Lord of the Northern Quadrant)

真武神像

Ming dynasty, first half 17th century
H. 10 in., W. 6 in.
Private Collection

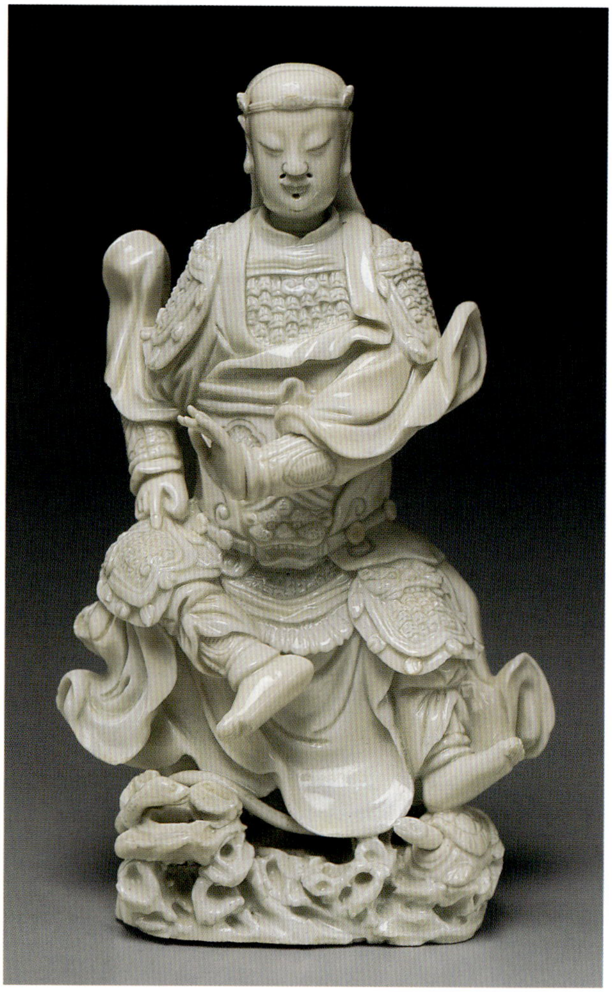

This warlike figure is seated on a rocky throne, his left arm raised in a gesture of deterrence, while a snake and the head of a tortoise project from the rocks below. He wears chest and thigh armor under his robe; on his head is a simple cap, and his characteristically long hair falls to his shoulders.

According to legend, Zhenwu (Xuantian shangdi) was successful in defeating the demon kings despite the intervention of a snake and a tortoise, which usually appear when he is depicted. He was thus accorded the titles of "First Lord of the Highest Heaven" and "Perfected Warrior," and subsequently became one of the most popular Daoist deities in Ming small-scale devotional sculpture for domestic use (Little 2000, pp. 291–97 and cat. nos. 105–6, illustrating examples in Longquan celadon and Jingdezhen blue-and-white ware). Appropriately, a temple dedicated to Zhenwu was built at the northernmost point of the Forbidden City in Beijing. An example of this model is in the Metropolitan Museum of Art, New York (with replaced hands); another is in the Virginia Museum of Fine Arts; see also Donnelly 1969, pl. 101A, and Kerr and Ayers 2002, no. 26.

42. Zhang Shoushan (17th century)
The Twin Genii of Mirth and Harmony (hehe erxian)

張壽山 和合二仙

Ming dynasty, early 17th century

H. 4 ½ in., W. 6 ¼ in., D. 3 ¼ in.

Square seal: *Zhang Shoushan yin*

Gourd-shaped seal: *Zhang Shoushan*

Anonymous Lender

The two laughing boys are seated together in genial conversation, wearing loose robes open to the waist. The figure on the right raises a finger to make a point. His crossed feet are bare whereas his companion wears shoes and has on his lap a box from which a bat, the emblem of happiness, is attempting to escape. Two marks of the modeler Zhang Shoushan, *Zhang Shoushan yin* in a square and the gourd-shaped *Zhang Shoushan*, are stamped on the back.

This immortal Daoist pair are the patron saints of merchants and of potters, and watch over their prosperity. Originally, they were historical figures: two irreverent priests who lived in the Tang period (618–907). A closely similar model by He Chaozong, bearing two of his seals, is in the Percival David Foundation, London (Donnelly 1969, pl. 149B; see also pl. 149A, for another less satisfactory version in the British Museum, bearing two more of his seals). Another He Chaozong-marked example of the subject is in the Hickley Collection in Singapore (Kerr and Ayers 2002, no. 23).

Published: Donnelly 1969, pl. 139 B.

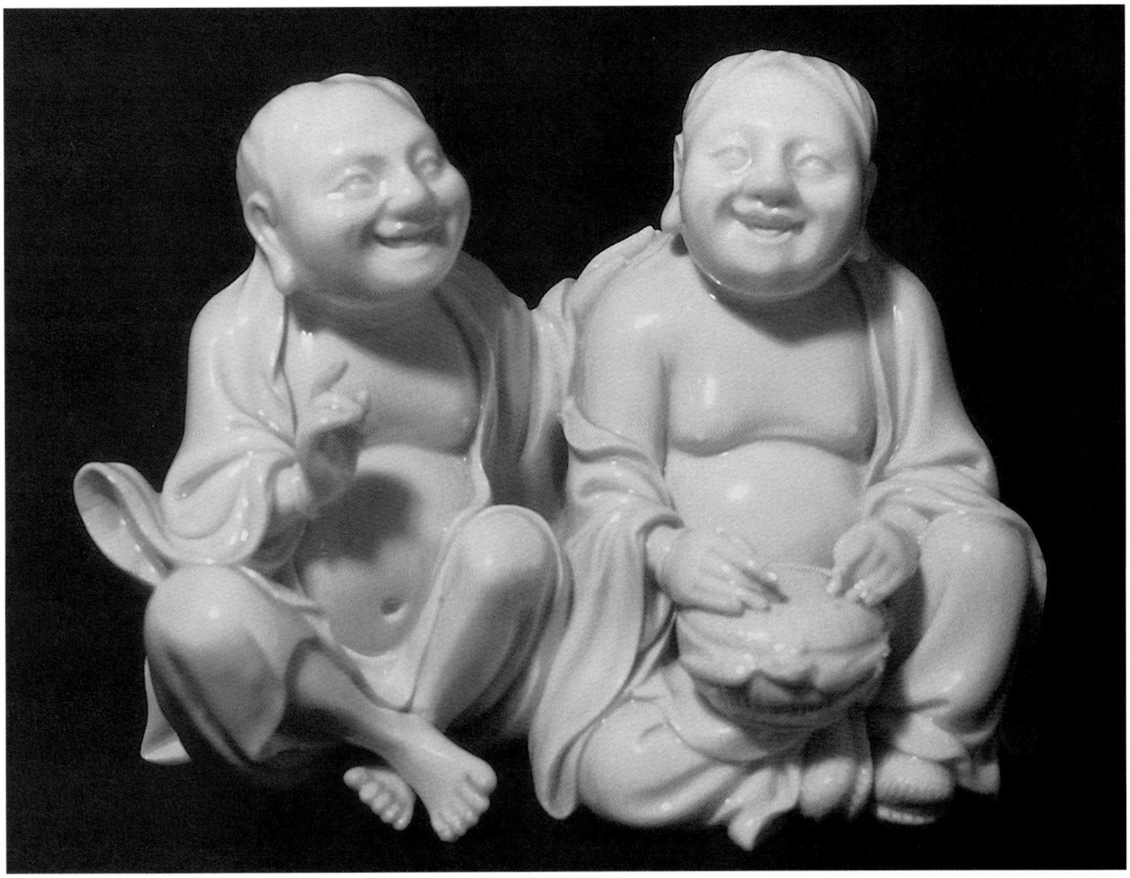

43. He Chaozong (early 17th century) The Poet Li Taibai

何朝宗 太白醉酒

Ming dynasty, early 17th century

H. 5 ¼ in., W. 4 ¾ in., D. 4 ¾ in.

Gourd-shaped commendation seal: *qianli miantan* (speak face to face though a thousand miles apart)

Square seal: *He Chaozong*

Robert H. Blumenfield Collection

Li Taibai (701–762) is asleep beside his wine jar. The poet's robes lie open and he is bare to the waist, his left hand resting on his knee.

The seal of the modeler He Chaozong, *He Chaozong* in a square, and above, *qianli miantan* (speak face to face though a thousand miles apart) in a gourd-shaped seal, are stamped on the back. For the use of the commendation mark elsewhere by He Chaozong, see the figure of Li Tieguai in the British Museum (Donnelly 1969, p. 258 and pl. 150C).

This great Tang poet was overly fond of the wine jar, and is said to have died while attempting to embrace the moon's reflection in the river. According to legend his spirit saved Dizang Wang, the Overlord of Hell, from drowning; hence, no doubt, his popularity in temples where devotions were paid to this deity.

Published: Blumenfield 2002, p. 134, pls. A, B.

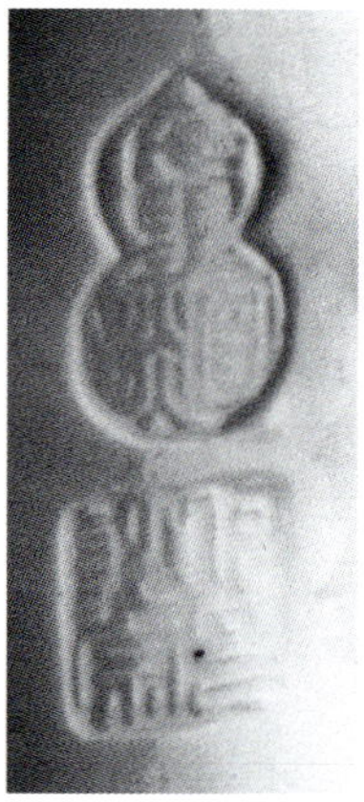

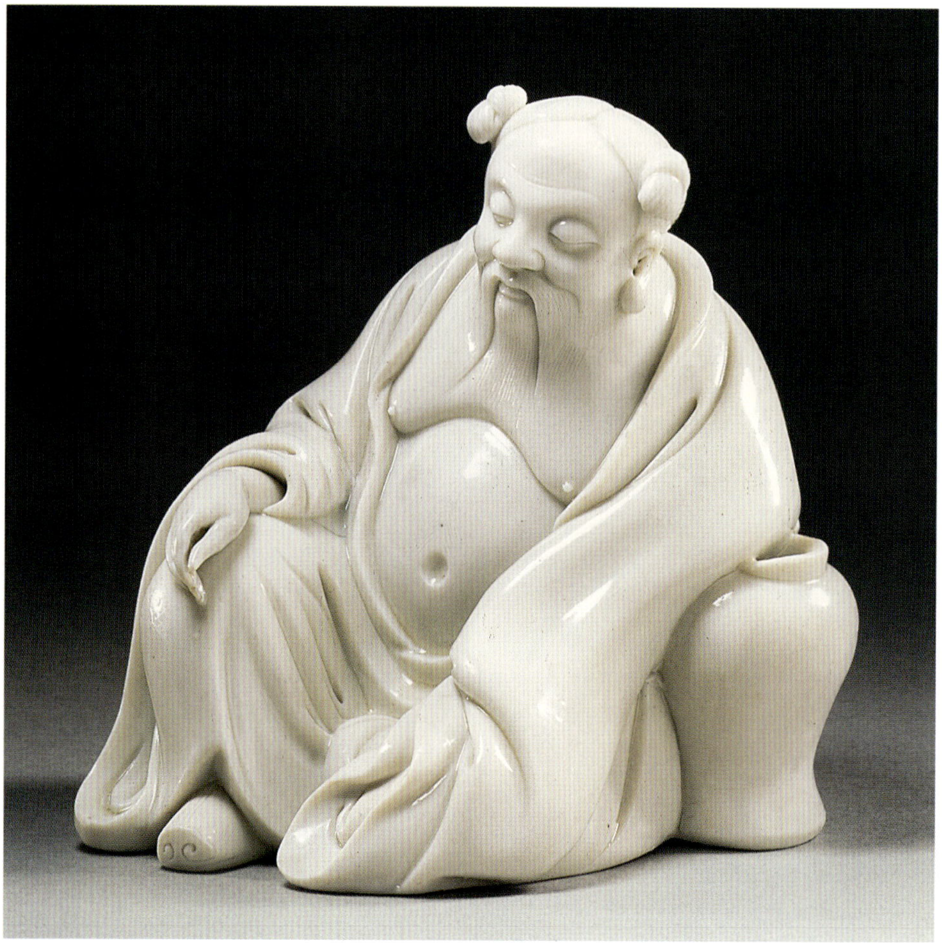

44. Deity with Four Attendants in a Rocky Landscape

登山仙人

Ming or early Qing dynasty, 17th century

H. 9 ¾ in., W. 6 in., D. 4 ¾ in.

Robert H. Blumenfield Collection

The deity is enthroned in a rocky bower with a scroll on a table among pointed and pierced rocks, accompanied below by a servant with a broom and three attendant figures in belted robes and scholar's hats.

In this rare model the deity, whose identity remains uncertain, wears a headdress of the kind seen in representations of the Daoist San Guan, or Three Rulers of Heaven, Earth, and Water, who function as judges of human fate; they are depicted in an illuminated manuscript in the Museum of Fine Arts, Boston (Little 2000, no. 72, p. 236).

Published: Blumenfield 2002, p. 59, pl. A.

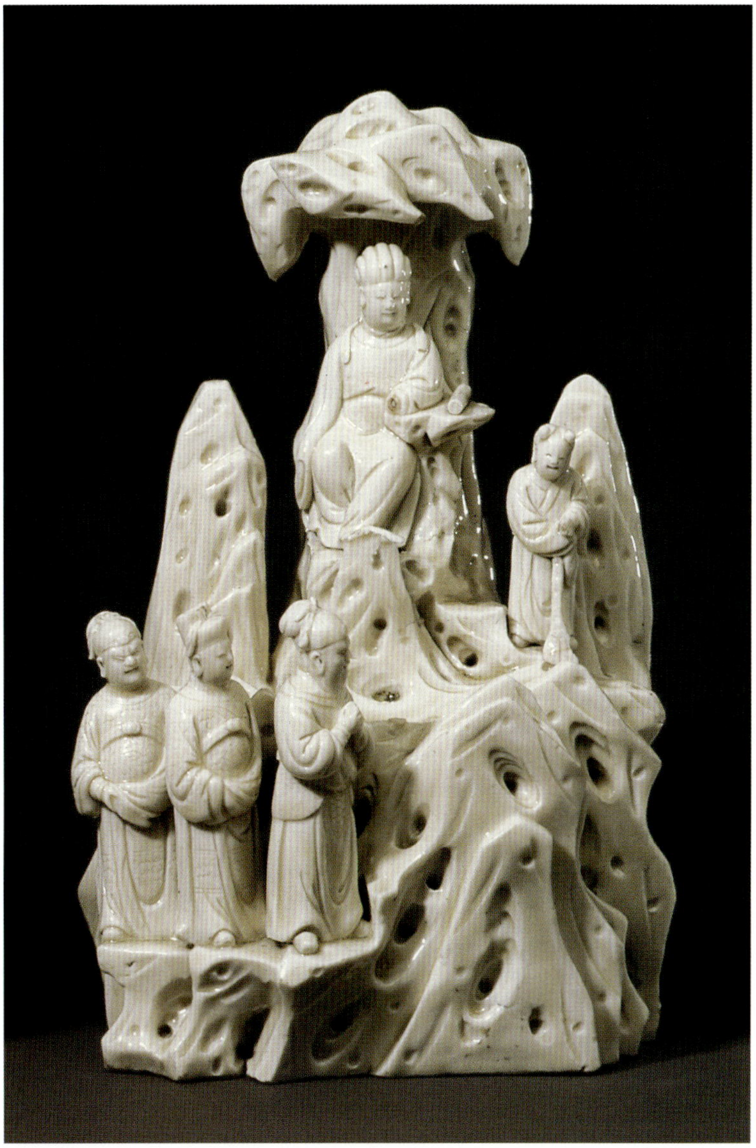

45. Shoulao (Shouxing, Star God of Long Life)

壽老（壽星）

Ming or early Qing dynasty, 17th century

H. 5 in., W. 4 ¾ in.

Richard Lehman Gray Collection

The god is seated between a stag and a crane. He has a long beard and bushy eyebrows, and wears on his domed head a cap with streamers falling behind to his shoulders; he holds a peach with both hands.

Shouxing was a popular domestic god in China, and the stag, crane, and peach, frequently associated with him in artistic representations, are all potent Daoist symbols of longevity. He is known also as "the Old Man of the Southern (Celestial) Pole" (see Little 2000, p. 269).

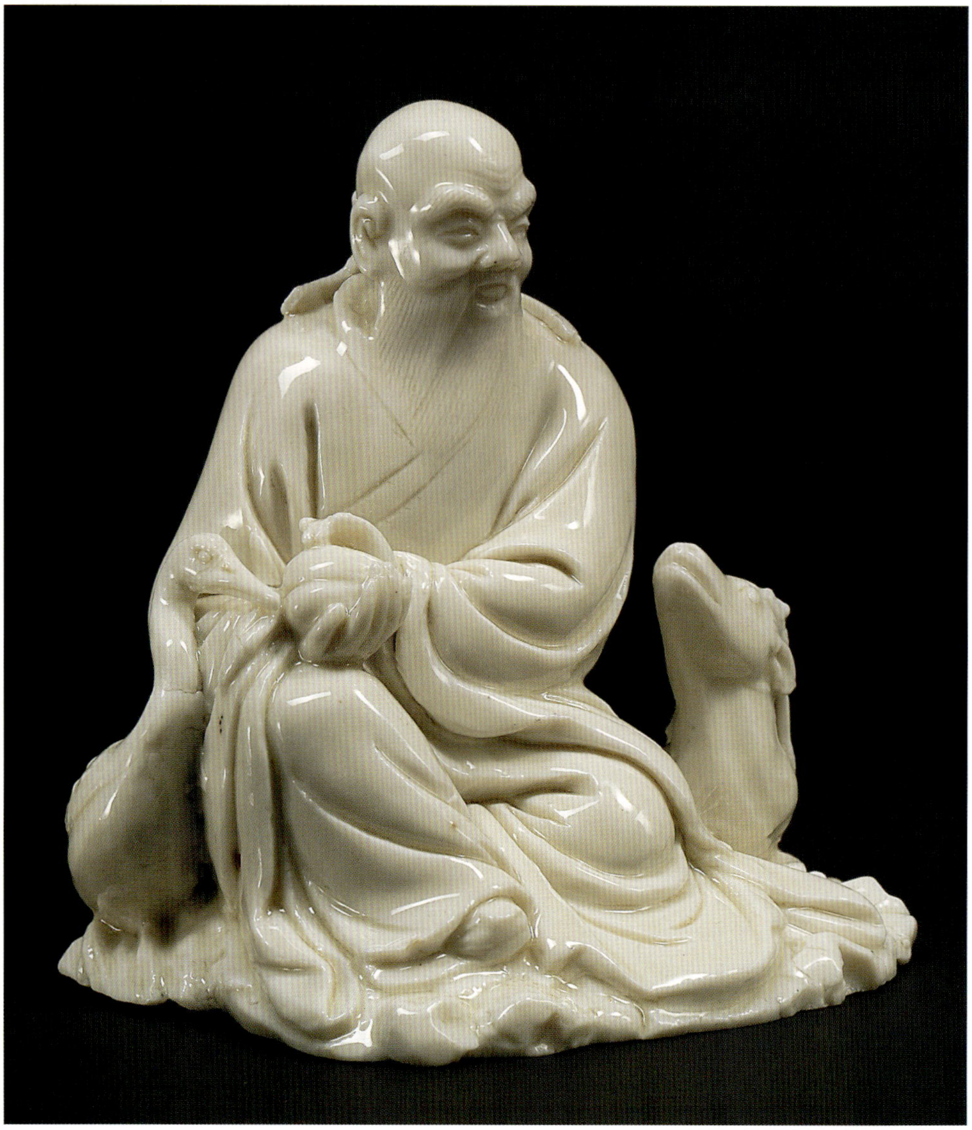

46. Wenchang Supported by his Demon Attendant, Kuixing

文昌與魁星

Ming or early Qing dynasty, 17th century

H. 10 ½ in., W. 3 ⅞ in., D. 3 ⅛ in.

Virginia Museum of Fine Arts, Richmond, Bequest of Forrest R. Brauer (85.1457)

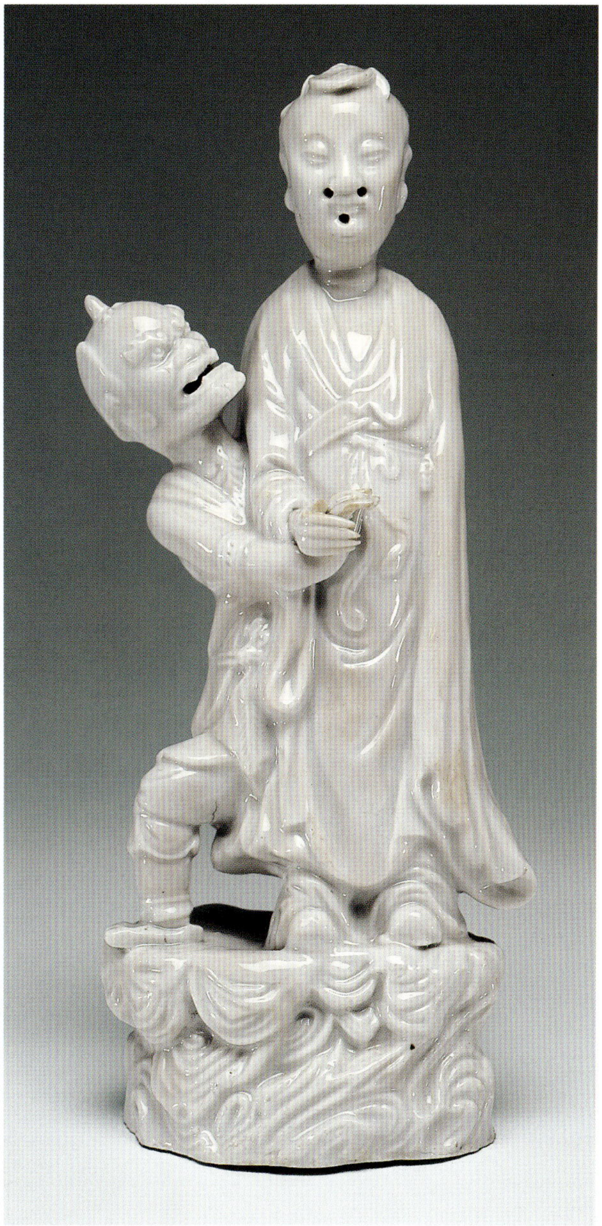

The God of Literature wears a belted robe and cap with tassels falling to the shoulder; his grinning companion has a pointed protuberance on his head. They are set on a rocky oval base.

For a similar model in carved and painted wood, see Gerard Hawthorn Ltd., *Gods and Mortals* (London, 1999), no. 12. For another late Ming porcelain model in the British Museum in which Wenchang is accompanied by a similar but smaller figure of Kuixing, see Harrison-Hall 2001, no. 17:10, p. 513.

47. General Guan Yu (Guandi, God of War) on his Charger

馬上關羽

Ming or early Qing dynasty, 17th century

H. 5 in., W. 3 in., D. 2 in.

The Koger Collection, The John and Mable Ringling Museum of Art, the State Art Museum of Florida (24.109)

A warlike figure, the general wears armor and a high cap with streamers falling to his shoulders; his cheeks are pierced for the insertion of hair, he rides with his left hand cupped as though holding a bridle, and his mount is supported by a pillar rising from an oval base molded with cloud scrolls.

Guan Yu was a military hero of the Three Kingdoms period who was eventually deified in 1594 by order of the Wanli emperor; many temples were erected in his honor, and trades elected him as their patron saint (see Little 2000, p. 258).

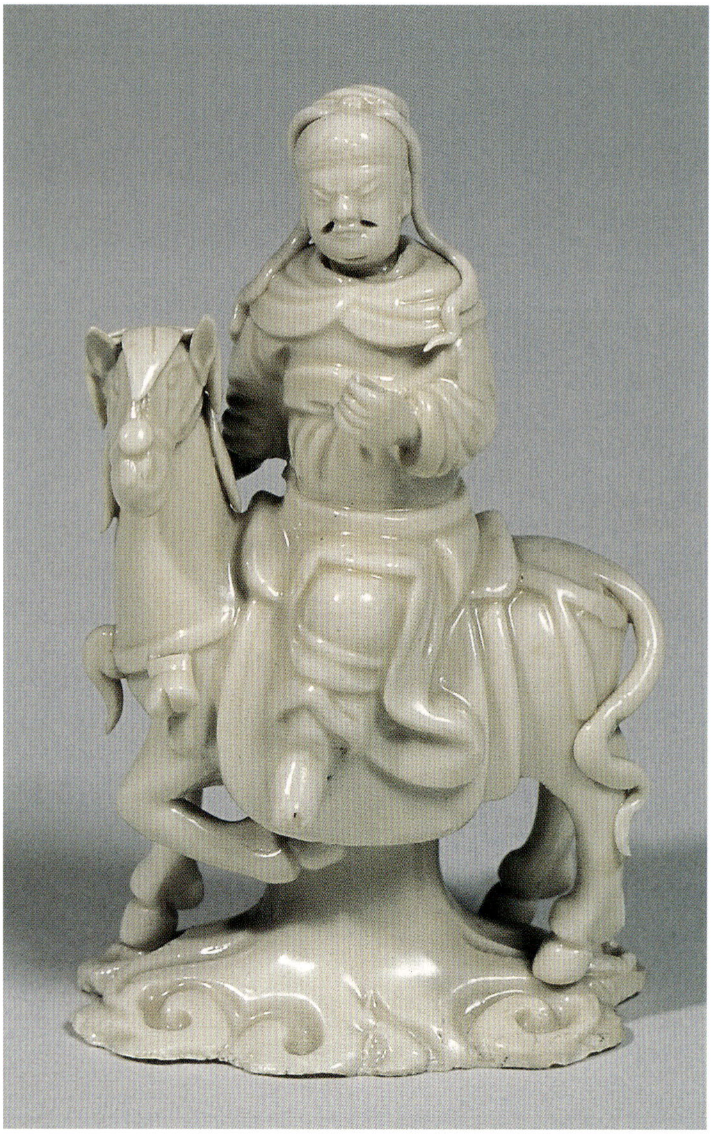

48. Tudi (Protecting Spirit of Rural Places)

土地公
Ming or early Qing dynasty, 17th century
H. 6 5⁄8 in., W. 3 1⁄4 in.
Richard Lehman Gray Collection

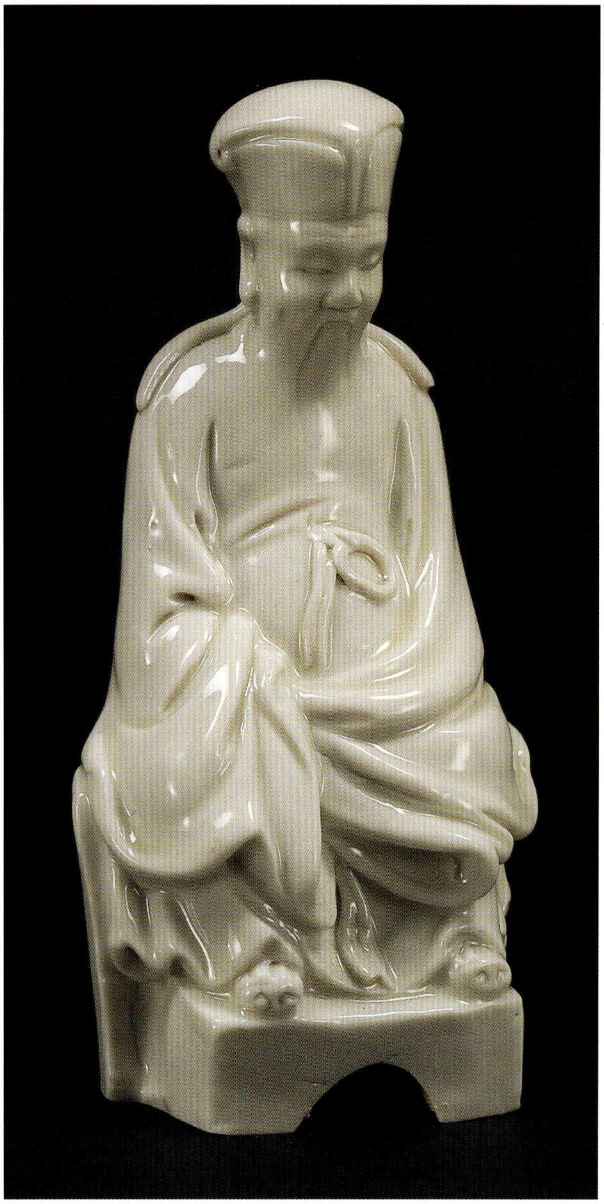

The bearded figure is seated on a low throne, his long robe tied with a belt at the waist. He wears a four-sided hat with tassels.

This much-respected deity, the Earth God, is widely seen in China in roadside shrines and was often set beside figures of Guanyin. The significance of the local Earth God in community life is discussed in Little 2000, pp. 49–50. For a comparable figure in the Fujian Provincial Museum see Hong Kong 1990, no. 120. Lang 1983, no. 235, illustrates a similar figure in the historic collection at Burghley House, England, which probably corresponds to the description of "figures sitting in Chaires" in an inventory made in 1688.

EXPORT FIGURES & WARES,
17TH TO EARLY 18TH CENTURIES

49. Pair of Buddhist Guardian Lions (Dogs of Fo)

佛獅

Ming or early Qing dynasty, 17th century

H. 10 ½ in., W. 3 ½ in., D. 5 in.

The Koger Collection, The John and Mable Ringling Museum of Art, the State Art Museum of Florida (32.205, 206)

The lions are fitted as joss-stick holders. They sit on their haunches on hollow rectangular plinths with tubular holders at their side, one paw resting on an openwork "embroidered ball," and their bushy tails resting on their backs.

Blanc-de-Chine "dogs of Fo" are among the commonest of all exports to the West in the seventeenth century, when "white lions" are often mentioned in inventories; they were still being imported into England in 1707 (see Godden 1979, p. 278). In China, pairs of these lions in stone are customarily seen at the entrance to temples and other important buildings.

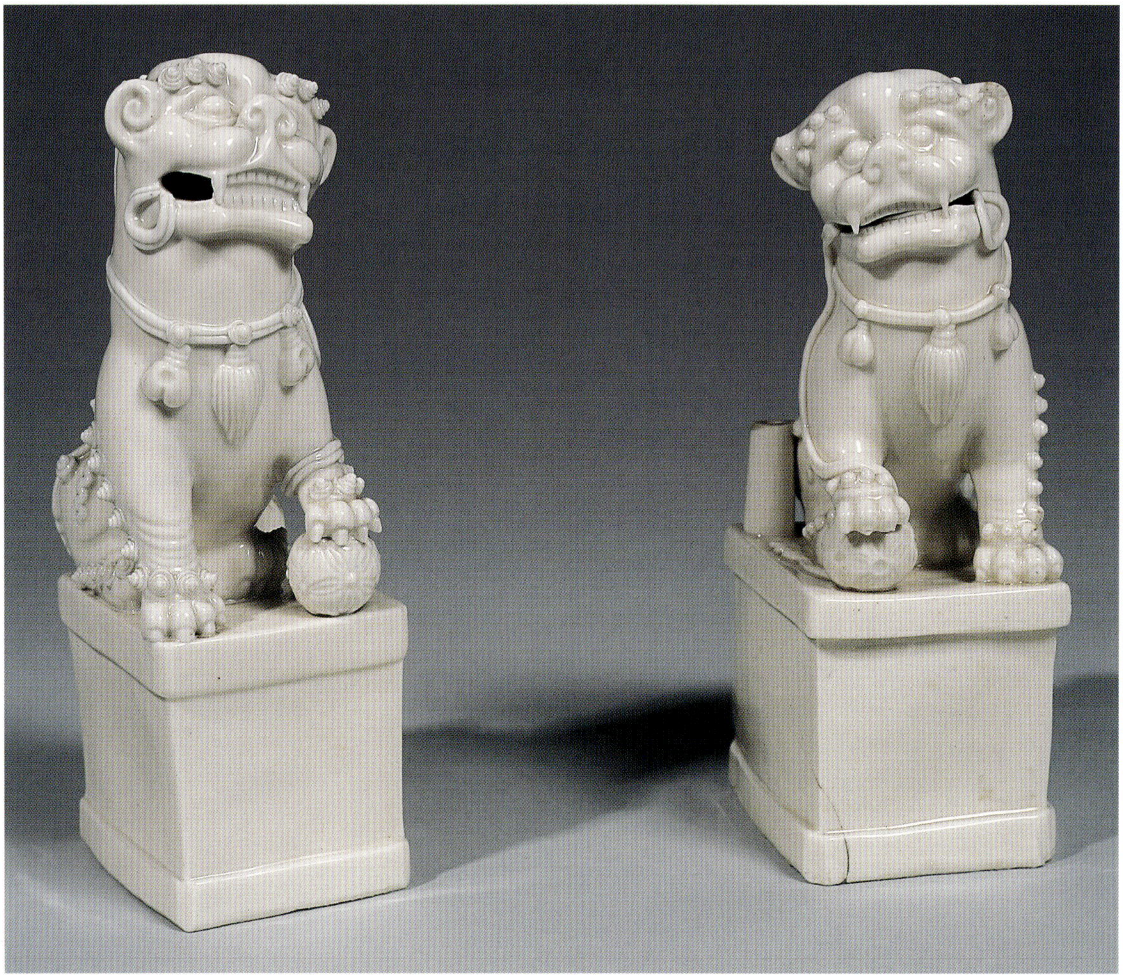

50. Guanyin Enthroned with her Acolytes

童子與觀音

Ming or early Qing dynasty, first half to mid-17th century

H. 9 ⅛ in., W. 4 ¾ in., D. 2 ⅜ in.

Virginia Museum of Fine Arts, Richmond, Bequest of Forrest R. Brauer (85.1502)

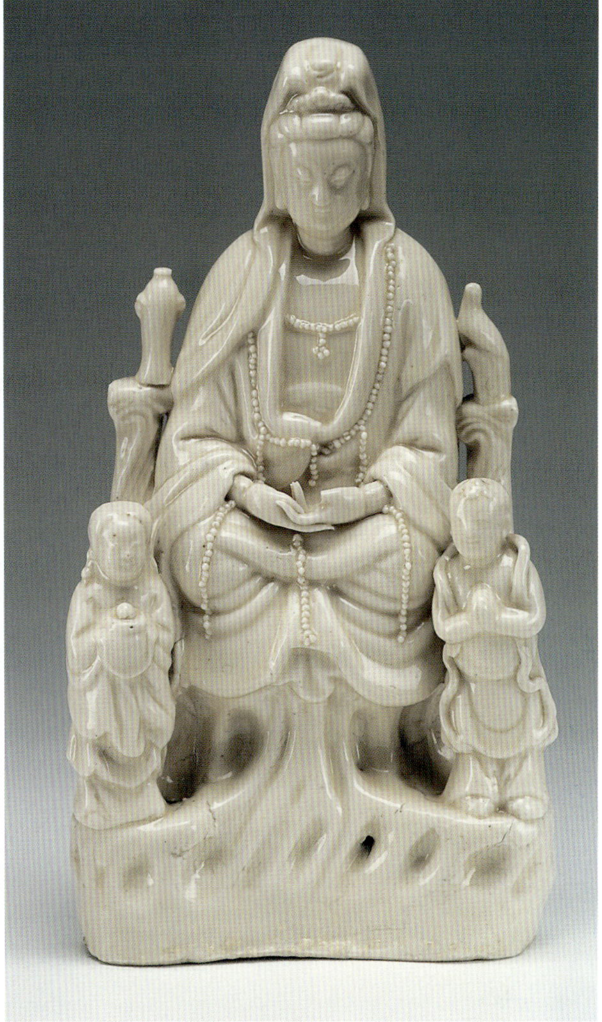

The Goddess of Mercy sits on a high-backed rocky throne with her legs folded and her hands in her lap. She is dressed typically in flowing robes and jeweled pendants, with a mantle over her head. The acolytes, Shancai and Longnü, stand below her on either side, and behind them are a bird and her flask of heavenly dew. The model is hollow and relatively thinly potted.

One of the earliest known Guanyin models from Dehua, this is apparently the group depicted in the margin of Blaeuw's *Nieuw Atlas* of 1655 (lower right). Various examples exist in the West (see Ayers 1986, pp. 29–30, figs. 17 and 18), and a number were almost certainly exported by the mid-seventeenth century.

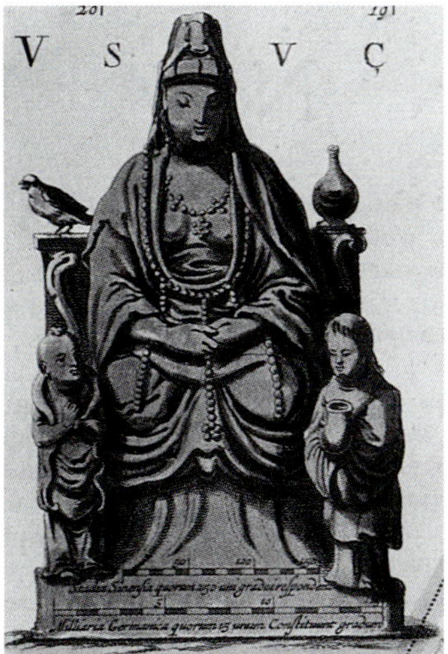

51. Puxian (Samantabhadra, Bodhisattva of Universal Benevolence)

普賢菩薩

Qing dynasty, late 17th century

H. 8 ¼ in., W. 4 ¼ in., D. 2 ⅛ in.

The Metropolitan Museum of Art, New York. Purchase, by subscription, 1879 (79.2.479)

This deity is characteristically shown seated on an elephant. The model is thinly potted and stands on a hollow base.

Often mistakenly identified as representing the bodhisattva Guanyin, this model found its way early to Europe and was in Augustus the Strong's Collection at Dresden (illustrated by Donnelly 1969, pl. 86B). The inventory of Queen Mary II's collection of porcelain at Kensington Palace included "two elophant with whomen on them in gold mantles." This piece was acquired by the museum in 1879.

Exhibited and published: Cooper-Hewitt Museum 1988, no. 195.

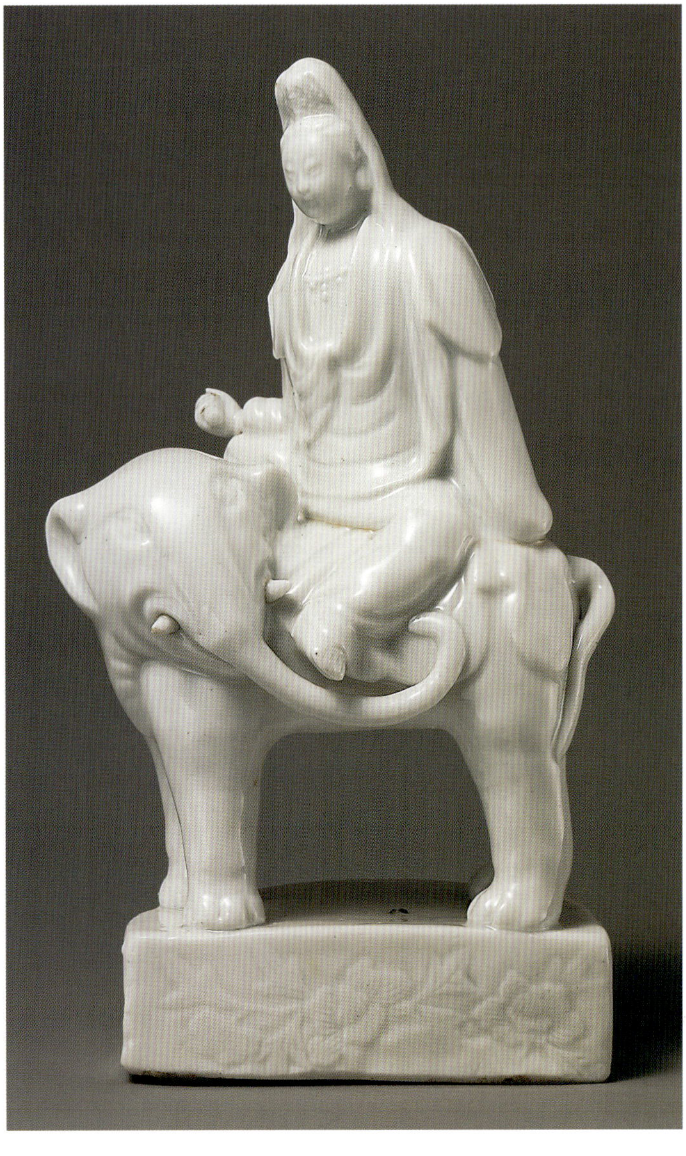

52. Dog

白瓷狗

Qing dynasty, late 17th–early 18th century

H. 9 in., W. 3 in., D. 4 in.

Robert H. Blumenfield Collection

The dog is seated on a rectangular plinth with a tubular taper holder at one side. It wears a collar with pendants round its neck.

Many models of animals were made for the European market. A large variety were in the cargo of the English East Indiaman *Dashwood* which was auctioned in London in 1703, including "5 Dogs" at a starting price of six pence each (Godden 1979, p. 267).

Published: Blumenfield 2002, p. 24, pl. A.

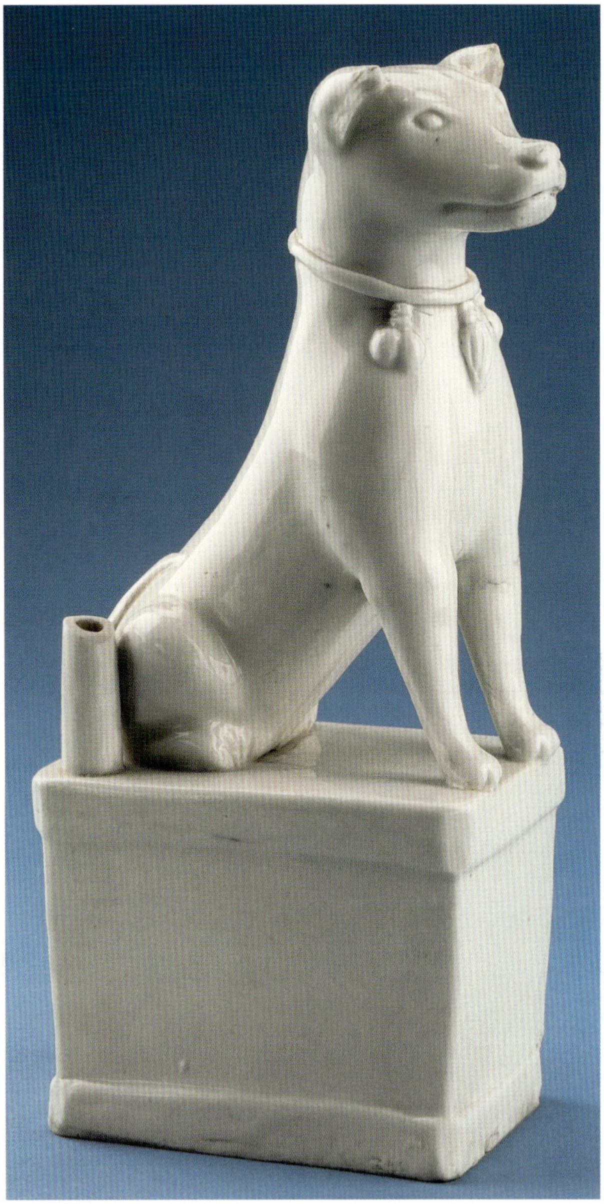

53. Crane

白瓷鶴

Ming or early Qing dynasty, 17th century

H. 7 in., W. 3 in., D. 3 ¼ in.

The Koger Collection, The John and Mable Ringling Museum of Art, the State Art Museum of Florida (30.189)

The crane, standing on long slender legs, is supported by the trunk of a prunus tree forming a joss-stick holder. An auspicious *lingzhi* fungus of longevity grows below.

In Chinese mythology the crane is the bird of long life, often found in company with Shoulao, the Longevity God, or Xiwangmu, Royal Mother of the West.

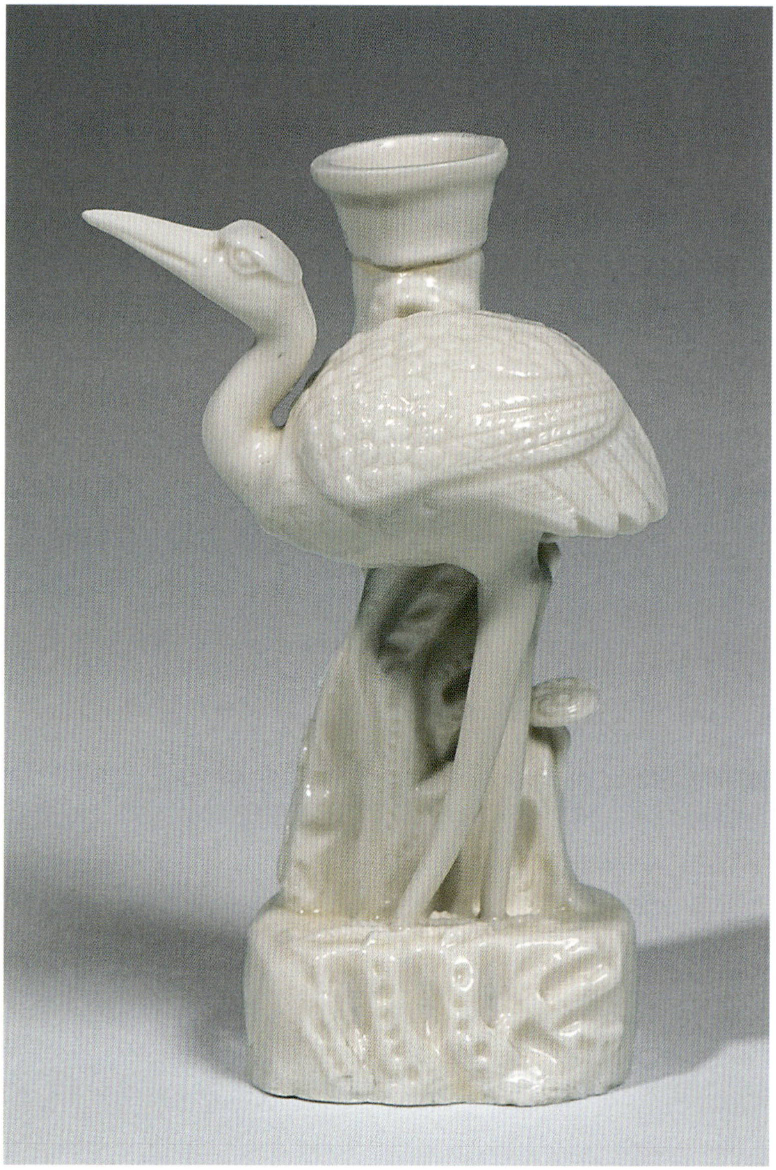

54. Hawk

白瓷鷹

Ming or early Qing dynasty, 17th century

H. 8 ½ in., W. 4 ¼ in., D. 5 ¼ in.

The Koger Collection, The John and Mable Ringling Museum of Art, the State Art Museum of Florida (30.203)

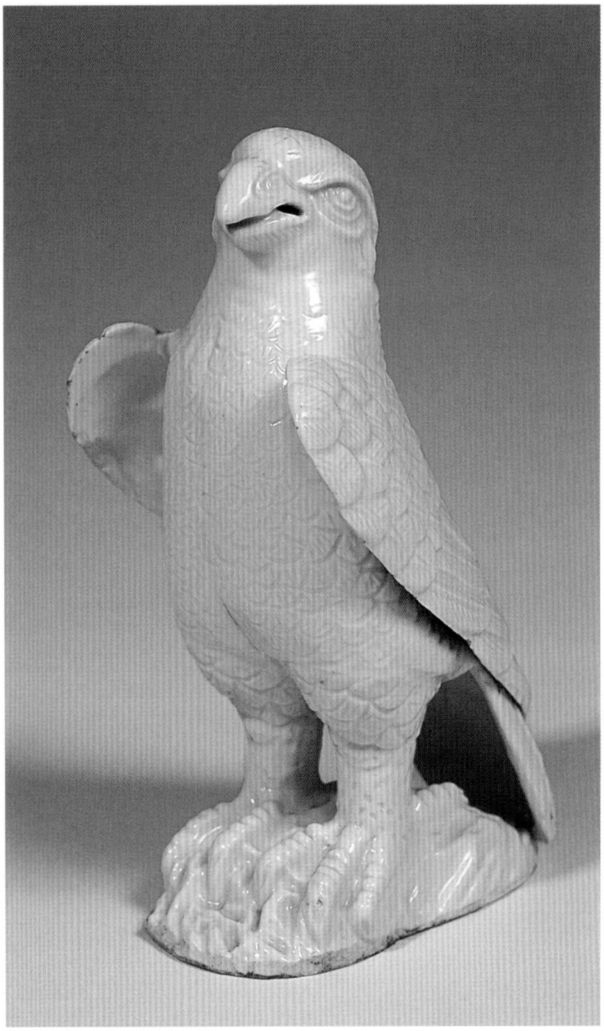

Large-eyed and with a curving beak, the bird stands spreading its powerful talons on a hollow rocky base. It is rather thinly molded, with a white glaze.

Lang 1983, no. 243, illustrates one of four comparable birds that seem to be identifiable with the "4 China ffaulcons" described in the 1688 inventory made at Burghley House in England.

55. Pair of Southeast Asian (?) Figures

南洋人像

Ming or early Qing dynasty, 17th century

Male figure: H. 8 ¾ in., W. 3 in., D. 2 ½ in.

Female figure: H. 9 in., W. 3 in., D. 2 ¼ in.

The Koger Collection, The John and Mable Ringling Museum of Art, the State Art Museum of Florida (33.232, 233)

These figures (sometimes called "Adam and Eve") are naked to the waist and stand on hollow rocky bases. Her long hair falls to her shoulders; his left arm is held across the body. Both models are supported from behind by tree stumps.

See Marchant 1994, no. 20, where David Freedman comments that the heads are purely Chinese in style. The reason for their production is not obvious; they were perhaps intended to represent unfamiliar racial types. Several examples of the female figure were in the royal collection at Dresden.

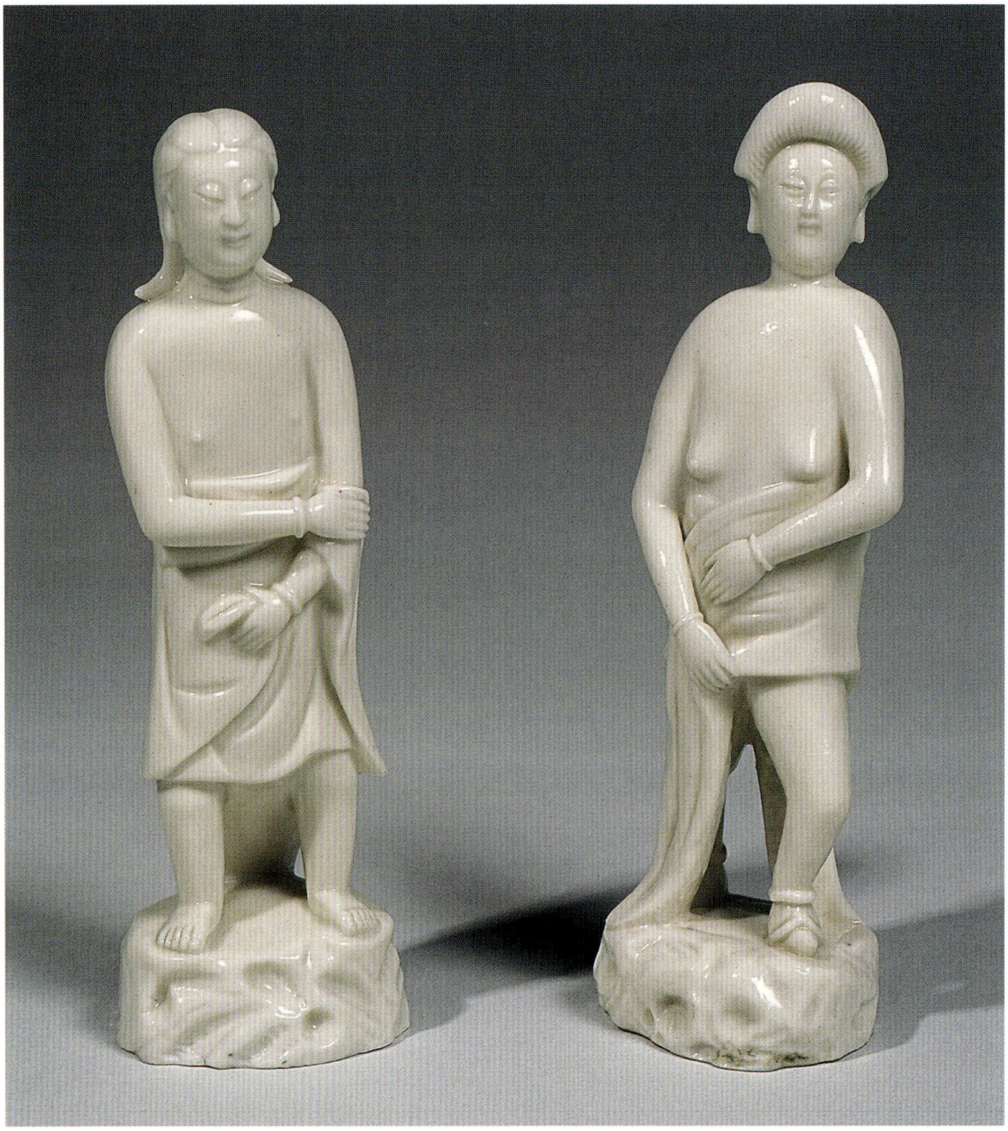

56. Madonna and Child

瑪當娜抱子

Qing dynasty, 17th–early 18th century

H. 13 ½ in., W. 3 ½ in., D. 3 in.

The Koger Collection, The John and Mable Ringling Museum of Art, the State Art Museum of Florida (33.229)

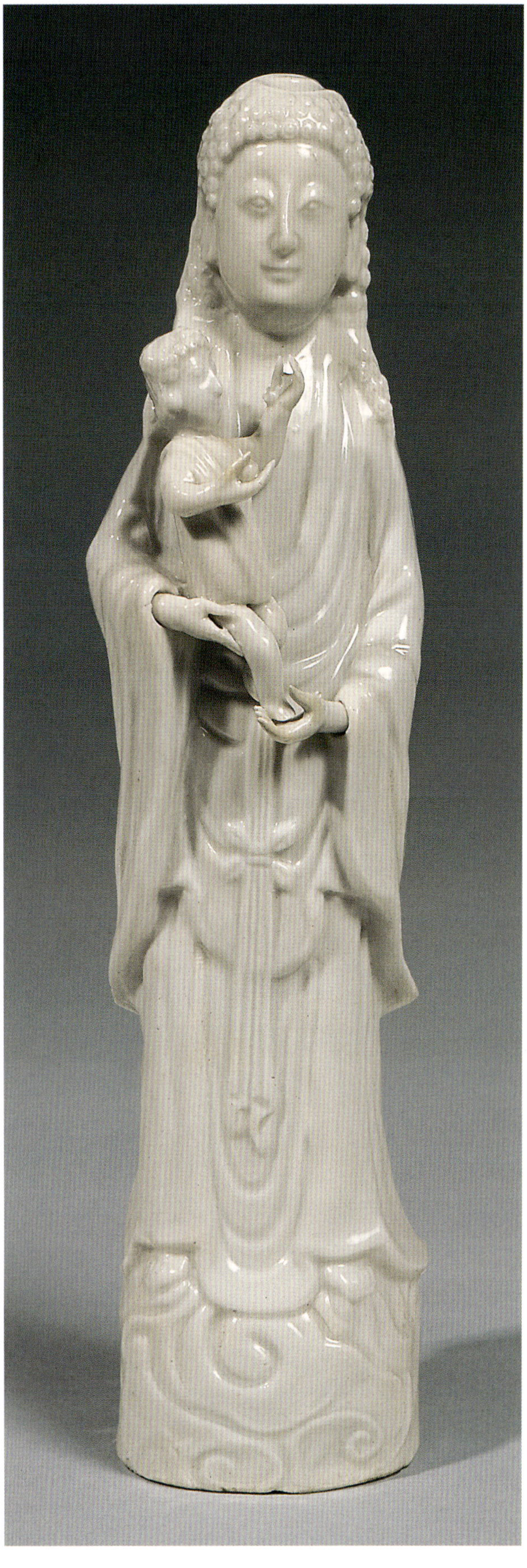

Standing on a hollow base molded with scrolling clouds, the female figure wears a long coat and a long robe with pendant ribbons in front, and holds the infant Jesus sitting on her right arm; her face is framed by the tight curls of her hair, which falls to her shoulders, and the features are Western and impassive.

Several variations of this model of a Christian subject are known (see Donnelly 1969, pl. 122 and pp. 195–96, where the existence of models of St Anthony of Padua is also noted). All were probably made to the order of Catholic missionaries brought to the East by the Portuguese or Spaniards, and perhaps copy carvings produced in Christian settlements in India or the Philippines. "Sancta Marias" are named in the list of cargo loaded by the English East Indiaman *Dashwood* at Amoy in 1701 and sold at auction in London in 1703 (Godden 1979, p. 266); a larger number—39 large Sancta Marias, distinguished from the comparable 170 women with children, who were probably Guanyin—were mentioned in a 1699 sale of the goods brought home on the *Nassau* (see ibid., p. 259).

57. Model of a Pulpit

教壇模型

Qing dynasty, late 17th–early 18th century

H. 4 ½ in., W. 3 in., D. 3 in.

The Koger Collection, The John and Mable Ringling Museum of Art, the State Art Museum of Florida (33.231)

This octagonal pulpit has an openwork balustrade molded with floral motives and steps on one side. The cylindrical stem is similarly decorated and rises from a hollow base.

Whether these pulpits were, like the madonna figures above, made to the order of Christian communities in the East is not clear; "pulpits with padries" from the cargo of the *Dashwood* were also sold at auction in London in 1703, but the "padries" (padres?) are missing and remain unidentified. The suggestion made with regard to a model in the Hickley Collection that the pulpits may be the bases for pagodas leaves us no further forward, as these too are unknown (Kerr and Ayers 2002, no. 47). It has also been suggested they were originally intended as candlesticks, although the pricket for the candle would have been impracticably thick; but this still does not explain the reference to "padries." In the Residenz, Munich, is a pulpit with a Guanyin model set on top, both parts being decorated with gilding added in Europe.

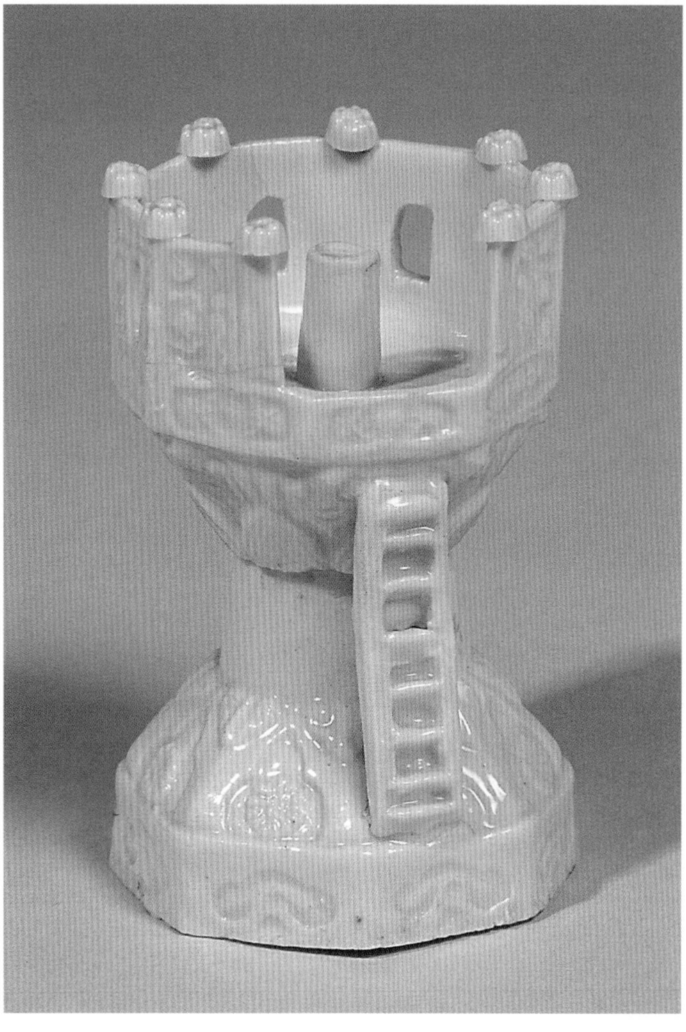

58. Dutch Family Group

荷人一家

Qing dynasty, late 17th–early 18th century

H. 6 ¼ in., W. 5 ¾ in., D. 3 ½ in.

The Koger Collection, The John and Mable Ringling Museum of Art, the State Art Museum of Florida (30.201)

The man and his wife sit on either side of a low table and raise their glasses; they are flanked by their son and daughter, and a plant stands in a pot on the ground between them. A dog and a monkey complete the group. The man and the boy wear typical Dutch coats, neckerchiefs, and tricorne hats, while the lady, who is more oriental in appearance, is seemingly bare to the waist and has a high pointed European-style headdress; the girl wears a jacket and pleated skirt and holds a fan. Standing on the table are a small cross and a bowl containing food. The group is set on a low, semicircular base.

The commonest of the export figure groups, it is one of those (in several variations, some having added enameling in colors that was often, if not invariably, put on in Europe) that were taken on board at Amoy in 1701 by the English East Indiaman *Dashwood* and sold in London as "Dutch familyes" two years later (Godden 1979, p. 266). The model is noted in the Dresden inventory, where characteristically the main figure was described as an "Indian."

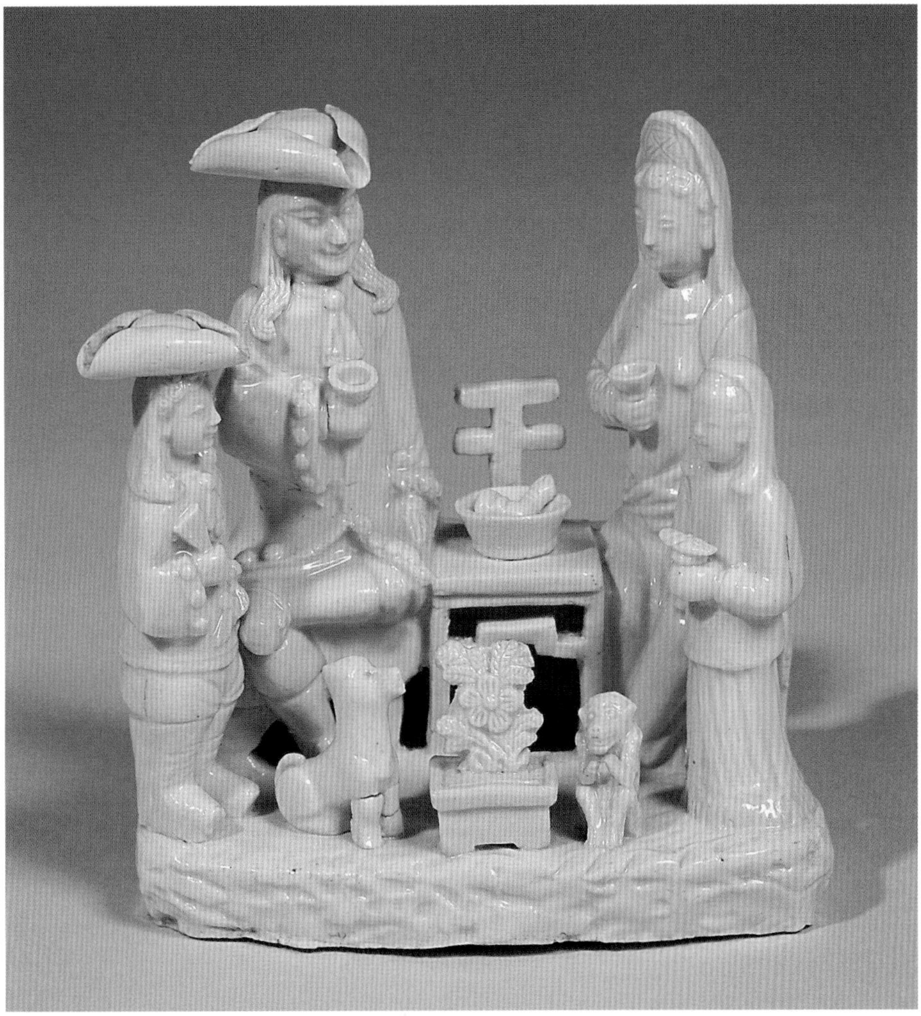

59. European on Horseback Presenting his Sword

馬上西人

Qing dynasty, late 17th–early 18th century

H. 11 ¾ in., W. 7 ½ in., D. 3 ¼ in.

The Koger Collection, The John and Mable Ringling Museum of Art, the State Art Museum of Florida (30.192)

He wears a long-sleeved, buttoned riding coat, neckerchief, leggings, and boots, and holds the hilt of a sword, perhaps intended to be of inserted metal, in his extended right hand, the left hand being clenched as if holding a bridle; a pistol holster hangs at his waist. His shoulder-length wig is topped by a wide-brimmed hat.

Possibly taken from a European print, the pose is reminiscent of that typically represented in contemporary portraits of successful military leaders. A similar model was listed in the Dresden inventory in 1721 (Beurdeley and Raindre 1987, fig. 337). For the same model with added enamels, see Howard and Ayers 1978, vol. 1, no. 59; also Marchant 1994, no. 33.

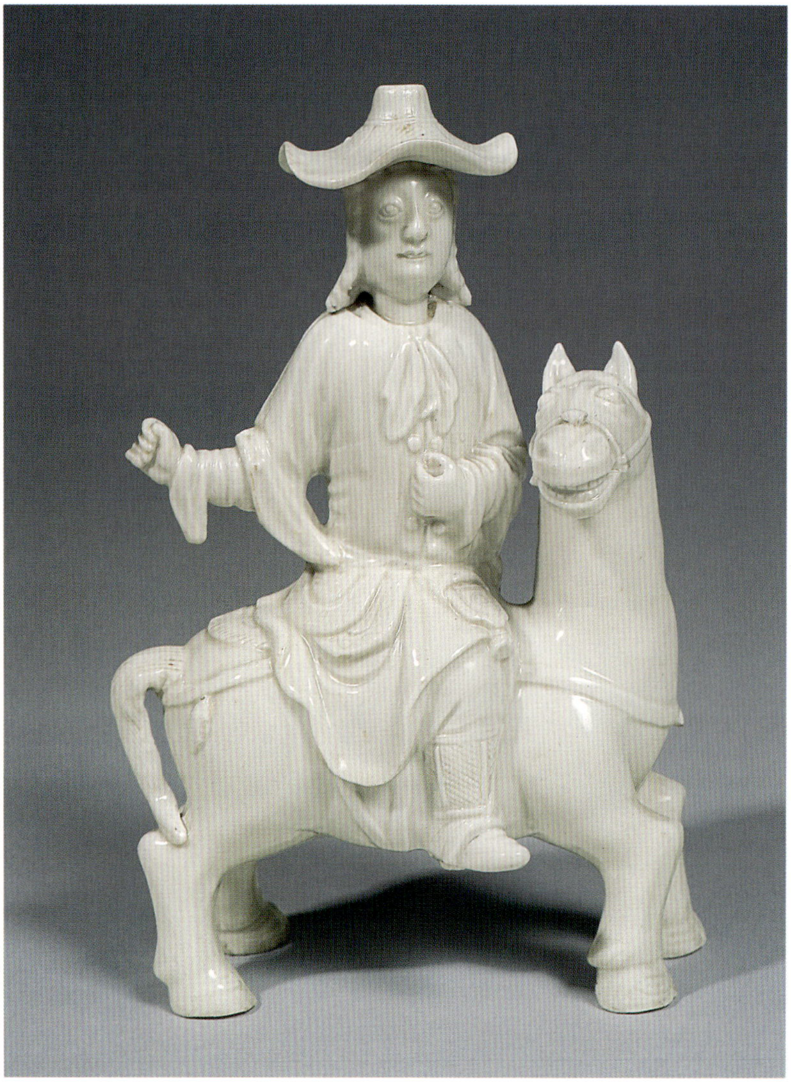

60. Group of Westerners on a Lion

騎獅西人

Ming or early Qing dynasty, 17th century

H. 11 ¾ in., W. 8 in.

Richard Lehman Gray Collection

A Westerner sits on the back of a fanciful lion with its head turned; beside him sit a lion cub and a woman with oriental features wearing a high European-style headdress. The lion is saddled and stands on a low, hollow oval base which also supports a Western groom holding a piece of cash, and behind him, two more lion cubs.

The inspiration behind this rather comical group is obscure. A version with the figures differently arranged is illustrated by Donnelly 1969, pl. 119A, p. 193; it is of especial interest in that it represents one of an "image pair" owned by the van Cortland family of New York and inventoried there in 1774. Donnelly dismisses the family history according to which they had been brought from Holland in 1638, finding the date probably rather too early for this kind of export model; however, this is the earliest recorded *blanc-de-Chine* figure in America. Other versions exist in which the animal is an elephant or a horse (e.g., Marchant 1994, no. 21).

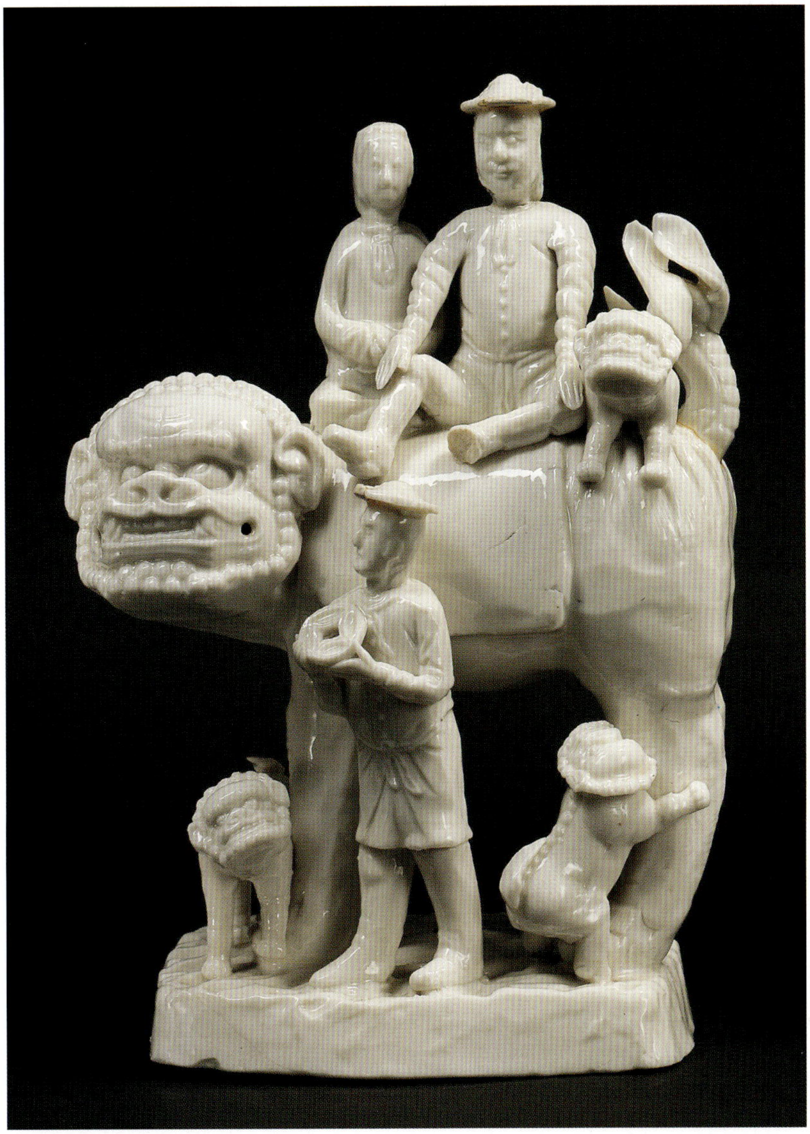

61. Group of Figures (The Assignation)

人像

Qing dynasty, late 17th–early 18th century

H. 6 ⅛ in., W. 4 in., D. 2 ½ in.

The Koger Collection, The John and Mable Ringling Museum of Art, the State Art Museum of Florida (24.110)

A well-dressed lady and her attendant appear on a balustraded terrace, below which a fully robed scholar stands to one side while a short, strangely dressed figure of foreign appearance gestures towards them. They are mounted on a low flat base together with a tubular joss-stick holder.

It seems likely that this and other related small groups with the same personnel depict amatory encounters inspired by popular scenes from the theater or in literature. For a variation of this model and others of the kind, see Marchant 1994, nos. 22–24.

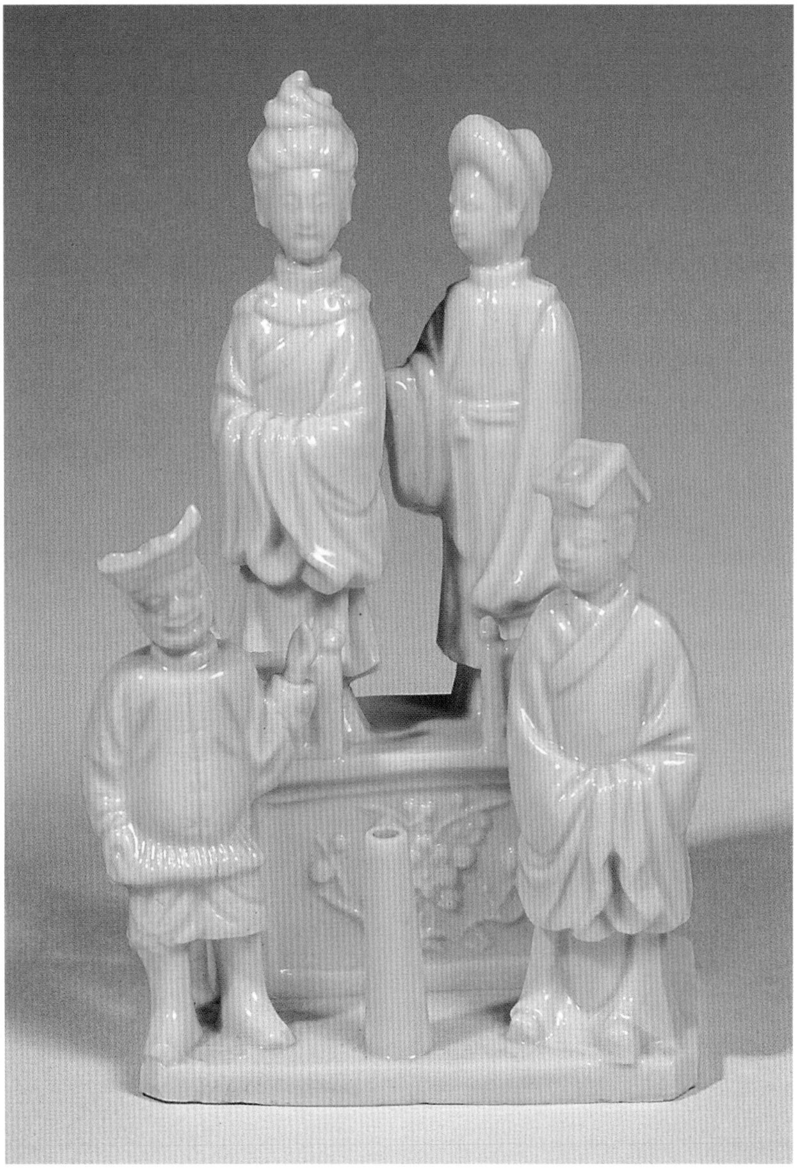

62. Westerner Riding the Mythical *Qilin*

騎麒麟西人

Qing dynasty, late 17th–early 18th century

H. 6 in., W. 5 ¼ in., D. 2 ¼ in.

The Koger Collection, The John and Mable Ringling Museum of Art, the State Art Museum of Florida (30.198)

The foreign-looking figure—grinning, bearded, and with round eyes—wears a long-sleeved, buttoned jerkin and a small flat-brimmed hat and sits sidesaddle on his mount, holding a stick; the *qilin* is a muscular creature having a stag's body with flaming haunches, a bushy tail, a dragon-like head, and a single horn.

The *qilin* is revered as a creature of good omen. Here it is adapted to provide an amusing curiosity for Western taste.

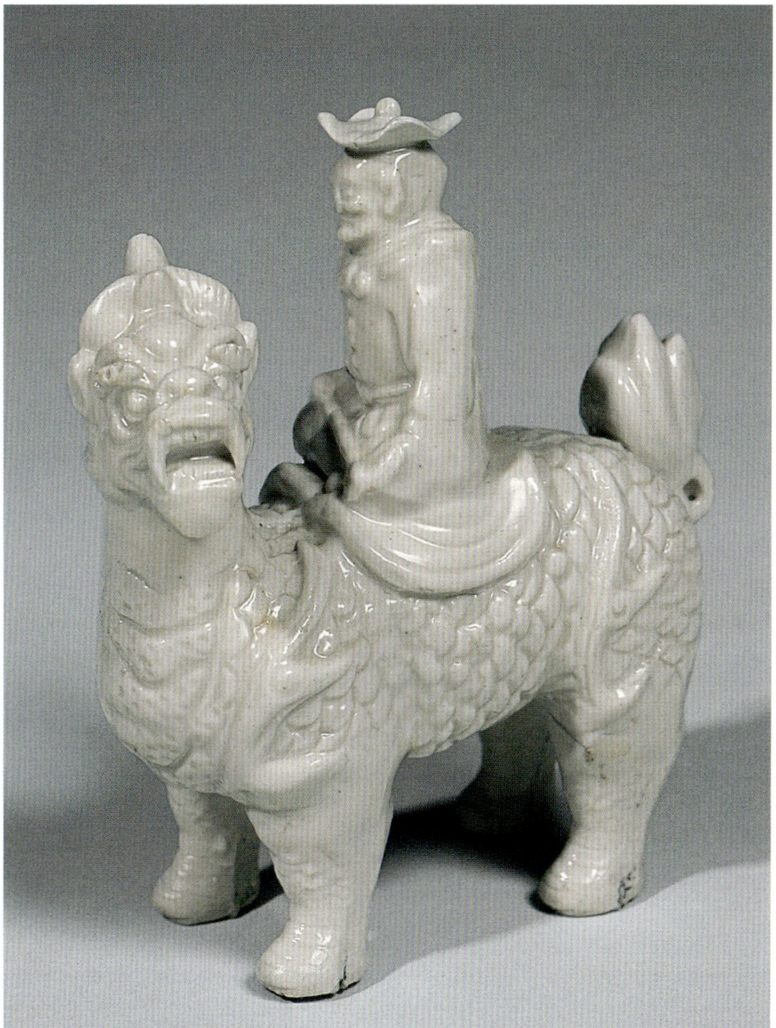

63. Water Dropper or Whistle in the Form of a European Fighting an Animal

西人鬥獸水注或哨

Qing dynasty, late 17th–early 18th century

H. 2 ¾ in., W. 1 ¾ in., D. 1 ¾ in.

The Koger Collection, The John and Mable Ringling Museum of Art, the State Art Museum of Florida (30.197)

The water dropper is hexagonal with a pouring hole at one corner and a stopping hole at the opposite end. A man is modeled standing on one leg and holding a sword and shield, his other leg on the back of an animal that resembles a large dog. He leans on a hollow post that serves practically as a whistle.

Donnelly 1969, p. 180, remarks that most such objects are clearly more ornamental than useful as water vessels; perhaps nearly all were designed purely for export.

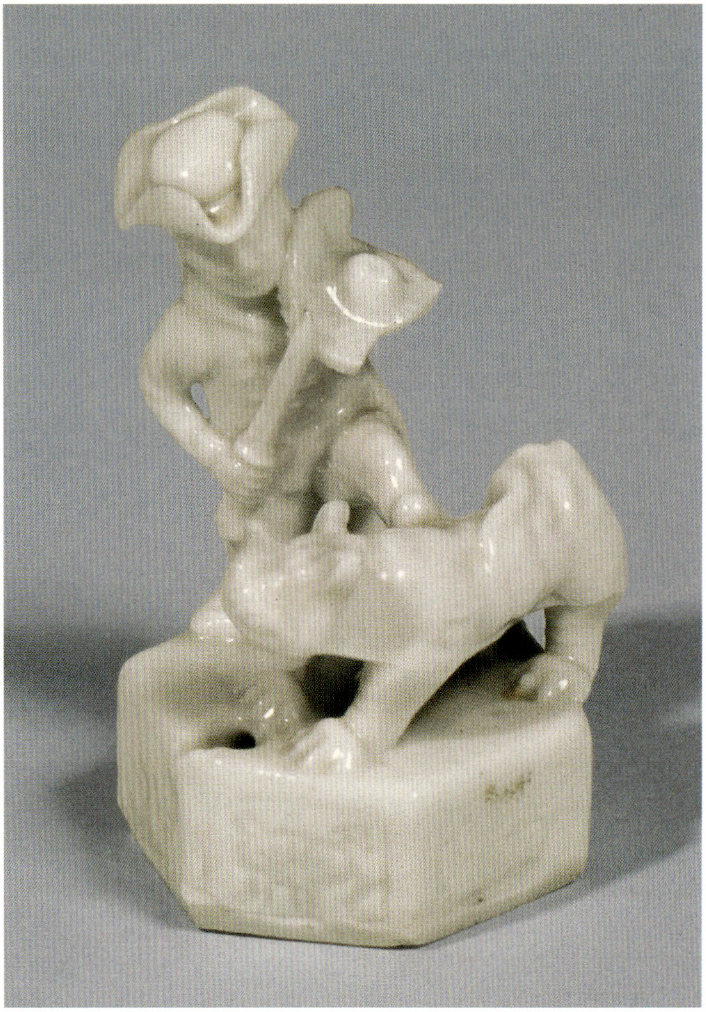

64. Mug in European Silver-gilt Mount

西式鑲銀瓷杯

Qing dynasty, late 17th century

European mount, ca. 1700

H. 6 ½ in., W. 5 ¾ in., D. 4 ¾ in.

The Koger Collection, The John and Mable Ringling Museum of Art, the State Art Museum of Florida (25.123)

The globular vessel with a ribbed cylindrical neck copies a German stoneware form. Its body is molded with floral scrolls; the mounts are applied to the rim and to the cover, which has been added.

Several European mug and cup forms were produced at Dehua (see Fichtner 1937), no doubt to order and after models supplied for the purpose. The practice of adding silver mounts to rare imported porcelains was long established.

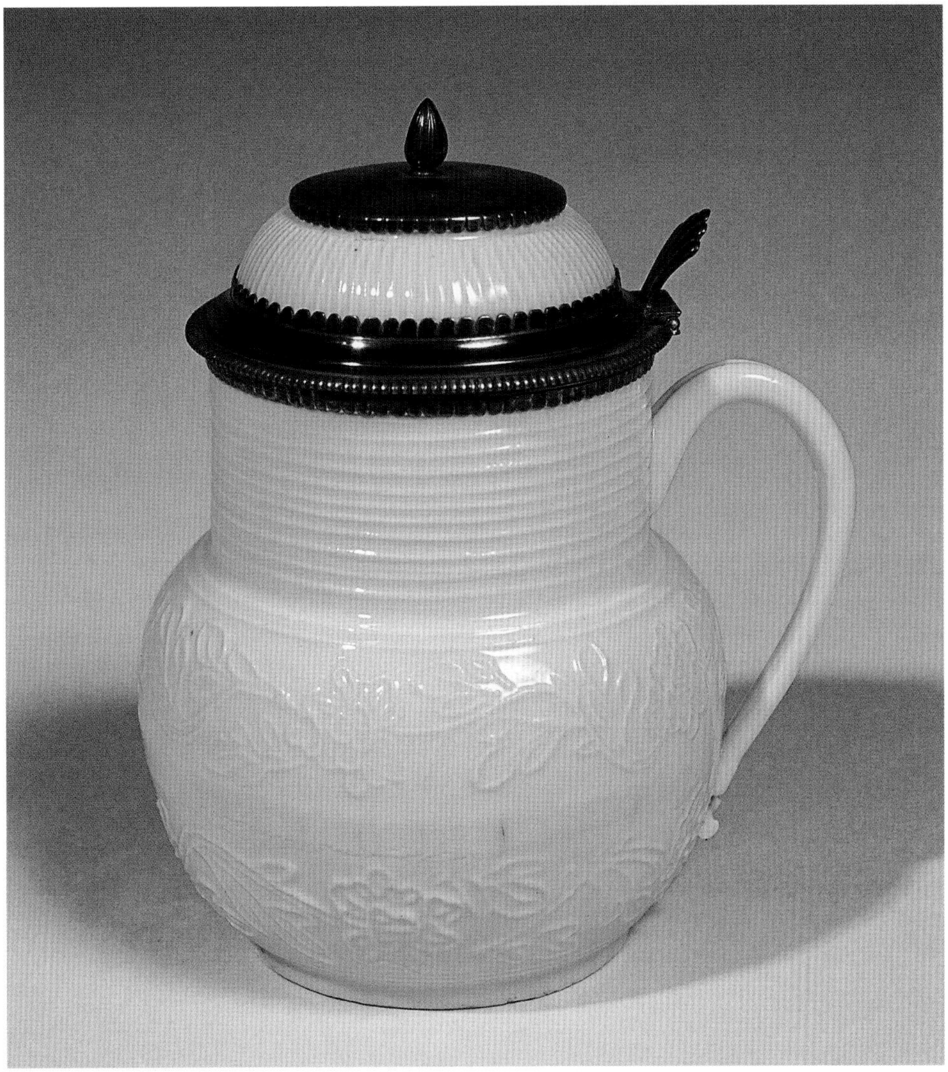

65. Teapot in European Silver-gilt Mount

西式鑲銀茶壺

Ming or early Qing dynasty, 17th century
European mount, late 17th century
H. 7 ½ in., W. 6 ¾ in., D. 5 ½ in.
Peabody Essex Museum, Salem, Massachusetts (E82868)

The teapot is globular with a square overhead handle, short spout, and lid attached by chains to leaf-shaped mounts embracing the spout and corners of the handle.

This rare, probably rather early vessel may have been made as a winepot but, like cat. no. 20, was regarded in Europe as a teapot. The chains were added to avoid breakage.

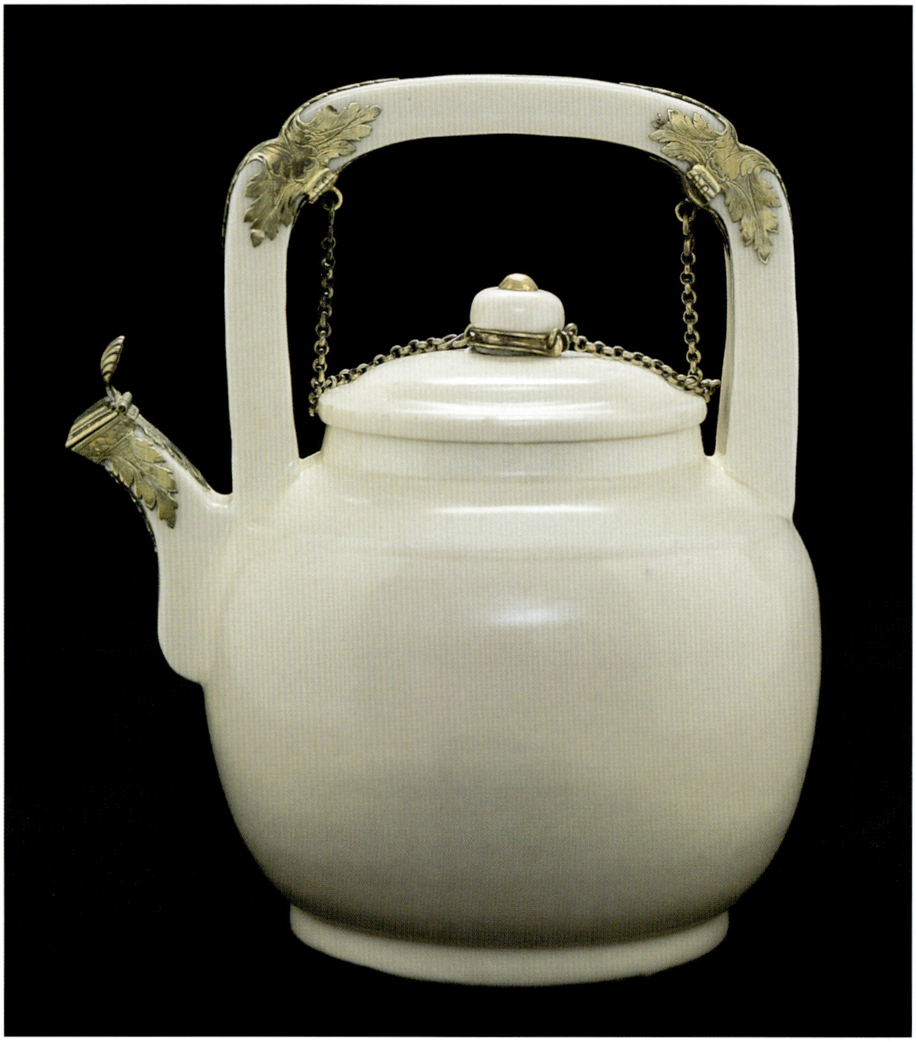

66. Elephant

白瓷象

Ming or early Qing dynasty, 17th century

H. 4 ½ in., W. 4 in., D. 7 ½ in.

Robert H. Blumenfield Collection

The elephant was rarely seen in China after ancient times, and when seen in art is most frequently associated with Buddhist deities of Indian origin (see Donnelly 1969, pl. 110 for various *blanc-de-Chine* models).

Published: Blumenfield 2002, p. 91, pl. B.

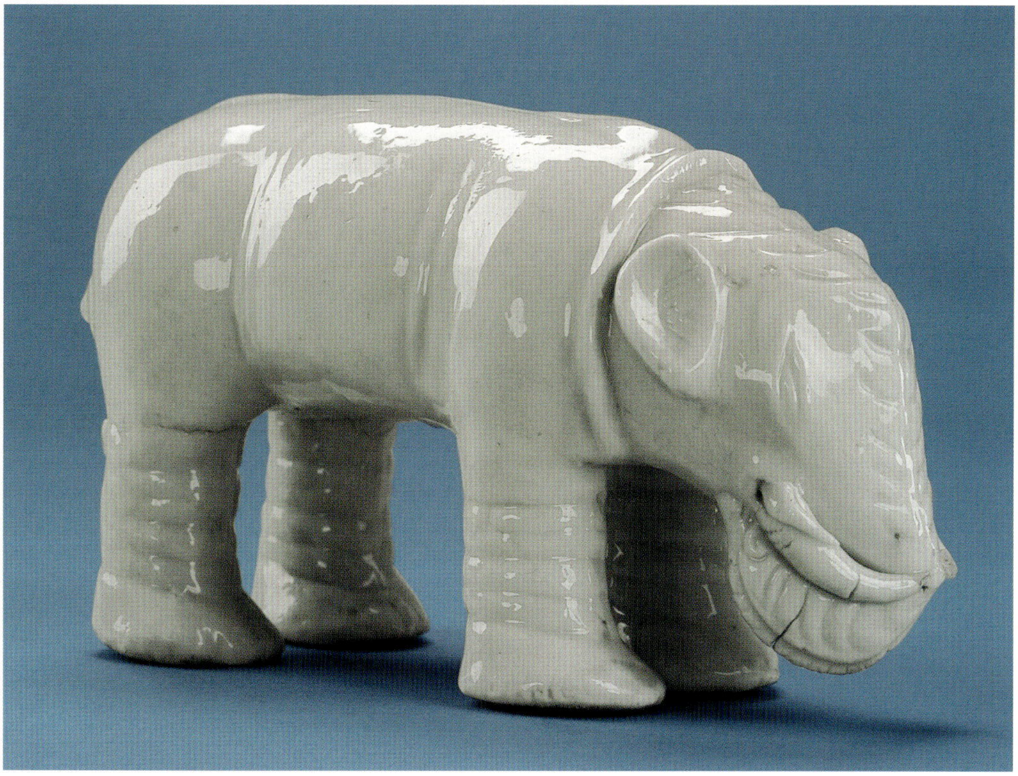

67. European-style Porringer

西式把杯
Qing dynasty, early 18th century
H. 2 ½ in., W. 7 in., D. 5 ¼ in.
Robert H. Blumenfield Collection

The vessel was painted in Holland in enamels with an armorial design on the inside. In Europe the majority of porringers were made of silver or pewter, and porcelain examples made to order in China would have been rare. As porcelain painted in colors became more popular in Europe, *blanc-de-Chine* wares grew in demand among the Dutch enamelers who profitably transformed them into more valuable items. A similar example in the British Museum having a cover is reproduced by Donnelly 1969, pl. 133A, p. 235.

Published: Blumenfield 2002, p. 92, pl. B.

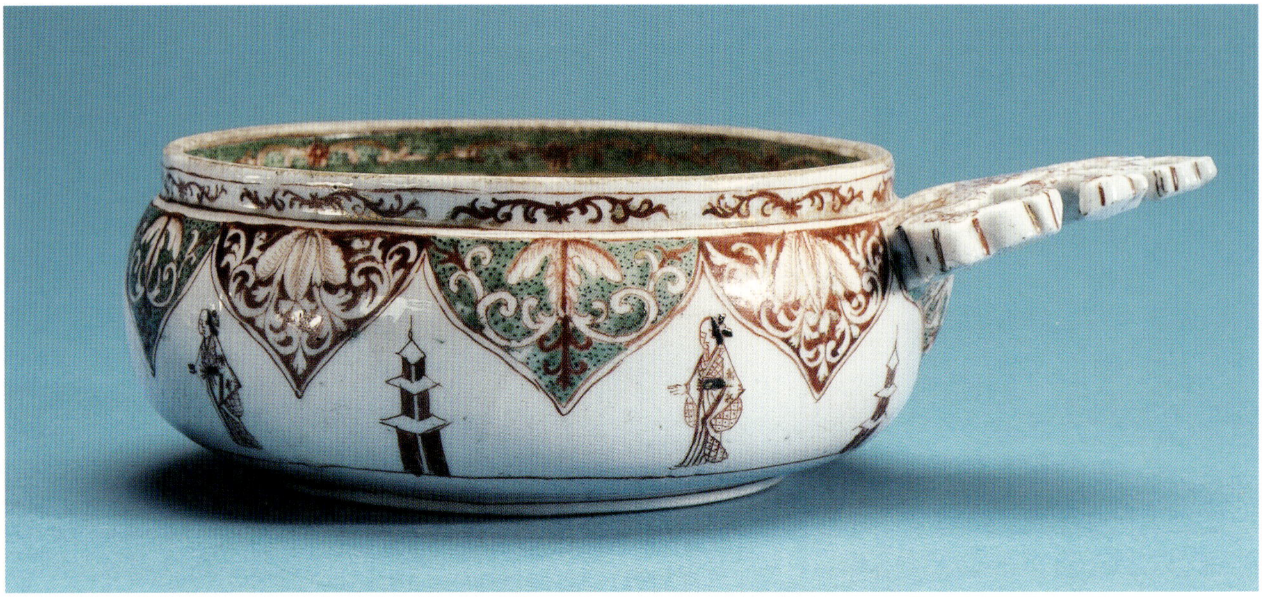

FIGURES OF THE LATE QING OR REPUBLIC PERIOD, ca. 1850–1940

68. Su Xuejin (1869–1919) Sakyamuni Buddha

蘇學金　坐禪釋迦牟尼
Qing dynasty, late 19th century
H. 10 ½ in., W. 5 ½ in., D. 4 ½ in.
Square seal: *boji yuren*
Virginia Museum of Fine Arts, Richmond, Bequest of Forrest R. Brauer (85.1478)

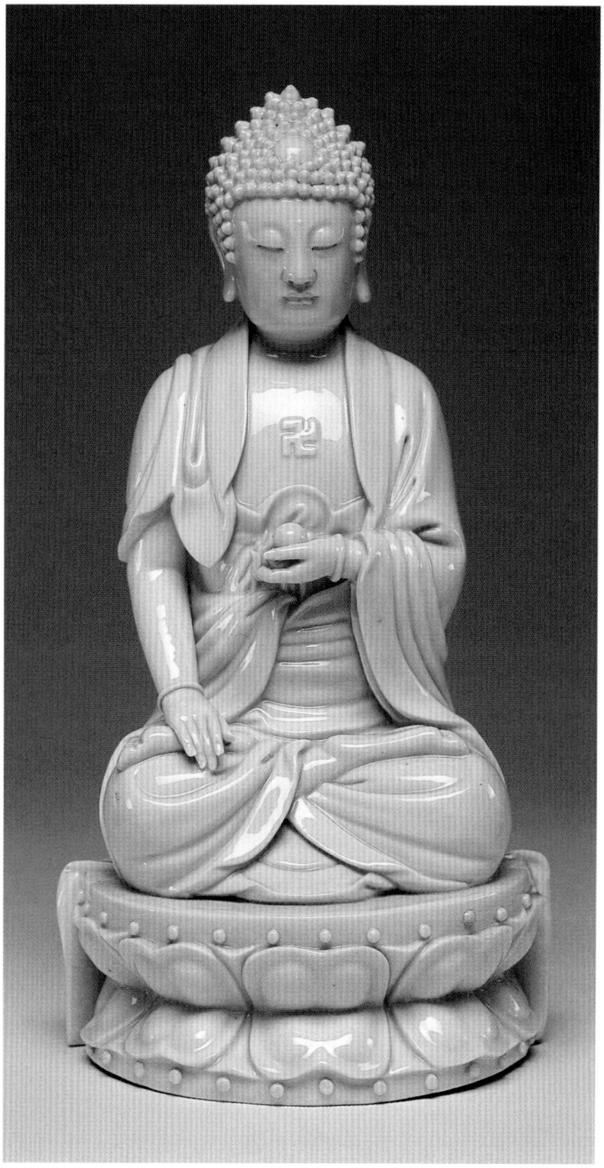

The Buddha is seated on a lotus base with his legs crossed in the *padmasana* pose. In his left hand he holds a jewel; on his breast in applied relief is his monogram, the swastika. His severe features are framed by the elongated earlobes and the tight coils of hair that rise to a point above the *usnisa*. The square seal *boji yuren*, as used by the potter Su Xuejin (1869–1919), is stamped on the back.

Over the centuries, images of the Buddha have become steadily more stylized. This late figure may be compared with the seventeenth-century model, cat. no. 32, which presents an unusually simplified image. No less distinctive are the cold white body and thin, greyish glaze that characterize much of the work of this potter and his followers.

Su Xuejin, several of whose models are exhibited here, was the leader of a major revival in the art of the porcelain figure model that took place towards the end of the nineteenth century. The mark *boji yuren* is one of a number that he is recorded to have used. It is an obscure punning reference to the skill of the fisherman which he appears to have adopted as his personal or factory motto; consequently, it is commonly referred to among specialists as the "fisherman" mark. A large number of his models are now in collections throughout the world, where Donnelly's dating of them to the late eighteenth or early nineteenth century is generally followed (Donnelly 1969, pp. 173, 259, and numerous illustrations). For Su Xuejin's career, see Zeng 1995 and Xu Yixing 1993.

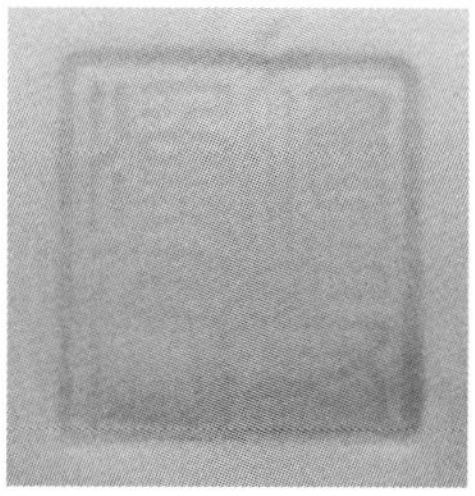

69. Su Xuejin (1869–1919) Liu Hai with his Three-legged Toad

蘇學金 劉海戲蟾

Qing dynasty or early Republic, late 19th–early 20th century

H. 12 in., W. 5 in., D. 4 in.

Square seal: *boji yuren*

The Koger Collection, The John and Mable Ringling Museum of Art, the State Art Museum of Florida (24.116)

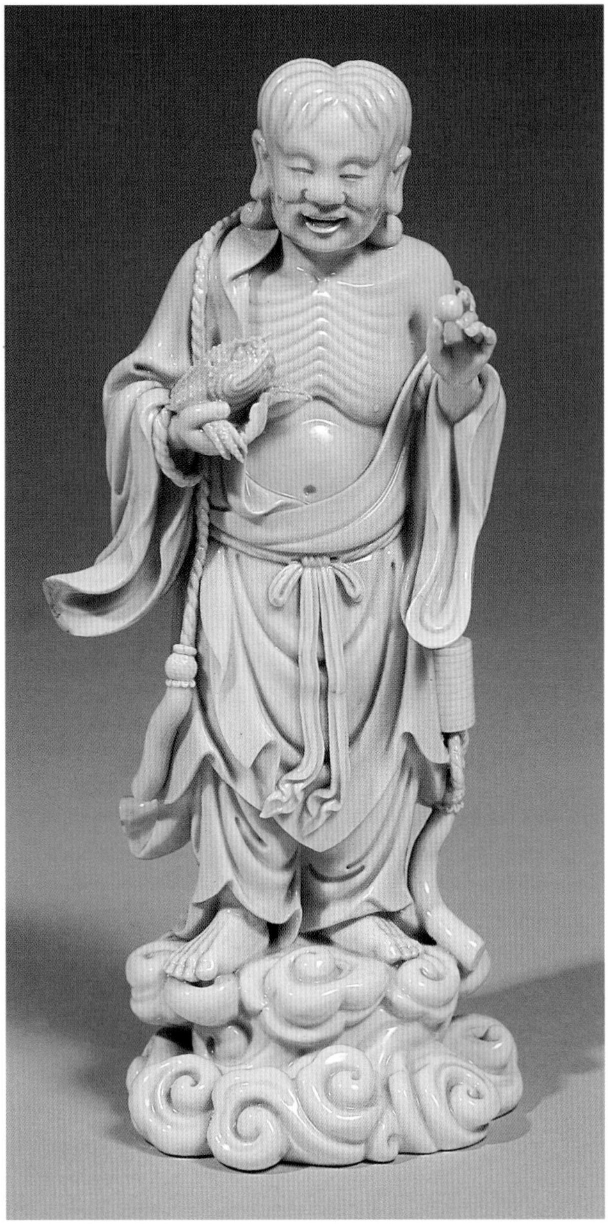

The Daoist immortal Liu Hai is represented as a tousle-haired youth, bare to the waist and with exposed ribs, standing on a base of cloud scrolls. He holds his three-legged toad in his right hand and a pearl in his left; his string of cash hangs at his left side. The square seal *boji yuren*, as used by the potter Su Xuejin (1869–1919), is stamped on the back.

On account of the control of the sacred three-legged toad afforded him by his precious string of cash, Liu Hai's aid was invoked by those involved in commercial transactions. A similarly marked model now in the British Museum is illustrated by Donnelly 1969, pl. 100D.

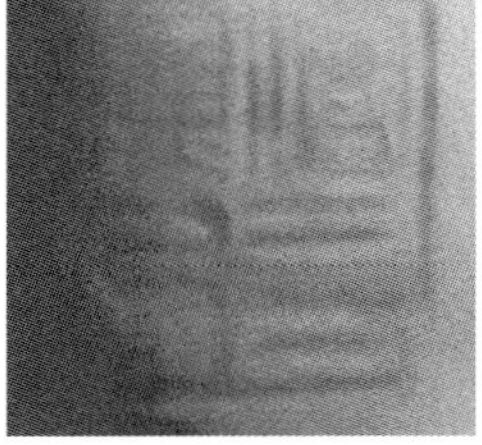

70. Su Xuejin (1869–1919)
Magu with a Fawn

蘇學金 麻姑傍鹿

Qing dynasty or early Republic,
late 19th–early 20th century

H. 15 ½ in., W. 5 in. at base, D. 4 in. at base

Square seal: *boji yuren*

The Metropolitan Museum of Art, New York.
Purchase, Anita M. Linzee Bequest, 1934 (34.13)

This deity wears long robes and stands on a flat base fretted with rockwork; the fawn at her side looks up and bears a vase of flowers. Her hair is dressed with flowers; in her right hand she holds a spray of the sacred *lingzhi* fungus. The square seal *boji yuren*, as used by the potter Su Xuejin (1869–1919), is stamped on the back.

The popular female immortal Magu is a composite deity (see Little 2000, p. 334, for a reference to her early biography and an early Ming painting depicting her in one of her guises). Her image is customarily presented to married couples on their silver and golden wedding anniversaries (Werner 1961, p. 299).

An identical model is in the Wadsworth Athenaeum, Hartford (Donnelly 1969, pl. 158); it is one of a group of eleven figure models received through the Ulman Gift in 1959, some of which were also modeled by Su Xuejin.

Published: *The Metropolitan Museum of Art Bulletin* 29 (August 1934), p. 137.

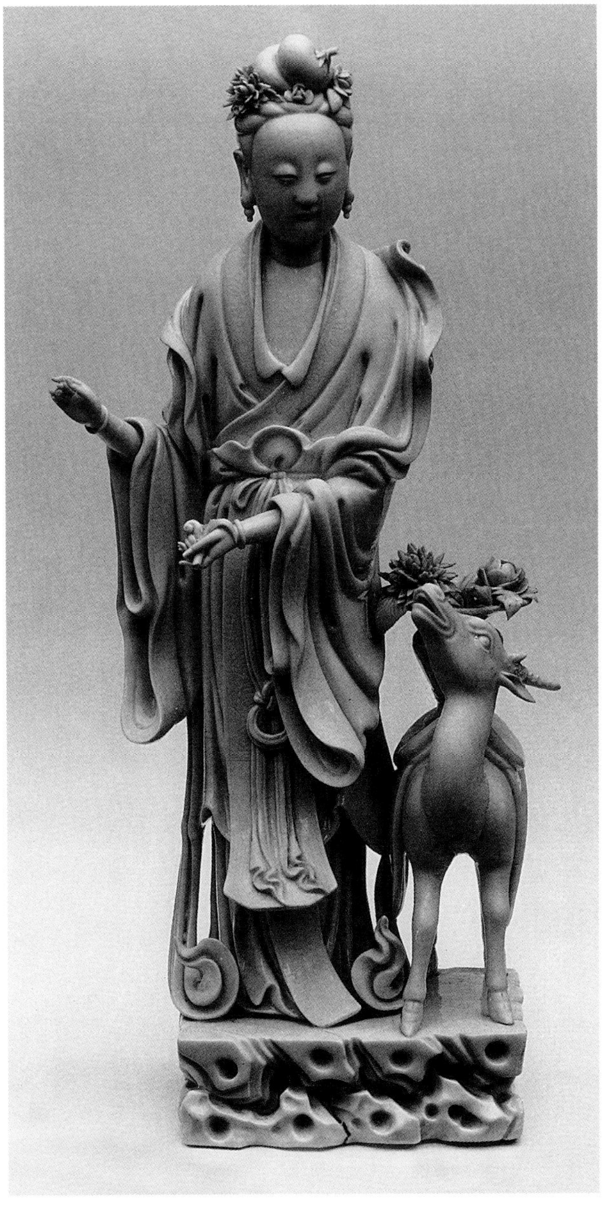

71. Su Xuejin (1869–1919)
Standing Guanyin
蘇學金 立觀音像
Qing dynasty, ca. 1895
Figure: H. 12 ¼ in., W. 5 ⅛ in., D. 3 ½ in.
Box: H. 14 ¾ in., W. 6 ⅞ in., D. 5 ⅛ in.
Square seal: *boji yuren*
Phillip Allen Collection

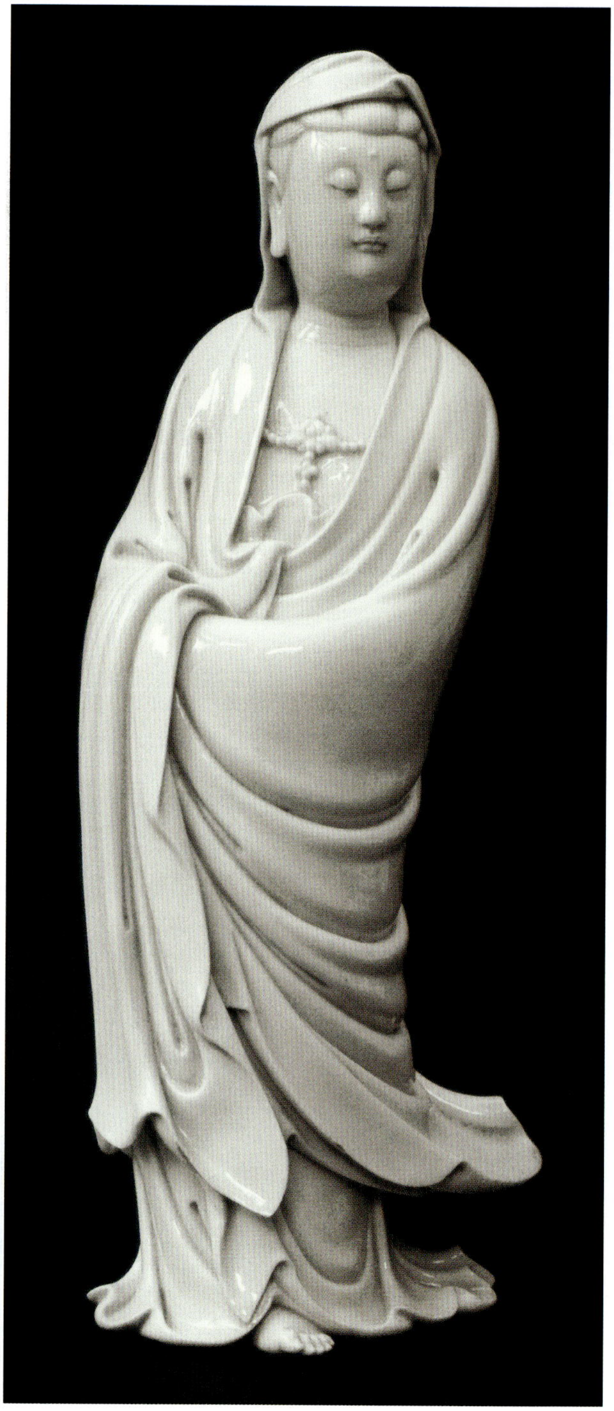

This deity, standing in flowing robes, still has its original fitted silk-lined box. The square seal *boji yuren*, as used by the potter Su Xuejin (1869–1919), is stamped on the back.

This marked example of the work of Su Xuejin is of unusual interest for having, according to the tradition of the owner's family, been presented in 1897 to his grandparents as a wedding gift, enclosed in its original Chinese box (lower left). It demonstrates the undeniable quality of Su's work as a porcelain modeler, which inspired a rapid rise in productivity at Dehua. Many models bearing his marks may have since been made there, although not by his hand.

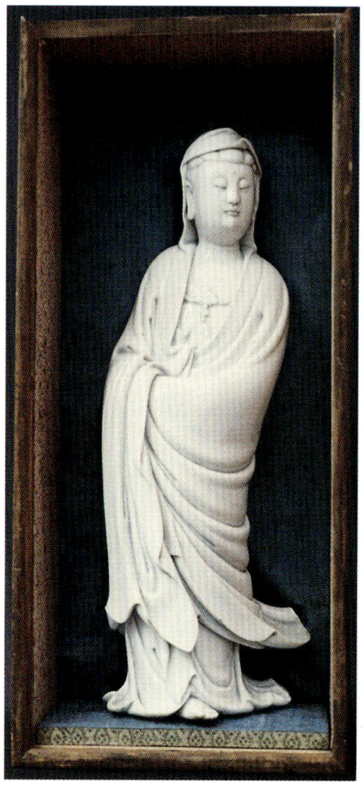

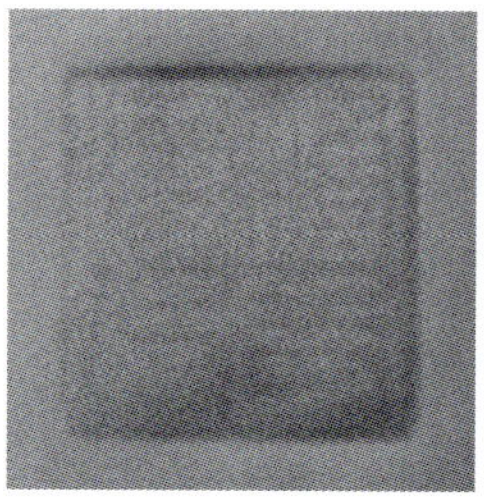

72. Xu Youyi (1887–1940)
Standing Buddha

許友義 立佛像

Late Qing or Republic period, early 20th century
H. 21 in., W. 7 ½ in.
Gourd-shaped seal: *Dehua*
Square seal: *Xu Yunlin zhi*
Richard Lehman Gray Collection

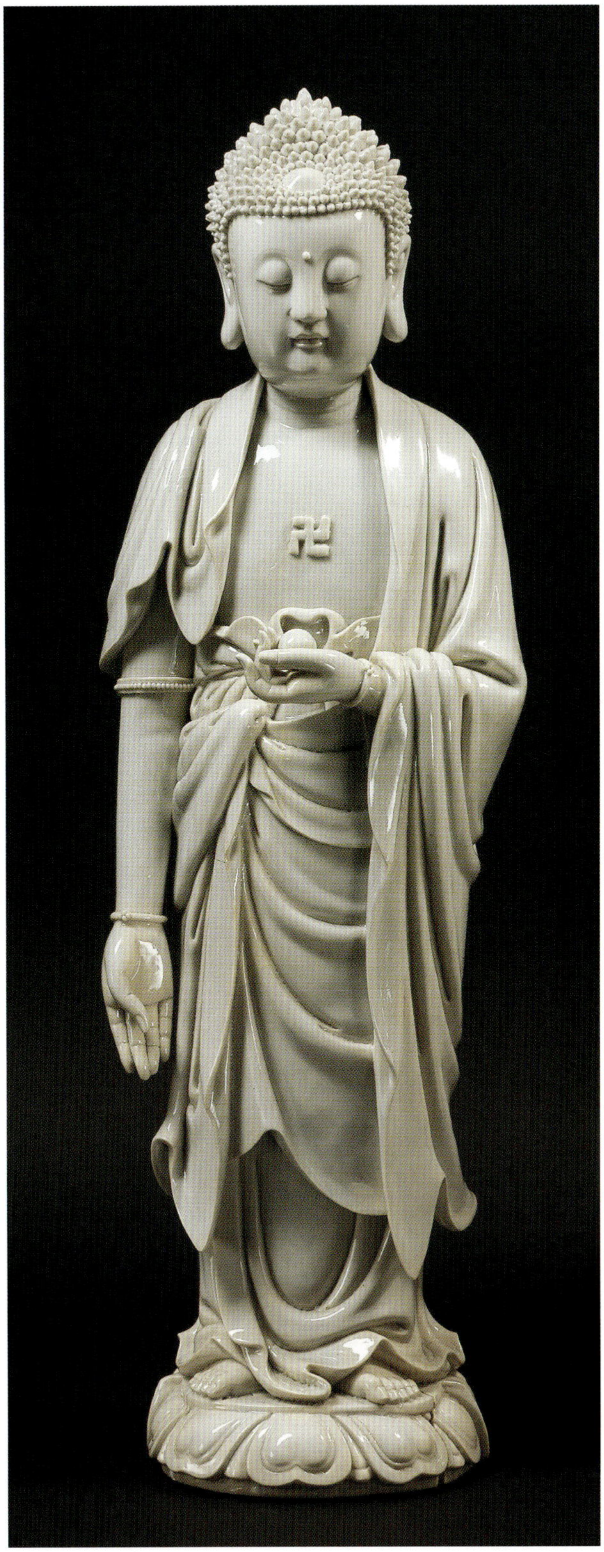

The Buddha stands with his right hand in the *bhumisparsa* (earth-touching) mudra; in his left hand is a jewel and on his breast is the swastika emblem. Beneath his feet, the low base is modeled with lotus petals. The square seal *Xu Yunlin zhi* of Xu Youyi (1887–1940) is stamped on the back.

Xu Youyi was the principal follower of Su Xuejin, as well as his pupil and associate. He came from a family of carvers of wood and clay images, and his work shows considerable versatility. For the bare outlines of his career and the marks he used, see Zeng 1995 and Xu Yixing 1993. Donnelly had considered him to be a late eighteenth-century potter.

For another example of the model with this mark, see Donnelly 1969, pl. 156B. A comparable standing Buddha with the mark of Zhang Shoushan, which may be regarded as its late Ming forerunner and possibly its original, is in the Percival David Foundation, London (see Donnelly 1969, pl. 138A).

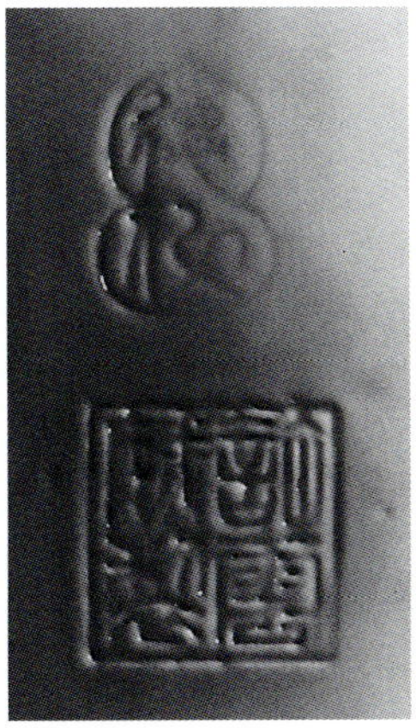

73, 74. Xu Youyi (1887–1940) Two Buddhist Temple Guardians, Duowen and Zengzhang

許友義 二天王像 多聞和增長

Late Qing or Republic period, early 20th century
H. 15 in., W. 6 ½ in.
H. 13 in., W. 6 ¼ in.
Gourd-shaped seal: *Dehua*
Square seal: *Xu Yunlin zhi*
Richard Lehman Gray Collection

These figures are two of the Four (Buddhist) Heavenly Kings (*lokapala*), guardians of the universe. Duowen (Vaisravana) holds a *vajra* (thunderbolt) across his chest, while Zengzhang (Virudhaka) raises a folded magic umbrella in his left hand. Both figures are dressed in full armor and stand on rockwork bases; they are surrounded by free-standing and swirling ribbons. In all probability they are based on bronze originals. The square seal *Xu Yunlin zhi*, belonging to Xu Youyi (1887–1940), and *Dehua* in a gourd-shaped cartouche are stamped on the back of each figure.

Another example of no. 73 is identified by Donnelly as Weituo (Viharapala), a *deva* or protector of the faith whose image was placed in Buddhist monasteries (Donnelly 1969, pl. 157 bottom right). The emergence of the second porcelain model, no. 74, suggests however that they are more likely to represent two of the Four Heavenly Kings. According to Werner, who outlines their complex history, these Buddhist deities were adopted by the Daoists and the two here were given the names of Moli Shou and Moli Hong (Werner 1962, pp. 455–57, 553). Yet another example of no. 73 is published by Blumenfield 2002, p. 59, pl. C.

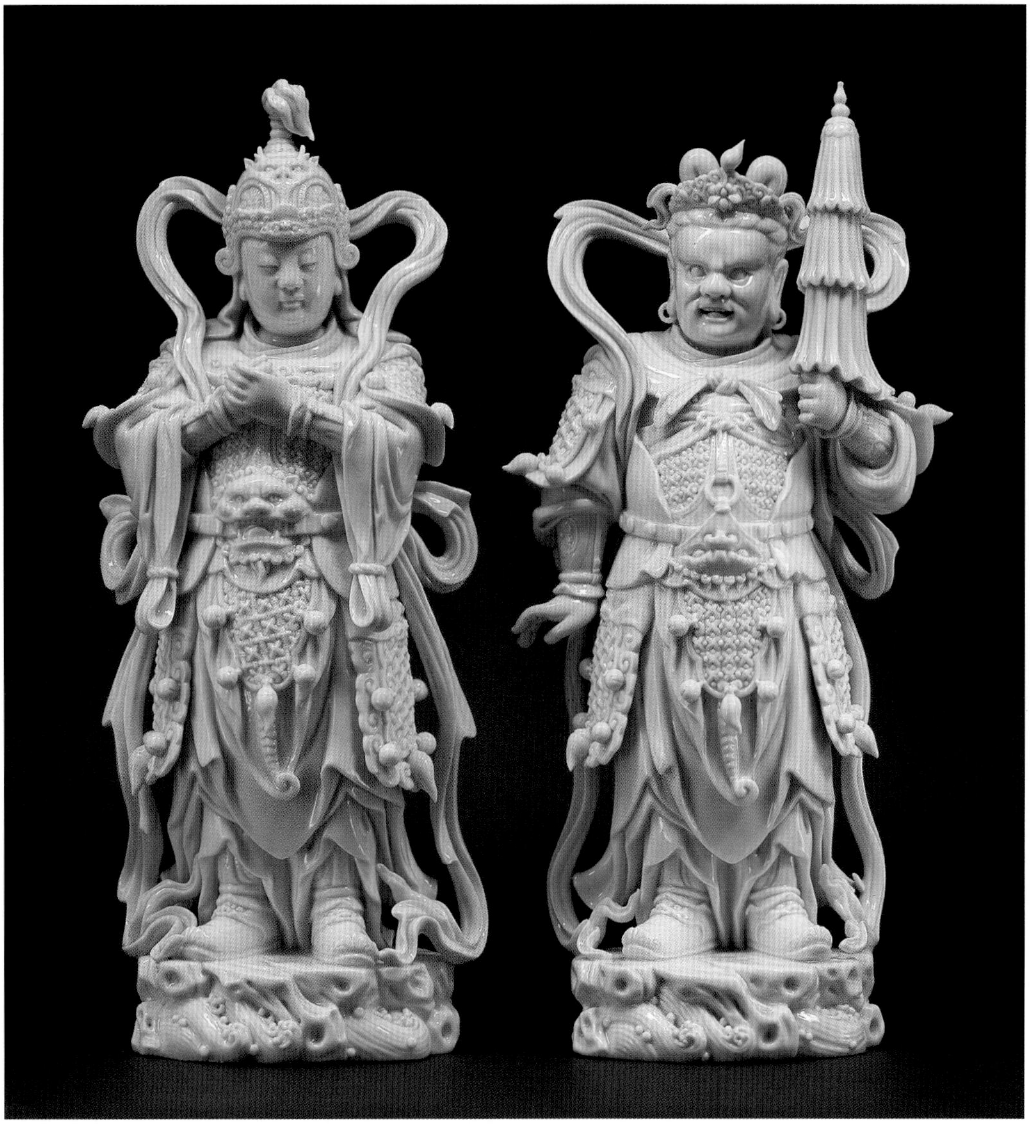

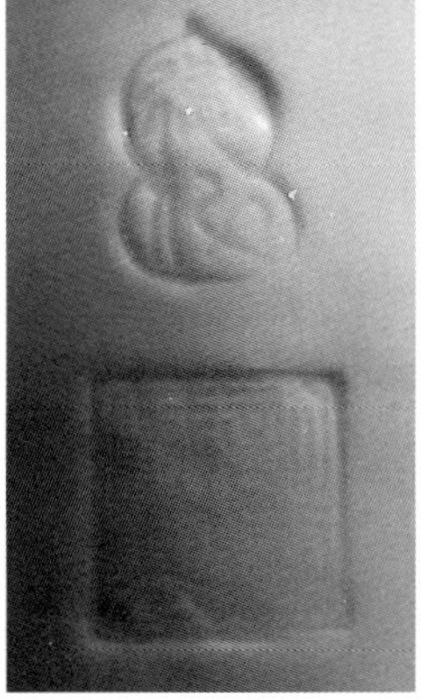

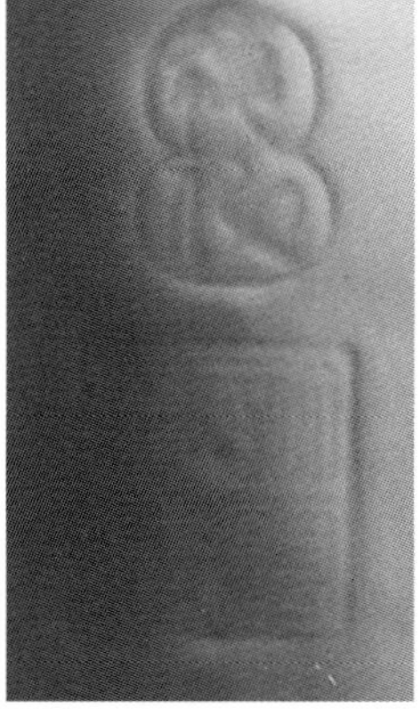

75. Damo Crossing the Yangzi

達摩一葦渡江

Qing dynasty or early Republic,
late 19th–early 20th century

H. 13 ¼ in., W. 4 ½ in.

Rectangular maker's mark: *taoya tang* (Elegant Pottery Hall)

Richard Lehman Gray Collection

Depicted as of Indian origin with prominent eyes and bushy eyebrows, and wearing full-length robes gathered in his hands at his chest, the patriarch stands on the legendary reed on top of a globular base with scrolling and foaming waves. The unattributed maker's mark *taoya tang* (Elegant Pottery Hall) in a rectangle is stamped on the back.

The significant role of Damo as the patriarch of meditative Buddhism has been mentioned above (see cat. no. 27, an outstanding model by He Chaozong); there is an evident relationship between this model and the one made up to three hundred years earlier. The superiority of the latter, notably in the modeling of both the head and draperies, is very marked. No less distinctive is the inferior quality of the glaze on the late figure. An example now in the British Museum is illustrated by Donnelly 1969, pl. E; another in the Hickley Collection is published in Kerr and Ayers 2002, no. 16.

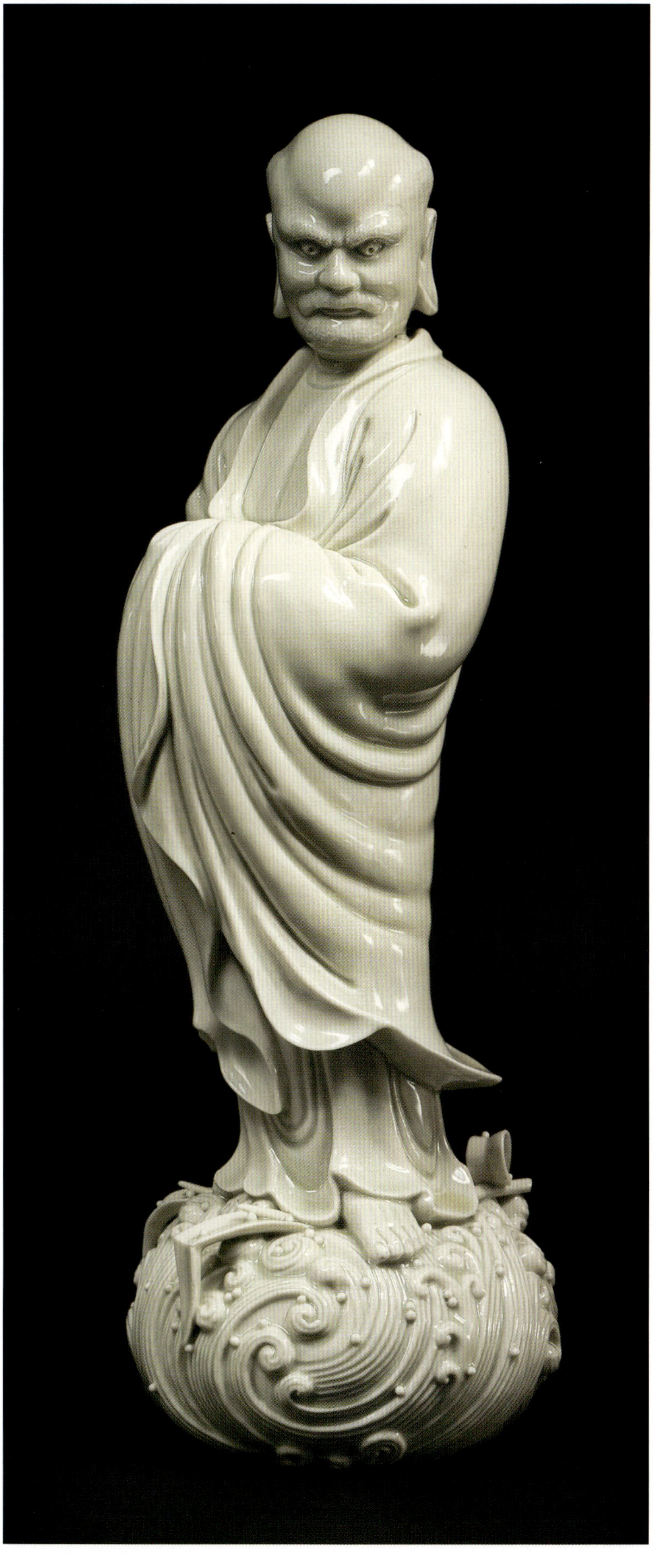

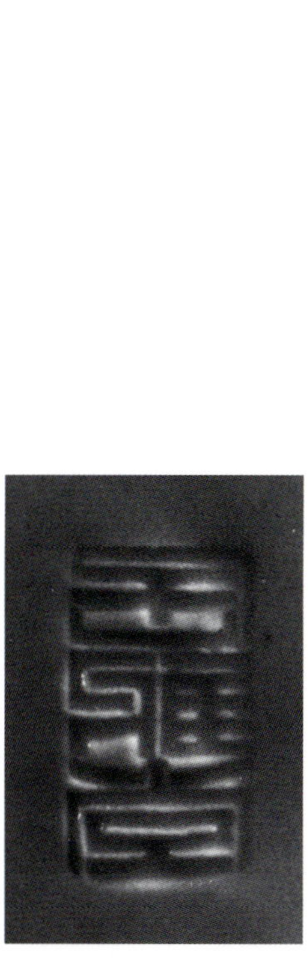

76. The Daoist Immortal Li Tieguai

八仙之一李鐵拐

Qing dynasty or early Republic,
late 19th–early 20th century
H. 5 in., W. 7 ½ in., D. 4 ¼ in.
Virginia Museum of Fine Arts, Richmond,
Bequest of Forrest R. Brauer (85.1455)

The gaunt, lame figure with an expression of suffering on his bearded face reclines on a low rocky plinth and leans against a rolled mat, holding his gourd in his left hand.

One of the Eight Daoist Immortals (*baxian*), this wandering lame beggar with his crutch and gourd of medicine is, as Werner puts it, "the emblem or type of sick people," and is revered as such (Werner 1961, p. 343). The late date of this artistically expressive but hardly devotional model is further indicated by the cold quality of its material and glaze.

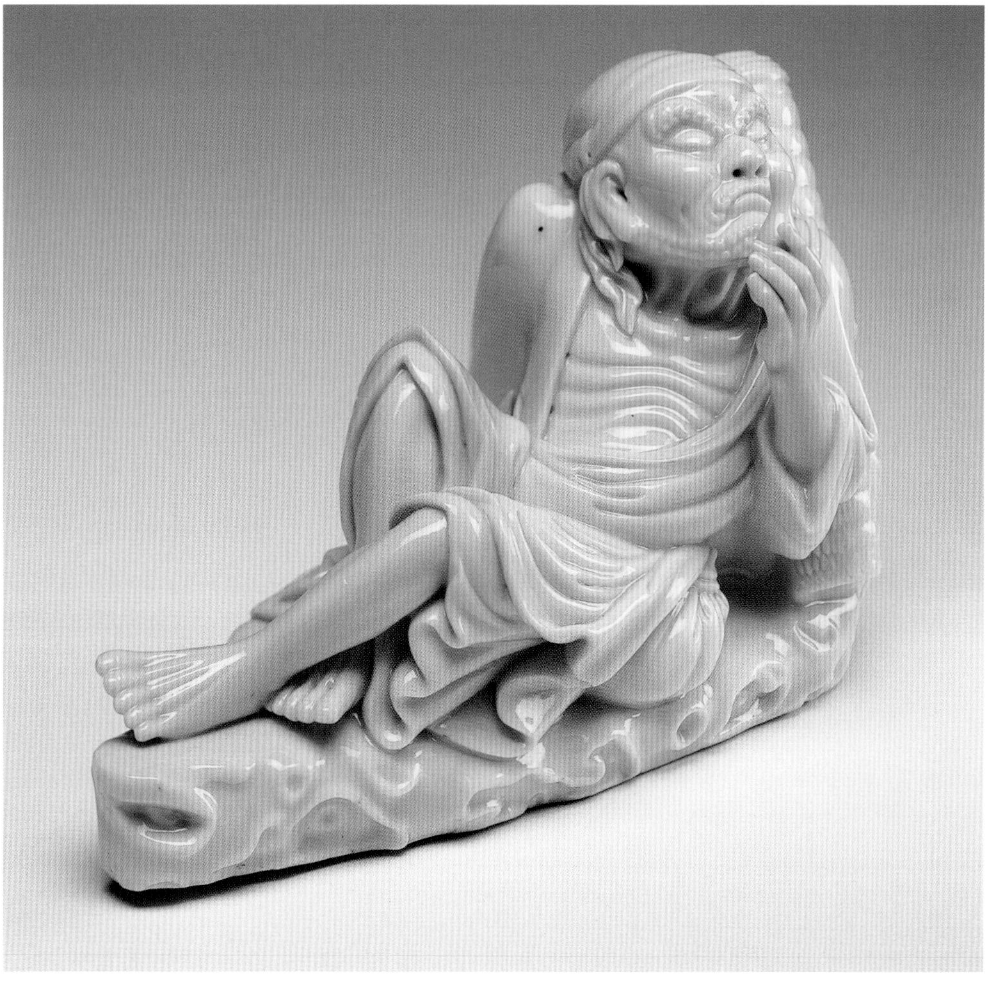

77. Xu Youyi (1887–1940)
Boat with Xiwangmu and her Companions

許友義 王母仙舟

Qing dynasty or early Republic,
late 19th–early 20th century
H. 13 ½ in., W. 12 in., D. 6 in.
Gourd-shaped seal: *Dehua*
Square seal: *Xu Yunlin zhi*
The Koger Collection, The John and Mable Ringling Museum of Art, the State Art Museum of Florida (32.213)

The generously sized rustic boat, set on an oval base of breaking waves, has a handle in the form of an over-branching peach tree on which is perched a monkey. Facing the goddess is her familiar mount, a large crane, and surrounding her are four musicians playing the *sheng* (mouth organ), *xiao* (flute), *qin* (zither), and *pipa* (lute). The square seal *Xu Yunlinzhi,* as used by the potter Xu Youyi (1887–1940), and the seal *Dehua* in a gourd-shaped cartouche are stamped on the back of her throne.

Xiwangmu, the Royal Mother of the West, occupies an important place in Daoist mythology and is repeatedly depicted in the decorative arts of China. She lives in the Kunlun mountains of China's far west, among gardens in which grow the peaches of immortality.

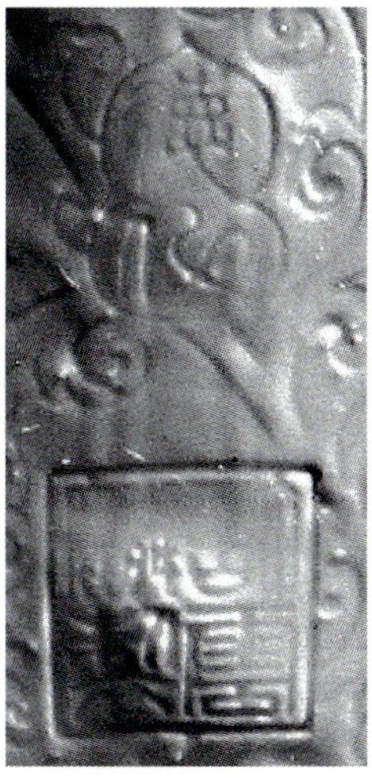

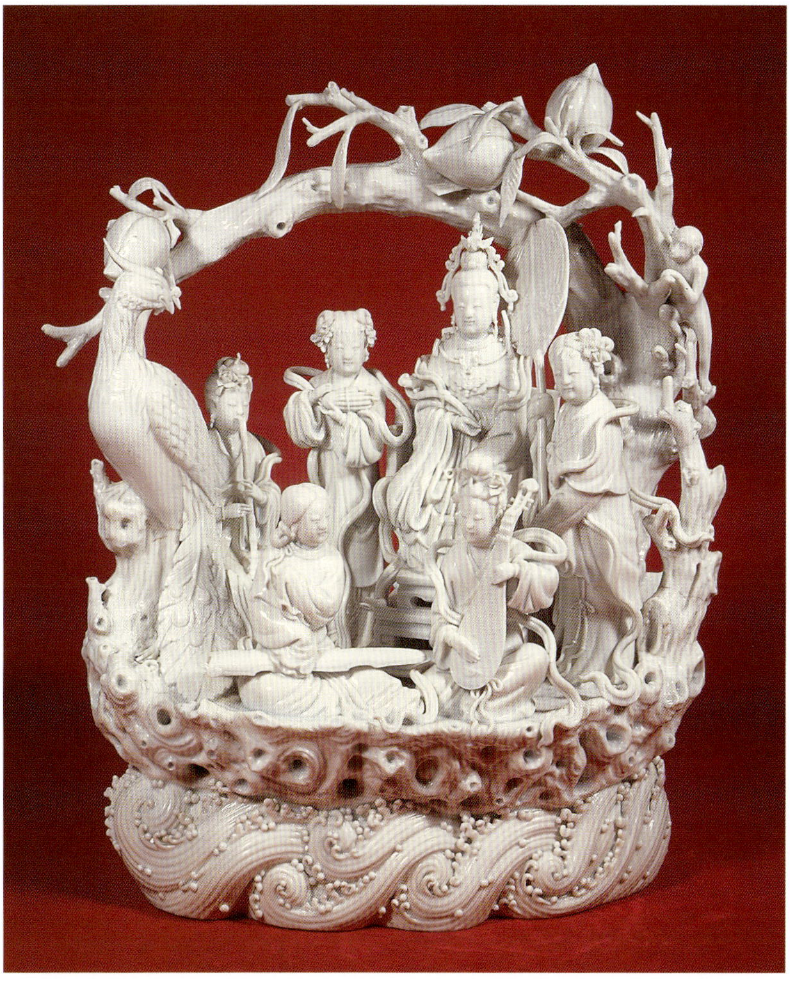

Selected Chinese Characters

Anhai	安海
Anpinggang	安平港
anqi zhuo	案啟桌
Anxi	安溪
Baijiao	白礁
Bailian	白蓮
Baosheng dadi	保生大帝
baxian zhuo	八仙桌
Baxian	八仙
Bixia yuanjun	碧霞元君
Boji yuren	博及漁人
Boshan	博山
Budai	布袋
Caishen	財神
Chan	禪
Changwu zhi	長物志
Chaozhou	潮州
Chen Jian Zhong	陳建中
Chen Jinggu	陳靖姑
Chen Nianshan	陳念山
Chen Shixin	陳氏信
Chen Wei	陳偉
Da Ming Wanli nianzhi	大明萬曆年制
Daiyun	戴雲
Damo	達摩
dan	担
Dehua	德化
Deng Xiang	鄧想
ding	鼎
Dongfang Shuo	東方朔
Dongyue miao	東岳廟
Doumu	斗母
fu	福
Fujian	福建
Fuzhou	福州
gu	觚
Guandi	關帝
Guanyin	觀音
Guanyu	關羽
Hehe erxian	和合二仙
gui	簋
Guo Shengwang	郭聖王
Guoxing ye (Coxinga)	國姓爺
Haicheng	海澄
Hanshan	寒山
He Chaochun	何朝春
He Chaozong	何朝宗
heshang	和尚
Housuo	後所
Jiangnan	江南
Jiangxi	江西
Jigong	濟公
jin	斤
Jingdezhen	景德鎮
Jingdezhen taolu	景德鎮陶錄
Jinjiang	晉江
Jiulong	九龍
kaiguang	開光
Kangxi	康熙
keting	客廳
Kuixing	魁星
Li Taibai	李太白
Li Tieguai	李鐵拐
Li Zhi	李贄
Lin Bing	林炳
Lin Chaojing	林朝景
Lin Jiesheng	林捷升
Lin Xiaozong	林孝宗
Lin Xizong	林希宗
Lin Zixin	林子信
lingzhi	靈芝
Liu Bingyuan	劉秉元
Liu Hai	劉海
Liu Yuan	劉元
Longnü	龍女
lu	祿
luohan	羅漢
Magu	麻姑
Mazu	媽祖
Mile fo	彌勒佛
mingjiao	明教
Mingshi	明史
mingzong	明宗
Minnan	閩南

Mulan	木蘭
Nan'an	南安
Nanyin	南音
pipa	琵琶
pusa	菩薩
Putian	莆田
Putuoshan	普陀山
Puxian	莆仙
Qin	琴
qingbai	青白
Qingshui zushi	清水祖師
Qitian dasheng	齊天大聖
Qu Yuan	屈原
Quanzhou	泉州
Quanzhou fuzhi	泉州府志
Qudougong	屈斗宮
Raozhou	饒州
ruyi	如意
Sanguan	三官
Shancai	善才
sheng	笙
Shengshi	盛世
Shide	拾得
shou	壽
Shoulao	壽老
Shouxing	壽星
Su Xuejin	蘇學金
Su Yunyu	蘇蘊玉
Sun Wukong	孫悟空
Taizu of Min	閩太祖
Taoxi	桃溪
Tiandu yuanshuai	田都元帥
tixi	剔犀
Tongan	同安
Tudi gong	土地公
Tudi	土地
wan bang	萬邦
Wang Bi	王弼
Wanli	萬曆
Wen Zhenheng	文震亨
Wenchang	文昌
wugong	五供
Wusheng laomu	無生老母
Xiamen	廈門
xiangzhuo	香桌
Xiao Mingwang	小明王
Xiao	簫
Xiwangmu	西王母
Xu Benzhang	徐本章
Xu Liangxi	許良西
Xu Youyi	許友義
Xu Yunlin	許雲麟
Xu Yuyuan zhi	許裕源製
Xuande	宣德
Xuannü	玄女
Xuantian shangdi	玄天上帝
Yangzi	揚子
Ye Wencheng	葉文程
yishu	藝術
Yongchun	永春
Yongle	永樂
Yuegang	月港
Yunlin	雲麟
Yunyu	蘊玉
Zeng Fan	曾凡
Zhang Shoushan	張壽山
Zhangzhou	漳州
Zheng Chenggong	鄭成功
Zheng Zhilong	鄭芝龍
Zhenwu	真武
Zulong gong	祖龍宮

Short Bibliography

Aga-Oglu 1975. Aga-Oglu, Kamer. *The Williams Collection of Far Eastern Ceramics: Tonnancour Section.* Ann Arbor: University of Michigan, Museum of Anthropology, 1975.

Aga-Oglu 1985. Aga-Oglu, Kamer. *The Williams Collection of East Asian Ceramics.* Detroit: Detroit Institute of Arts, 1985.

Ayers 1985. Ayers, John. *Chinese Ceramics: the Koger Collection.* London: Sotheby, 1985.

Ayers 1986. Ayers, John. "Blanc-de-Chine: Some Reflections." *Transactions of the Oriental Ceramic Society 1986–87*, vol. 51 (1988), pp. 13–36. Reprinted in Kerr and Ayers 2002, pp. 19–34.

Beurdeley and Raindre 1987. Beurdeley, Michel and Guy Raindre. Qing Porcelain: Famille Verte, Famille Rose, 1644–1912. London: Thames and Hudson, 1987.

Blumenfield 2002. Blumenfield, Robert H. *Blanc de Chine: The Great Porcelain of Dehua.* Berkeley: Ten Speed Press, 2002.

Brinkley, Frank. *China: its History, Arts and Literature.* Vol. 9 of *Oriental Series.* Boston: J.B. Millet, 1902.

Chapman 1999. Chapman, Jan. *The Art of Rhinoceros Horn Carving in China.* London: Christie's, 1999.

Chen 1999. Chen Jianzhong. *Dehua min yao qing hua* (Dehua Folk Blue-and-White Wares). Beijing: Wenwu, 1999.

Chinese Porcelain Company 1999. Chinese Porcelain Company. *Spring Brochure.* New York, 1999.

Chinese Porcelain Company 2000. Chinese Porcelain Company. *17th & 18th Century Chinese Porcelain from Distinguished Private Collections.* New York, 2000.

Christie's Amsterdam 1984. Christie's Amsterdam. *Fine and Important Late Ming and Transitional Porcelain: the Property of Captain Michael Hatcher.* 2 vols. Amsterdam, 1984. Catalogue of an auction held at Christie's Amsterdam, 14 March 1984; "the second and final part" 12–13 June 1984.

Christie's Amsterdam 1985. Christie's Amsterdam. *The Private Collection of Captain M. Hatcher.* Amsterdam, 1985. Catalogue of an auction held at Christie's Amsterdam, Thursday 14 February 1985.

Christie's Amsterdam 1992. Christie's Amsterdam. *The Vung Tao Cargo: Chinese Export Porcelain.* Amsterdam, 1992. Catalogue of an auction held at Christie's Amsterdam, Tuesday 7 April and Wednesday 8 April 1992.

Cooper-Hewitt Museum 1988. Cooper-Hewitt Museum, New York. *Courts and Colonies: The William and Mary Style in Holland, England, and America.* New York: Cooper-Hewitt Museum; Seattle: Distributed by University of Washington Press, 1988.

Donnelly 1969. Donnelly, Patrick J. *Blanc de Chine: The Porcelain of Tehua in Fukien.* London: Faber and Faber, 1969.

Fichtner 1937 Fichtner, Fritz. "Chinesische Porzellane aus der Provinz Fukien unter europaischen Einfluss." Offprint from *Keramische Rundschau* (Berlin 1937) no. 4, pp. 33–35; no. 5, pp. 47–50.

Fong 1990. Fong, Mary H. "Dehua Figures: A type of Chinese Popular Sculpture." *Orientations* 21 (Jan. 1990).

Franks 1876. Franks, A.W. *Catalogue of a Collection of Oriental Porcelain and Pottery Lent for Exhibition at Bethnal Green Branch Museum.* London, 1876.

Freedman 1985. Freedman, David S. "Some Thoughts on the Dating of Blanc de Chine." In Marchant 1985.

Freedman 2000. Freedman, David S. "The Porcelain of the Tek Sing." In *Tek Sing Treasures.* Stuttgart: Nagel Auktions, 2000.

Godden 1979. Godden, Geoffrey A. *Oriental Export Market Porcelain and its Influence on European Wares.* London; New York [etc.]: Granada, 1979.

Harrison-Hall 2001. Harrison-Hall, Jessica. *Catalogue of late Yuan and Ming ceramics in the British Museum.* London: The Museum, 2001.

Hinton and Impey 1998. Hinton, Mark and Oliver Impey. *Kensington Palace and the Porcelain of Queen Mary II: Essays in association with the Exhibition "China Mania."* London: Historic Royal Palaces, 1998.

Ho Chuimei 2002. Ho Chuimei. "Blanc de Chine in Archaeological Perspective: a Tribute to Donnelly." In Kerr and Ayers 2002, pp. 35–43.

Hobson 1915. Hobson, R.L. *Chinese Pottery and Porcelain.* 2 vols. London; New York: Cassell, 1915.

Honey 1945. Honey, W.B. *The Ceramic Art of China and Other Countries of the Far East.* London: Faber and Faber, 1945.

Hong Kong 1975. Chinese University of Hong Kong, Art Gallery. *An Exhibition of Te Hua Porcelain.* Hong Kong, 1975. Exhibition held at the Art Gallery, Institute of Chinese Studies, Chinese University of Hong Kong, January to June 1975.

Hong Kong 1990. Fung Ping Shan Museum, University of Hong Kong. *Dehua Wares.* With an introduction by Zeng Fan. Hong Kong, 1990. An exhibition at Fung Ping Shan Museum, Hong Kong, from 17 Oct.–13 Dec. 1990.

Howard and Ayers 1978. Howard, David S. and John Ayers. *China for the West: Chinese porcelain and other decorative arts for export illustrated from the Mottahedeh Collection.* 2 vols. London: Sotheby Park Bernet, 1978.

Joerg 1982. Joerg, C.J.A. *Porcelain and the Dutch China Trade.* The Hague: Nijhoff, 1982.

Kerr and Ayers 2002. Kerr, Rose, John Ayers, et. al. *Blanc de Chine: Porcelain from Dehua, A Catalogue of the Hickley Collection.* Singapore: Asian Civilisations Museum, 2002.

Kilburn 1998. Kilburn, Richard. "Chinese Porcelain in late 17th Century English Inventories." In Hinton and Impey 1998, pp. 69–78.

Krahl 1986. Krahl, Regina. *Chinese Ceramics in the Topkapi Saray Museum, Istanbul.* Edited by John Ayers. London: Sotheby's Publications, 1986.

Krahl 1994. Krahl, Regina. *Chinese Ceramics from the Meiyintang Collection.* 2 vols. London: Azimuth Editions, 1994.

Kwok 1993. Kwok, Kenson. "Blanc de Chine: The Hickley Collection." *Arts of Asia* 23, no. 6 (Nov.–Dec. 1993).

Kwok 2002. Kwok, Kenson. "A Note on the Construction of Dehua Figures." In Kerr and Ayers 2002, pp. 45–50.

Lane 1949. Lane, Arthur. "Queen Mary II's Porcelain Collection at Hampton Court." In *Transactions of the Oriental Ceramic Society 1949–50*, vol. 25.

Lisbon 2001. Museu Calouste Gulbenkian. *Exotica: The Portuguese Discoveries of the Renaissance Kunstkammer.* Lisbon, 2001.

Lang 1983. Lang, Gordon. *The Wrestling Boys: an Exhibition of Chinese and Japanese Ceramics in the Collection at Burghley House.* Stamford, Lincs.: Burghley House Preservation Trust, 1983.

Little 2000. Little, Stephen. *Taoism and the Arts of China.* Chicago: The Art Institute of Chicago, 2000.

Locsin 1967. Locsin, Leandro and Cecelia. *Oriental Ceramics Discovered in the Philippines.* Rutland and Tokyo: Tuttle, 1967.

Locsin 1968. Locsin, Cecilia Y. *A Group of White Wares from Te-hua.* Vol. 7 of *Manila Trade Pottery Seminar: introductory notes.* Manila: Research Foundation in Philippine Anthropology and Archaeology, [1968].

Marchant 1985. S. Marchant and Son. *Blanc de Chine.* London, 1985. Exhibition from 8 Dec.–20 Dec. 1985.

Marchant 1994. S. Marchant and Son. *Exhibition of blanc de chine to be held from ... 3rd June 1994 until ... 24th June.* London, [1994].

Oriental Ceramic Society 1984. Oriental Ceramic Society. *Chinese Ivories: from the Shang to the Qing: an exhibition organized by the Oriental Ceramic Society jointly with the British Museum.* London, 1984. Catalogue with essays by James Watt, Derek Gillman, and Craig Clunas.

Pope 1956. Pope, John Alexander. *Chinese Porcelains from the Ardebil Shrine.* Washington, D.C.: Freer Gallery of Art, 1956.

Priestley and Ferraro 1996. Priestley and Ferraro Chinese Art. *Chinese art: exhibition dates 16–23 December 1996, 6–17 January 1997.* London, 1996.

Reidemeister 1932. Reidemeister, L. "Der Grosse Kurfurst und Friedrich III als Sammler ostasiatisches Kunst." *Ostasiatische Zeitschrift*, n.s., 8 (1932).

Sheaf and Kilburn 1988. Sheaf, Colin and Richard Kilburn. *The Hatcher Porcelain Cargoes: the complete record.* Oxford: Phaidon, 1988.

Stroeber 2002. Stroeber, Eva. "Dehua Porcelain in the Collection of Augustus the Strong in Dresden," in Kerr and Ayers 2002, pp. 51–58.

Sullivan 1957. Sullivan, Michael. "Kendi." *Archives of the Chinese Art Society of America* 11 (1957).

Sullivan 1962. Sullivan, Michael. "Notes on Chinese Export Wares in South-East Asia." *Transactions of the Oriental Ceramic Society 1960–62*, vol. 33, pp. 61–77.

Tan 2002. Tan, Heidi. "Pamela Hickley: a Connoisseur's View." In Kerr and Ayers 2002.

Valenstein 1989. Valenstein, Suzanne. *A Handbook of Chinese Ceramics.* Rev. ed. New York: Metropolitan Museum of Art, 1989.

Volker 1954. Volker, T. *Porcelain and the Dutch East India Company.* Leiden: E.J. Brill, 1954.

Werner 1961. Werner, E.T.C. *A Dictionary of Chinese Mythology.* New York: Julian Press, 1961.

Wilson, Ming. *Rare Marks on Chinese Ceramics.* London: The School of Oriental and African Studies, University of London, in association with the Victoria and Albert Museum, 1998. Catalogue of exhibition held at the Percival David Foundation and the Victoria and Albert Museum.

Wood 1995. Wood, Frances. *Did Marco Polo go to China?* London: Secker & Warburg, 1995.

Xu and Chen 1996. Xu Benzhang and Chen Jianzhong. "Ancient Dehua Porcelain." *Transactions of the Oriental Ceramic Society 1995–96,* vol. 60, pp. 17–23.

Xu and Ye 1993. Xu Benzhang and Ye Wencheng. *Dehua cishi yu Dehua ya.* Fujian, 1993.

Xu Yixing 1993. Xu Yixing, ed. *Dehua taoci lishi renwu* (Historical Figures concerned with Dehua Ceramics). Dehua, 1993.

Ye and Xu 1980. Ye Wencheng and Xu Benzhang. *The Extensive International Market for Dehua Porcelain.* Translated by Rose Kerr. Chinese Translations, no. 10. London: Oriental Ceramic Society, [ca. 1984]. Paper originally published in *Haiwai Jiaotongshi Yanjiu*, 1980, no. 2.

Zeng 1990. Zeng Fan. "An Archaeological Study of Ceramics from the Dehua Kilns in Fujian." In Hong Kong 1990.

Zeng 1995. Zeng Fan. "Additional Comments on the Dehua Kilns." *Transactions of the Oriental Ceramic Society 1995–96,* vol. 60, pp. 25–27.

PHOTO CREDITS

© 2002 The Metropolitan Museum of Art	1, 51, 70
©2002 The Detroit Institute of Arts	2
Photography by Brian Shrum	3, 4, 6, 8, 12-18, 23, 26, 26b, 33, 36, 38-40, 40b, 47, 49, 53-59, 61-64, 69, 69b, 77, 77b
Courtesy of Robert H. Blumenfield Collection	5, 10, 22, 24, 37, 43, 43b, 44, 52, 66, 67
Photography by Maggie Nimkin	7, 11, 19, 20, 29, 29b, 35, 35b, 45, 48, 60, 72-75, 72b-75b
Photography by Katherine Wetzel © Virginia Museum of Fine Arts	9, 21, 46, 50, 68, 68b, 76
Photography by Richard Goodbody, Courtesy of The Chinese Porcelain Company	25, 25b, 28, 28b, 31, 32
Courtesy of Priestley & Ferraro Chinese Art	27, 27b
Photograph by Schecter Lee, ©1986 The Metropolitan Museum of Art	30
Photography by Katherine Wetze	34, 34b, 41
Anonymous	42
Courtesy of Peabody Essex Museum	65
Courtesy of John Ayers	71, 71b
The Treasury of St. Mark, Venice	Fig. 1
© Copyright The British Museum	Fig. 2, 4
Courtesy of Chen Jainzhong, Dehua Ceramics Museum	Fig. 3
The Royal Collection ©2002, Her Majesty Queen Elizabeth II	Fig. 5
The Walters Art Museum, Baltimore	Fig. 6
Courtesy of Yuan Bingling	Fig. 7, 8

China Institute Gallery Exhibitions: 1966–2002

** 1. SELECTIONS OF CHINESE ART FROM PRIVATE COLLECTIONS IN THE METROPOLITAN AREA
November 15, 1966–February 15, 1967
Curator: Mrs. Gilbert Katz

** 2. ART STYLES OF ANCIENT SHANG
April 5–June 11, 1967
Curator: Jean Young

** 3. ANIMALS AND BIRDS IN CHINESE ART
October 25, 1967–January 28, 1968
Curator: Fong Chow

** 4. GARDENS IN CHINESE ART
March 21–May 26, 1968
Curator: Wan-go H.C. Weng

** 5. CHINESE JADE THROUGH THE CENTURIES
October 24, 1968–January 26, 1969
Curator: Joan M. Hartman

** 6. FOREIGNERS IN ANCIENT CHINESE ART
March 27–May 25, 1969
Curator: Ezekiel Schloss

** 7. CHINESE PAINTED ENAMELS
October 23, 1969–February 1, 1970
Curator: J.A. Lloyd Hyde

**8. ALBUM LEAVES FROM THE SUNG AND YUAN DYNASTIES
March 26–May 30, 1970
Curator: C.C. Wang

** 9. MING PORCELAINS: A RETROSPECTIVE
October 29, 1970–January 31, 1971
Curator: Suzanne G. Valenstein

**10. CHINESE SILK TAPESTRY: K'O-SSU
March 24–May 27, 1971
Curator: Jean Mailey

** 11. EARLY CHINESE GOLD AND SILVER
October 21, 1971–January 30, 1972
Curator: Dr. Paul Singer

** 12. DRAGONS IN CHINESE ART
March 23–May 28, 1972
Curator: Hugo Munsterberg

** 13. WINTRY FORESTS, OLD TREES: SOME LANDSCAPE THEMES IN CHINESE PAINTING
October 26, 1972–January 28, 1973
Curator: Richard Barnhart

** 14. CERAMICS IN THE LIAO DYNASTY: NORTH AND SOUTH OF THE GREAT WALL
March 15–May 28, 1973
Curator: Yutaka Mino

** 15. CHINA TRADE PORCELAIN: A STUDY IN DOUBLE REFLECTIONS
October 25, 1973–January 27, 1974
Curator: Claire le Corbeiller

** 16. TANTRIC BUDDHIST ART
March 14–May 24, 1974
Curator: Eleanor Olson

** 17. FRIENDS OF WEN CHENG-MING: A VIEW FROM THE CRAWFORD COLLECTION
October 24, 1974–January 26, 1975
Curators: Marc F. Wilson and Kwan S. Wong

** 18. ANCIENT CHINESE JADES FROM THE BUFFALO MUSEUM OF SCIENCE
April 3–June 15, 1975
Curator: Joan M. Hartman

** 19. ART OF THE SIX DYNASTIES: CENTURIES OF CHANGE AND INNOVATION
October 29, 1975–February 1, 1976
Curator: Annette L. Juliano

** 20. CHINA'S INFLUENCE ON AMERICAN CULTURE IN THE 18TH AND 19TH CENTURIES
April 8 –June 13, 1976
Curators: Henry Trubner and William Jay Rathburn
(Exhibition traveled to the Seattle Art Museum, October 7–November 28, 1976.)

21. CHINESE FOLK ART IN AMERICAN COLLECTIONS: EARLY 15TH THROUGH 20TH CENTURIES
October 27, 1976–January 30, 1977
Curator: Tseng Yu-Ho Ecke

22. EARLY CHINESE MINIATURES
March 16–May 29, 1977
Curator: Dr. Paul Singer

** 23. I-HSING WARE
October 28, 1977–January 29, 1978
Curator: Terese Tse Bartholomew
(Exhibition traveled to the Nelson Gallery of Art, Kansas City, February 19–May 21, 1978, and the Asian Art Museum of San Francisco, June 16–September 21, 1978.)

**24. EMBROIDERY OF IMPERIAL CHINA
March 17–May 28, 1978
Curator: Jean Mailey

** 25. ORIGINS OF CHINESE CERAMICS
October 25, 1978–January 28, 1979
Curator: Clarence F. Shangraw

** 26. ART OF THE HAN
March 14–May 27, 1979
Curator: Ezekiel Schloss

27. TREASURES FROM THE METROPOLITAN MUSEUM OF ART
October 25–November 25, 1979
Curator: Clarence F. Shangraw

** 28. CHINESE ART FROM THE NEWARK MUSEUM
March 19–May 25, 1980
Curators: Valrae Reynolds and Yen Fen Pei

29. CHINESE PORCELAINS IN EUROPEAN MOUNTS
October 22, 1980–January 25, 1981
Curator: Sir Francis Watson

* 30. FREEDOM OF CLAY AND BRUSH THROUGH SEVEN CENTURIES IN NORTHERN CHINA: TZ'U-CHOU TYPE WARES 960–1600 A.D.
March 16–May 24, 1981
Curator: Yutaka Mino
(Exhibition originated at Indianapolis Museum of Art.)

31. THE ART OF CHINESE KNOTTING
July 29–September 21, 1981
Curator: Hsia-Sheng Chen

**32. MASTERPIECES OF SUNG AND YUAN DYNASTY CALLIGRAPHY FROM THE JOHN M. CRAWFORD JR. COLLECTION
October 21, 1981–January 31, 1982
Curator: Kwan S. Wong, assisted by Stephen Addiss
(Exhibition traveled to the Spencer Museum, University of Kansas, March 14–April 18, 1982.)

33. THE COMMUNION OF SCHOLARS: CHINESE ART AT YALE
March 20–May 30, 1982
Curator: Mary Gardner Neill
(Exhibition traveled to the Museum of Fine Arts, Houston, June 22–August 22, 1982, and the Yale Art Gallery, New Haven, October 5, 1982–April 17, 1983.)

* 34. CHINA FROM WITHIN
November 4–December 12, 1982
A Smithsonian Institution Travelling Services Exhibition, organized by the International Photography Society in cooperation with the China Exhibition Agency, Beijing, and the Chinese Embassy, Washington, DC

**35. BAMBOO CARVING OF CHINA
March 18–May 29, 1983
Curators: Wang Shixiang and Wan-go H.C. Weng
(Exhibition traveled to The Nelson-Atkins Museum of Art, Kansas City, July 24–September 11, 1983, and the Asian Art Museum of San Francisco, October 3, 1983–January 15, 1984.)

36. CHINESE CERAMICS OF THE TRANSITIONAL PERIOD: 1620–1683
October 21, 1983–January 29, 1984
Curator: Stephen Little
(Exhibition traveled to the Kimbell Art Museum, Fort Worth, May 26–August 26, 1984.)

* 37. MASTERPIECES OF CHINESE EXPORT PORCELAIN AND RELATED DECORATIVE ARTS FROM THE MOTTAHEDEH COLLECTION
February 10–March 7, 1984
U.S.–China 200 Bicentennial Exhibition, organized by Anita Christy

38. CHINESE TRADITIONAL ARCHITECTURE
April 6–June 10, 1984
Curator: Nancy Shatzman Steinhardt
(A permanent travelling exhibition of China Institute. Shown at Allegheny College, Meadeville, PA, March 28–April 19, 1985; Marlboro College, Marlboro, VT, September 11–October 31, 1985; State University of New York, Binghamton, January 7–February 27, 1986.)

** 39. CHINESE RARE BOOKS IN AMERICAN COLLECTIONS
October 20, 1984–January 29, 1985
Curator: Soren Edgren

40. THE SUMPTUOUS BASKET: CHINESE LACQUER WITH BASKETRY PANELS
March 20– June 3, 1985
Curator: James C.Y. Watt

** 41. KERNELS OF ENERGY, BONES OF EARTH: THE ROCK IN CHINESE ART
October 26, 1985–January 26, 1986
Curator: John Hay

* 42. PUPPETRY OF CHINA
April 19–June 29, 1986
Curator: Roberta Helmer Stalberg
Organized by the Center for Puppetry Arts, Atlanta

43. SELECTIONS OF CHINESE ART FROM PRIVATE COLLECTIONS
October 18, 1986–January 4, 1987
Exhibition celebrating the 60th Anniversary of China Institute and the 20th Anniversary of China Institute Gallery, organized by James C.Y. Watt and Annette L. Juliano.

* 44. 1987 NEW YEAR EXHIBITION

* 45. FOLK ART
April 4–May 30, 1987
Curator: Nancy Zeng Berliner

46. RICHLY WOVEN TRADITIONS:
COSTUMES OF THE MIAO OF
SOUTHWEST CHINA AND BEYOND
October 22, 1987–January 4, 1988
Curator: Theresa Reilly

* 47. 1988 NEW YEAR EXHIBITION
February 4–February 24, 1988

** 48. RITUAL AND POWER:
JADES OF ANCIENT CHINA
April 23–June 19, 1988
Curator: Elizabeth Childs-Johnson

* 49. STORIES FROM CHINA'S PAST
September 17–November 12, 1988
Curator: The Chinese Culture Center of San Francisco

* 50. 1989 NEW YEAR EXHIBITION: LANTERNS
January 28–February 25, 1989

* 51. MIND LANDSCAPES:
THE PAINTINGS OF C.C. WANG
April 3–May 27, 1989
Curator: Jerome Silbergeld

**52. CHINA BETWEEN REVOLUTIONS:
PHOTOGRAPHY BY SIDNEY D. GAMBLE, 1917–1927
June 29–September 9, 1989
Curator: The Sidney D. Gamble Foundation for China Studies and China Institute in America

* 53. VIEWS FROM JADE TERRACE:
CHINESE WOMEN ARTISTS, 1300–1912
October 5–December 2, 1989
Organized by Indianapolis Museum of Art

* 54. 1990 NEW YEAR EXHIBITION:
THE CHINESE EARTH–VIEWS OF NATURE
January–March 1990
Curator: Anita Christy

55. CLEAR AS CRYSTAL, RED AS FLAME:
LATER CHINESE GLASS
April 21–June 16, 1990
Curator: Claudia Brown and Donald Robiner

56. THE ECCENTRIC PAINTERS OF YANGZHOU
October 20–December 15, 1990
Curator: Vito Giacalone

* 57. 1991 NEW YEAR EXHIBITION:
CHILDREN IN CHINESE ART
January 26–March 2, 1991
Organized under the auspices of the China Institute Women's Association

58. ANCIENT CHINESE BRONZE ART:
ASTING THE PRECIOUS SACRAL VESSEL
April 20–June 15, 1991
Curator: W. Thomas Chase

59. EARLY CHINESE CERAMICS FROM
NEW YORK STATE MUSEUMS
October 19–December 14, 1991
Curator: Martie W. Young

60. TREASURES OF THE LAST EMPEROR:
SELECTIONS FROM THE PALACE MUSEUM, BEIJING
February 1–March 7, 1992
Curator: Lawrence Wu

61. LAMAS, PRINCES AND BRIGANDS:
PHOTOGRAPHS BY JOSEPH ROCK OF THE
TIBETAN BORDERLANDS OF CHINA
April 15–July 31, 1992
Curator: Michael Aris

62. WORD AS IMAGE:
THE ART OF CHINESE SEAL ENGRAVING
October 21–December 12, 1992
Curator: Jason C. Kuo

63. A YEAR OF GOOD FORTUNE:
LEGENDS OF THE ROOSTER AND
TRADITIONS OF THE CHINESE NEW YEAR
January 19–March 6, 1993
Curator: Willow Weilan Hai

* 64. DISCARDING THE BRUSH:
GAO QIPEI, 1660–1734
April 17–June 12, 1993
Curator: Klass Ruitenbeek
Organized by the Rijksmuseum Amsterdam

65. AS YOU WISH: SYMBOL AND MEANING ON
CHINESE PORCELAINS FROM THE TAFT MUSEUM
October 23–January 15, 1994
Curator: David T. Johnson

* 66. SENDING AWAY THE OLD,
WELCOMING THE NEW
February 5–March 5, 1994
Curator: Karen Kane

* 67. CAPTURING A WORLD:
CHINA AND ITS PEOPLE–
PHOTOGRAPHY BY JOHN THOMSON
March 26–June 11, 1994
Curator: organized by the British Council, catalogue by the British Council

* 68. AT THE DRAGON COURT:
CHINESE EMBROIDERED MANDARIN
SQUARES FROM THE SCHUYLER V.R.
CAMMANN COLLECTION
October 20–December 22, 1994
Brochure from similar show which took place at Yale Univ. Art Gallery
Curator: John Finlay

69. ANIMALS OF THE CHINESE ZODIAC: CELEBRATING CHINESE NEW YEAR
January 20–March 4, 1995
Curator: Willow Weilan Hai

70. CHINESE PORCELAINS OF THE SEVENTEENTH CENTURY: LANDSCAPES, SCHOLARS' MOTIFS AND NARRATIVES
April 22–August 5, 1995
Curator: Julia B. Curtis

71. ABSTRACTION AND EXPRESSION IN CHINESE CALLIGRAPHY
October 14–December 21, 1995
Curator: H. Christopher Luce
(Exhibition traveled to the Seattle Art Museum, Washington, November 21, 1996 to March 23, 1997.)

* 72. CALLIGRAPHY AS LIVING ART: SELECTIONS FROM THE JILL SACKLER CHIENSE CALLIGRAPHY COMPETITION
Feburary 3–March 9, 1996
Curator: Willow Weilan Hai, in conjunction with the A. M. Sackler Foundation, Washington, D.C.

* 73. HARE'S FUR, TORTOISESHELL AND PARTRIDGE FEATHERS CHINESE BROWN- AND BLACK-GLAZED CERAMICS, 400–1400
April 20–July 6, 1996
Curator: Robert Mowry
Organized by the Harvard University Art Museum, Massachusetts

74. THE LIFE OF A PATRON: ZHOU LIANGGONG (1612–1672) AND THE PAINTERS OF SEVENTEENTH-CENTURY CHINA
October 23–December 21, 1996
Curator: Hongnam Kim

*75. ADORNMENT FOR ETERNITY: STATUS AND RANK IN CHINESE ORNAMENT
February 6-July 14, 1997
Curators: Julia White and Emma Bunker
Organized by the Denver Art Museum

76. POWER AND VIRTUE: THE HORSE IN CHINESE ART
September 11 - December 13, 1997
Curator: Robert E. Harrist, Jr.

*77. SCENT OF INK: THE ROY AND MARILYN PAPP COLLECTION OF CHINESE ART
February 5 – June 20, 1998
Curator: Claudia Brown
Organized by the Phoenix Art Museum

*78. CHINESE SNUFF BOTTLES FROM THE PAMELA R. LESSING FRIEDMAN COLLECTION
September 16 – December 13, 1998
Organized by the Asian Art Coordinating Council

79. A LITERATI LIFE IN THE TWENTIETH CENTURY: WANG FANGYU—ARTIST, SCHOLAR, CONNOISSEUR
February 11-June 20, 1999
Curator: H. Christopher Luce

80. THE RESONANCE OF THE QIN IN EAST ASIAN ART
September 17-December 12, 1999
Curator: Stephen Addiss

81. THE STORY OF RED: CELEBRATE THE CHINESE NEW YEAR IN 2000
January 12 - February 11, 2000
Curator: Willow Weilan Hai Chang

82. DAWN OF THE YELLOW EARTH: ANCIENT CHINESE CERAMICS FROM THE MEIYINTANG COLLECTION
March 21-June 18, 2000
Curator: Regina Krahl

83. THE CHINESE PAINTER AS POET
September 14-December 20, 2000
Curator: Jonathan Chaves

*84. LIVING HERITAGE: VERNACULAR ENVIRONMENT IN CHINA
January 25-June 10, 2001
Curator: Kai-yin Lo

85. EXQUISITE MOMENTS: WEST LAKE & SOUTHERN SONG ART
September 25-December 9, 2001
Curator: Hui-shu Lee

86. CIRCLES OF REFLECTION: THE CARTER COLLECTION OF CHINESE BRONZE MIRRORS
February 7-June 2, 2002
Curator: Ju-hsi Chou
Organized by The Cleveland Museum of Art

For information on availability of these titles and others, please contact China Institute in America at (212) 744–8181

** No catalogue or exhibition catalogue published by another institution*

*** Catalogue out of print*

China Institute

FRIENDS OF THE GALLERY

Juanzhu (Benefactor)
Robert T. and Kay F. Gow
Howard and Mary Ann Rogers
Oscar L. Tang

Zanzhu (Patron)
Jane DeBevoise and Paul Calello
William M. Lipton
H. Christopher Luce and Tina Liu

Zizhu (Sponsor)
Robert M. and Renee Beningson
Susan L. Beningson
Catherine Gamble Curran
Alice King
Margro R. Long
Jeannette N. Rider
David Solo
Diane H. Schafer and Jeffrey Stein
John S. and Susy Wadsworth

Pengyou (Friend)
M. Leon Canick and Josephine Berger-Nadler
Arnold Chang
Maie Lee N. Chen
Herbert J. and Jeanine Coyne
John R. and Julia B. Curtis
Richard M. and Peggy Danziger
Bruce B. and Ruth A. Dayton
Elizabeth De Cuevas
Richard A. and Ruth Dickes
The Honorable and Mrs. C. Douglas Dillon
Ivan Y.T. and Laurette S. Feng
Michael E. and Winnie Feng
Hart and Nancy B. Fessenden
Rachelle R. Holden
Charlotte Horstmann
Ta Chun Hsu
Yue-Sai Kan
William W. Karatz
Younghee Kim-Wait and Jarrett F. Wait

Angela H. King
Yvonne Wong Koslow
James J. and Helen D. Lally
Marie and Shau Wai Lam
John Jody and Yue Tao Lee
William E. and Helen Y. Little
Robert W. and Virginia Riggs Lyons
Clare Tweedy and Howard McMorris
Theresa M. Reilly
James and Joanne Quan Reynolds
Daniel Shapiro
Abel and Sophia Sheng
Linda R. Shulsky
Stuart Skalka
Anthony M. Solomon
Ronald P. and Mei Wu Stanton
Charles J. Tanenbaum
Henry and Patricia P. Tang
Theow-Huang Tow
Mary J. Wallach
Chi-Chuan Wang
Shao F. and Cheryl L. Wang
Charlotte C. Weber
Marie-Hélène and Guy A. Weill
Wan-go H.C. and Virginia Dzung Weng
Yvonne C. and Frederick Wong
Robert P. and Barbara Youngman
Ivan D. Zimmerman and Taryn L. Higashi

Academic
Norris and Henriette Darrell
Annette L. Juliano and Joseph L. Geneve
Laura Whitman

List in formation

GALLERY COMMITTEE

John R. Curtis, Jr., *Chair*

Susan L. Beningson
Maggie Bickford
Claudia G. Brown
Robert Harrist
Maxwell K. Hearn
Annette L. Juliano
David Sensabaugh
Marie-Hélène Weill

GALLERY

Willow Hai Chang, Director
Pao Yu Cheng, Assistant
Elaine Smollin, Associate & Registrar

DOCENTS

Nora Ling-yun Shih, *Senior Docent*
Susan Klein
Stephanie Lin
Helen Wang

VOLUNTEERS

Kelly Chan
John J. Chang
Zhen Zhen Lu
Pamela May
Yvonne Wong Koslow
Mary McFadden